at

To
VICTORIA
With Love

by Simon Mort

HOW TO WRITE A
SUCCESSFUL REPORT

BUSINESS BOOKS
London Melbourne Sydney Auckland Johannesburg

Business Books Ltd
An imprint of the Hutchinson Publishing Group
17–21 Conway Street, London W1P 6JD

Hutchinson Group (Australia) Pty Ltd
PO Box 496, 16–22 Church Street, Hawthorne,
Melbourne, Victoria 3122

Hutchinson Group (NZ) Ltd
32–34 View Road, PO Box 40–086, Glenfield, Auckland 10

Hutchinson Group (SA) (Pty) Ltd
PO Box 337, Bergvlei 2012, South Africa

First published 1983
Reprinted 1984

Photoset in Times

Printed and bound in England by
Anchor Brendon Ltd, Tiptree, Essex

British Library Cataloguing in Publication Data
Mort, Simon
  How to write a successful report.
  1. Report writing
  I. Title
  808'.066658   HF5719

ISBN 0 09 151790 7 (cased)
     0 09 151791 5 (paper)

Contents

Preface and acknowledgements

This book seeks to guide, to advise and – above all – to stimulate. A civil servant on one of my recent courses said at the close of business: 'I never thought that I would come to look on report writing as an art form'. It was a charming expression of the sort of attitude that this book aspires to provoke.

Some readers may sometimes be surprised at the wide range of some of the illustrations. Comparisons are made, from time to time, with forms of written communication other than reports. Sometimes examples are even drawn from unwritten types of communication. This breadth of view is deliberate and important. Nobody just sits and writes reports. People go around communicating with each other in all sorts of interesting ways (and some pretty boring ones too). It is therefore essential to see the subject in the whole context of communication and to note the adjustments that must be made to produce a successful report.

If report writing is believed to be some specialist esoteric skill that can be considered in isolation, the report is likely to be brittle and certainly boring. One of the most important bits – if not the most important bit – of advice in the book is that the report writer must use breaks in his task to read other material. He should read as widely as possible: novels, periodicals, broadsheet newspapers or anything else that will take his mind off the task in hand. Even if it is only a few pages on the way home or a chapter in bed, it will help him to reappraise the report in the morning. It is the same if a technical writer never reads anything outside his own field. His style becomes clichéd, stale and repetitive.

I make no apology for the frequent references to articles and correspondence in the *Spectator* – except to the editor of that august organ. Indeed any report writer wishing to take his mind off the minutiae of his report would do well to spend an hour or two reading it. Its contributors demonstrate how serious matters can be described in a readable, informative and frequently entertaining way without distracting from the importance of the subject matter.

It has proved expedient to refer to the report writer as *he*. It could equally have been *she*, I suppose, but it wasn't. To have alternated between the two sexes would have been wearying and silly. (*Pace* the Editor of *Naked Ape*.)

Each chapter in the book is based on a particular line of inquiry, so that each is self-contained. Each is quite frequently cross-referenced to other chapters for the benefit of the selective reader. I hope that this does not irritate anyone.

My debt to other people is extensive as it is bound to be in a book that adopts the descriptive (as opposed to prescriptive) approach to techniques. My thanks are due to the following who gave me permission to reproduce material:

John Leach (American Airlines)
Chris Gebbie (Argos Distributors Ltd)
Richard Pulford (Arts Council of Great Britain)

S. A. Anfield (Bank of America)

M. C. Ansher (S & W Berisford Ltd)

Neil Nelson (British Caledonian Airways Ltd)

R. H. Sellers (British Vita Plc)

Elizabeth Bryant (Centre for British Teachers Ltd)

S. Plant (Chemical & Allied Products Industry Training Board)

John Norton, Torres Carlos, Pat de Jager, Raymond Langmead, Cephas Nyambauro and Peter Pritchard (Citibank NA)

Maurice Tull (Coca-Cola Southern Bottlers Ltd)

Brian Maclean (The Colt Car Company Ltd)

Stephen Connell (Communication Studies and Planning Ltd in respect of a report produced in conjunction with the Equal Opportunities Commission)

A. R. Young and S. J. Dickenson (Currys Ltd)

N. Brown [Dornay Foods (Division of Mars) Ltd]

Gary Lawson (Engineering Industry Training Board)

C. Tomkins (Esso Petroleum Company Ltd)

B. W. Parkes (Ford Motor Company Ltd)

David Gambles and John Joyce (General Council of British Shipping)

Frederic Drake and Judy Stanfield [General Electric Company (USA)]

Arnold Beech (Grattan Plc)

John Hawkins (Johnson Matthey Chemicals Ltd)

Clive Mathison (Miles Laboratories Ltd)

D. F. Drakes (National Nuclear Corporation Ltd)

Robin Wright (The National Trust)

N. Crawford (North British Properties Plc)

Michael Moynihan (Organisation for Economic Co-operation and Development)

R. Mellor (Overseas Containers Ltd)

Mike Phillips (Price Waterhouse)

Dennis Roper (The Prudential Assurance Company Ltd)

Mike Bishop (QANTAS Airways Limited)

Philippe Schiever (Schering Corporation USA: Sentipharm AG)

Felicity Beech (Shannon Free Airport Development Company Ltd)

Ian Taylor (The Stock Exchange)

F. D. Claridge (Trustee Savings Bank Central Executive)

K. Leigh (Trustee Savings Bank Group Computer Services Ltd)

Philip Hare (UAC Ltd)

Ron Foley (Warner-Lambert)

Philip Gibson and John Macfarlane for their personal permissions.

I also record thanks to the Copyright Department of the Oxford University Press for their permission to reproduce Figures 48, 62 and 63; and the Controller of Her Majesty's Stationery Office (with particular thanks to Jill Ward).

I am especially indebted to Lord Bullock for his particularly valuable thoughts and experiences and for his detailed comments on the relevant part of the manuscript. Thanks are also due to Tony Augarde (Senior Editor Oxford Dictionaries), Patrick Hanks (Editor of *Collins English Dictionary* at the time of its publication and now at the University of Essex), Betty Kirkpatrick (Editor of Chambers Dictionaries) and Deborah Biber (Annual Reports Ltd).

I am grateful to all my colleagues at Guardian Business Services for their interest in this book, in particular my masters Michael Milton and Chris West for their very practical encouragement and Tom O'Sullivan, Frank Gaunt and Alan Claridge for their various specialist comments. I thank Margaret Farren for preparing the typescript with such care and attention to detail and Joan Power and Sharon Lander for typing the extensive correspondence involved in the preparation of the book.

Finally I am enormously grateful to my wife for her support and to my children, Harriet and Justin, for their help in carrying out various tedious but important arithmetical and research tasks. (*Note:* Sir James Murray, *q.v.* later, started working his children in his scriptorium at the age of 6.)

This book has been fun to write. I hope that it is fun to read. If a report is a bore to write then it is a non-starter with the reader.

MICHAELMAS 1982   SIMON MORT

PART ONE

COMMUNICATIONS

CHAPTER ONE

Introduction: meeting the reader's requirements

'Acting is a craft to which there is no end: you always have to learn more.'[1]

The actress Liv Ullmann interviewed on television explained that acting is an infinite profession. The number of situations that can be represented has no limit. So it is with managerial reports. The infinite number of subjects that can be covered combines with the infinite number of report writers and report readers. All of these have different levels of knowledge, different attitudes and even different prejudices. This gives the subject its fascination. It also creates many problems.

The variety of purposes of writing reports is examined in detail in Chapter 2. The basic purpose of any report, common to all the functions, is to convey ideas from one mind to another. As every individual is slightly different, differing approaches are going to be appropriate on every occasion.

The readers' vocabularies will differ. Some reports will include distribution to a foreign readership, which does not have English as its first language. In many reports, elements of technical vocabulary – in its loosest sense – will be suitable. Technical vocabulary develops as a form of shorthand to describe complicated processes or equipment. Yet some readers will be innocent of it.

The amount of detail will vary from reader to reader. Some will be happy with a simple decision. Others will need reams of justification in respect of the same decision. The amount of detail required by one reader and one situation will be different with another reader and even a slightly different situation. Length will be constrained by the time available to the writer and that available to the reader.

The tone and style of a report will be dictated by the relationship between the reader and the writer. With one a friendly, matey style will be in order and anything more formal will seem strained and unnatural. Colloquialisms will seem out of place where most serious subjects are treated.

Elaborate systems of headings will help to get one sort of message across in one case but will hinder another. Some readers will dislike headings in any context: others will like a short telegraphic type of presentation. The number of illustrations, the cost, the precedents for previous reports of a similar kind are other factors that will vary from one occasion to another.

This book will set out generally admissible guidelines to act as a framework for most reports. On that framework report writers must embroider:

1   First, the requirements of their own house style to ensure local acceptability.
2   Secondly, the constraints of the subject matter. Some topics may call for elaborate and profuse illustrations; others will deserve a more Spartan treatment.
3   Finally, the individual preferences of the reader if they are known.

The danger of academic rules

The most important of all the criteria mentioned up to now is the reader's preference. All other requirements must be subject to this. Whatever the precedent, whatever the natural predelictions and preferences of the writer, if the message is not in a form, a language and a layout that is acceptable to the reader it is not going to get through. The report is going to fail.

However, every reader is a bit different from the next. So the question arises, how is it possible to lay down rules and conventions of report writing? Indeed, there are serious dangers of laying down prescriptive rules and suggesting that they are going to be suitable for all and sundry. The problems of this authoritarian approach are evident in the wider field of the English language as a whole. Managers, and training managers in particular, look for simplistic standards to satisfy glib training objectives. In the opening paragraphs of his analysis of levels of literacy, Sir Alan (later Lord) Bullock[2] reminds his readers that employers have always looked back longingly to a 'golden age' now gone. Employers always feel that their generation performed more reliably, more honestly and more industriously than their new intake. Yet, 50 years before, the authors of the Newbolt Report[3] had had the same complaints as Bullock received.

The golden age is a myth. It is an illusion born of nostalgia and the limitations of human memory. Likewise definitive rights and wrongs of English language and any topic related to it are subjective and dangerous. Yet easy answers have always had their appeal. The 'false idea of correctness'[4] was criticised by Logan Pearsall Smith in 1928, 40 years before the liberalism of the 1960s made linguistic iconoclasm so fashionable.

In a wonderfully comprehensive and yet descriptive book about Australian English, Baker[5] says:

> The odd idea that there is a definable something called Good English which is pure and beautiful and eternal . . . seems to have grown out of man's puny illusion that he can stop evolution in its tracks.

He goes on to describe 'Good English' as a 'clumsy misshapen monster patched up by all the petty Frankensteins who infest classrooms and pulpits and editorial chairs'. Two particularly important points emerge from Baker's observations. First, many people delude themselves that there is, or has been, a point at which the standard of the written word reached an unsurpassable standard. This has also given Latin its appeal over the last two or three centuries.[6] Because it has run its course, Latin offers standards that are permanent and unchanging. They are, however, standards that are entirely irrelevant. This is now being made abundantly clear as business affairs come to be controlled by a generation of managers who are largely ignorant of the principles of Latin grammar. Secondly, it is inevitable that in certain environments, such as the classroom and newspaper offices that Baker describes, rules will be inevitable in the interests of consistency. Newspaper style books will lay down criteria to be respected by all correspondents. *The Times* style book, for instance, specifies the level of a disaster before it can be described as a shambles.[7]

Yet there is a danger that people will become too subservient to academic rules regardless of practical influences. If it is too rule-bound, writing will lose touch with its subject-matter and its reader. It will become irrelevant. A contributor to *The Times Educational Supplement* described this as 'writing in a vacuum'. There is a danger of writers becoming too worried about 'getting it right' and being 'on their best behaviour'.[8]

The insistence on rules persists nonetheless. There can be no absolutes however. There is no Holy Grail of perfect English or of an ideal report. The comments of Professor Ayer in a slightly wider communicational context are appropriate:

> ... what is irrational is to work for a guarantee where none can be forthcoming; to demand certainty where probability is all that is obtainable.[9]

David Henshaw, the producer of the programme *Brass Tacks*, explained:

> ... I find it hard not to envy anyone – from Ken Livingstone to Milton Friedman – who feels himself in possession of 'the truth'. For me, life remains too complex and contradictory to share such whole-hearted convictions.[10]

Writing a report to meet the reader's requirements is not like the act of catching a train. Arrive at Paddington at 17.59 and 30 minutes later the traveller is halfway to Oxford. Arrive at Paddington at 18.01 and 30 minutes later he is still at Paddington. It is less predictable. To run the risk of overdoing the analogy, it is more like a traveller setting off from London Bridge to get to Paddington for the 18.00 train. He takes into account whether he can afford a taxi, whether a taxi will be quicker or slower than the Tube, which way he will invite the taxi to travel. Are there likely to be obstructions in the City of London? Is there a Buckingham Palace garden party or a state visit that will make travel almost impossible through Whitehall and the Royal Parks? Only the extremes are certain. If he leaves a quarter of an hour to get there he will be too late. If he leaves two hours he will be all right. However he probably cannot afford two hours.

This may seem rather evasive and negative. It amounts to saying: 'Its all too difficult. There aren't really any rules about writing reports.' Yet there must be some. The newspaper editors mentioned just now have to produce style books to prevent their publications looking like a rag-bag of bits and pieces, which would be unpalatable and unacceptable to the reader. Dr Johnson said that the concept of twilight does not invalidate the facts of day and night.[11]

John Rae, Headmaster of Westminster, wrote an article in *The Observer* early in 1982[12] in which he was mildly critical of the attitudes that regarded grammatical rules as an infringement of personal freedom. In the ensuing correspondence the authors of most letters completely missed Mr Rae's point that some conventions were inescapable in written communications just to get the message across to the reader. He saw such a grounding also as:

> ... a filter through which half-truths and misleading generalisations cannot pass. It is an essential tool for survival in a world dominated by communications.[13]

In other words some common understandings of principle are essential to ensure that the reader's requirements are met and the message gets across to him.

The prescriptive and descriptive approaches

Guidelines must therefore be based not on arbitrary principles. They must be directly related to the reader's needs.

The late Professor Barbara Strang, who was Professor of English Language and General Linguistics at Newcastle, makes a distinction between rules and observable rules.[14] Rules must be derived from what has been seen to work. The best approach is therefore to record and analyse what has been seen to work.

Baker's record of Australian English is so comprehensive and so valuable because it describes how people have found it appropriate and necessary to use English in Australia. It does not attempt to judge or quantify.

Commentators who judge just make the communication unnecessarily removed from what people need to say. Perhaps the essays of Safire[15] in the *New York Times* (and sometimes elsewhere[16]) are a useful brake on unjustified extensions of language. On the other hand Simon's[17] almost paranoic opposition to linguistic innovation is repressive and unhelpful. To resist the actual practice of writer and reader is unrealistic.

Quantifying is equally restrictive. Graves and Hodge writing in 1944 produced percentages to measure comparatives: 15 per cent was said to equal a small part, 20 per cent a part, 30 per cent a considerable part and 35 per cent quite a large part.[18] These discrete distinctions are clearly a serious over-simplification. A series of quotations illustrating uses of 'a small part', 'a considerable part' and so on would give a better indication of good usage.

This book therefore carries out a descriptive rather than a prescriptive analysis of report-writing practice. Examples are given of successful technique. Judgement is passed and opinion is given solely against the criterion of whether a report is likely to get its message across to its readership and to satisfy the reader's needs.

Layout of the book

The chapters that follow set out to answer the questions report writers most frequently ask. To this end, Chapter 2 starts by examining the purposes of reports and the way in which the reader's interest in the subject matter will suggest different formats of presentation. In this chapter reports are considered as complete entities. Thereafter, different facets or special problems are tackled.

Chapter 3 analyses what makes a report different from a letter or a memorandum. As the principal differences are a report's length and complexity, it is useful to consider how all the detailed information can be made more digestible to the reader. Stemming out of this is the structure and design of a report. Various useful formats have evolved. The most generally accepted are described, and compared with common variations, in Chapter 4. The structure and design are of particular importance as they give the reader his first impression of the report. Not everyone will wish or be able to read the whole report. Various expedients exist to permit reading the document at greater or lesser length and these are covered in Chapter 5.

Words, the subject of the next chapter, are the fundamental raw material of a report. The labels of tabulations, the headings and titles are all made up of words just as much as the prose itself is. Ill-chosen words and ignorance of the need for precision in this respect may cause ambiguity and, frequently, serious misunderstanding. At best, it is likely to result in an unnecessarily long paper which fails to make economical use of the language.

Chapter 7 takes word use a stage further and considers what variations in language and terminology are required from one report to another. There are further problems if the report is aimed at a wide readership with differing vocabularies.

Report style is a very nebulous area. It is probably the field in which the reader's wishes will be most varied and will be most difficult to pin down precisely. Here therefore the descriptive approach is particularly suitable and prescriptive dogmatism especially unhelpful. A range of examples is given in Chapter 8 including important contrasts with styles of written communication that are not appropriate to reports.

By this stage it will have emerged that many reports would be greatly clarified and enhanced by pictures of various kinds. There are dangers that tabulations, diagrams and other visual illustrations can be distracting, puzzling, mischievous or dishonest. Chapter 9 makes suggestions for ensuring that they are clear and relevant.

The mechanics of preparing and writing the report must not be forgotten. Chapter 10 outlines ten stages that will apply to the preparation of most reports and illustrates their application. Chapter 11 suggests ways of preparing the script for typing or printing so that it is free from confusion and consistent. Chapter 12 comments on binding, presentation and circulation of the finished document.

The principles discussed up to this point will be applicable to all reports. Some are so esoteric, so different from any others, that they call for special treatment. The next four chapters cover these specialised difficulties in relation to appraisal reports, accident/incident reports, abstracts and telexed reports.

Finally the book ends on a glance at reports of the future. Some comments are included on the effect that modern office equipment is likely to have on the information it transmits.

The paramount criterion: the reader's needs

In this way a plethora of examples will be given and criticised. As a result, some useful generalisations on good and bad practice will emerge. Far and away more important than all these is the reader's requirement. The writer must always keep returning to the reader: who he is, in terms of expertise and attitude, and why he wants the report. This is easier if the writer is well known to the reader. It is easier if there is only one reader. However, it is no less important if the report is going to 100 complete strangers.

Mozart is said to have defended *Don Giovanni* against adverse criticism by saying that he wrote it for himself, not for the public. The same temptation arises in the drafting of a report. Many writers distort a subject by their own prejudices and tell the readers what they think they ought to know rather than what they have asked to be told.

A well known leader writer for a national newspaper was telephoned one evening by a sub-editor about a leading article he had written. 'I can't understand a word of this' the sub-editor protested. 'You aren't meant to' replied the writer. 'That article was written for three people and you aren't one of them.' Many reports are written in arcane terminology or at a level of explanation that is completely unsuitable to the report.

It is the reader's requirements that must be mirrored in the report and which will dictate its purpose and design. The reader must avoid the inclination to:
1 Patronise and bore the reader by telling him what he knows already. A regular connection between writer and reader makes this easier. Sophia Loren explained that her close working relationship with Vittorio da Sica meant that he could direct her acting with the very minimum of instructions.
2 Ride his own hobby-horse at the expense of the reader's interest in the subject.
3 Include peripherally relevant details to try to impress the reader (or justify the time taken or, if there is one, the fee).

4   Provide excessive reasoning when all that is required is a simple recommendation.

A report is nothing in its own right. It depends on its interpretation by its reader.

As Berlo insists 'Meanings are in people, not in the message'.[19] The report should be designed in such a way that it is acceptable to the reader and he can interpret it in the way the writer wants.

CHAPTER TWO

The purpose of reports

In many cultures the sheer volume of words is as important as what is said. This type of impressionist communication is a vital part of many societies. Rapping, colourful exaggerated abuse or flattery is an entertaining and essential part of spoken communication in many West Indian communities.[1] Neapolitans keep a similar flow of words regardless of, and perhaps oblivious of, the precise significance of individual expressions.[2]

More formal communications in British commerce and industry sometimes operate on the same principles. At meetings and in briefings, weight of words and general impression often count for more than the exact details of what is said. George Woodcock[3] is quoted as saying: 'Facts sometimes get in the way of argument'.[4]

Written communication, however, calls for a more deliberate, economical approach. A report is not supported by the theatre of a meeting or an oral briefing. The report's message stands or falls on the black and white of the print read by the addressee at a time of his choosing. He may be tired. He may be in a hurry. He may be impatient or irascible. Yet the writer has no further control over how the reader assimilates this information. He can't put him right if he misinterprets a sentence or a diagram. He can't take questions at the end. He can't ask questions to check that the message has sunk in and to eliminate ambiguity. He can't pop up a visual aid or two if it seems that his original explanation is inadequate.

It is essential then, at the outset, to define the characteristics that distinguish written communication, including report writing, from other forms of communication.

Types of communication

A rudimentary division of communications will provide a tripartite division:
1 Written.
2 Oral.
3 Non-verbal. *Verbal* is here used in the first and original sense: 'of or concerned with words' (as opposed to the newer secondary sense 'oral, not written').[5]

Non-verbal communication includes all those forms of gesture and grimace with which everyone communicates (sometimes involuntarily) the whole time; unless they are asleep, or under the influence of drugs. These are grins, frowns and all the gestures with arms and hands that form an inevitable part of everyday communication, equally in commerce as in private life. The distance apart that two speakers choose[6] to stand,[7] and where they cast their eyes,[8] all add differing emphasis to the message.

Differences between written communication and the other forms

Compared with the other two forms, written communication:
1   Is more concise.
2   Should be more discreet.
3   Will often be more accurate.
4   Will be more deliberate.
5   Suffers from the disadvantage that response and feedback are less immediate.

Some languages, e.g. French, have developed two separate languages: one oral and one written. This has not happened in the United Kingdom and this probably enables the written word to be more natural and less stilted.[9]

Conciseness

At a meeting, an agenda item may be discussed for 40 or 45 minutes. During this time, gesture and histrionics constitute entirely proper communicational tools. The table will be thumped, papers will be shuffled and spectacles adjusted. Above all, repetition will be used for emphasis. However, when all this is reduced to minutes it will probably take up no more than 10 lines of typescript.

Consider, for example, this exchange from the oral evidence of the Welsh Development Agency to the Wilson Committee:[10]

Sir David Orr: What calibre of people have been coming along to you? Are they all entrepreneurs who have started young in setting up their own business? Are they people who have had experience in larger companies who now want to branch out on their own? What sort of people are coming along?

Mr Loveland: I think there is a fair mix, but most of them are entrepreneurs who have started up on their own at various times of life and are that peculiar breed of independent small to medium sized businessmen. If I may expand on that, they are more often than not very expert in their field. Equally, more often than not they are lacking generally in commercial expertise. They may be super engineers, they may be super product innovators, they may have a particular knowledge of a particular market. But in the totality of business in one element or more they are lacking.

The whole of this might be consolidated in minutes as:

All sorts of people sought help, but more were from small or medium businesses. They had specialist expertise, but lacked general commercial acumen.

There is, of course, an important distinction between an accurate account taken down in detail and one that is written up – inevitably in general terms – after the event. Dame Judith Hart has pointed out the greater accuracy of the accounts of Barbara Castle, who does shorthand, over those of Richard Crossman.[11]

A selection interview may last 30 minutes, an hour or – for a senior appointment – two days and a dinner party. In this process the most minute hesitation or uneasiness will be noted and interpreted. Every facet of the candidate's performance will be scrutinised and will contribute to the decision. However the memorandum to the personnel director giving the selected nomination will probably cover no more than one A4 sheet.

A spoken instruction to a seminar may need to be repeated a number of times. It is important to allow for distraction, inattention and forgetfulness. A written joining instruction would make the point only once and would do so in as few words as may be commensurate with clarity.

Perhaps the routine spoken exchanges of everyday life are unnecessarily verbose. There are now many influences that stimulate vacuous communication. A lot of exchanges are essentially phatic; deliberate, but not to be taken at their face value. Such conversations do much to promote goodwill in an office or on the shop-floor. Woolly answers to poignant questions help to delay grasping the nettle until the relevant information is to hand.

Human relationships require the inclusion of civility formulae in everyday exchanges. Embarrassment, lack of confidence or a shortage of vocabulary may be compensated by expressions such as 'like' or 'you know'. Individual phatic words or phrases may have more directly important functions. They may take the form of a single word, as when a ticket collector prefaces his request emphatically with 'All . . . tickets please' to gain attention. Nobody seriously suggests that he is ever likely to want to see only certain tickets. The reply 'Good question' to a fast ball at an oral briefing serves to keep the lines of communication open while a reply is concocted and, quite possibly, by flattering the questioner, to prepare him for rubbish.

Allerton (Manchester University)[12] likens the luxury of spoken communication to the need for flags on the sticks employed in semaphore. In many circumstances the sticks might be visible. Equally certainly there will be many situations in which they cannot be seen. The flags are an insurance to make sure that the message gets through.

All this forms an inevitable and not unwelcome part of communication in the 1980s. However, the temptation for written communication to imitate this extravagant banter must be resisted. Written communication is permanent. It is available for reference until it is thrown away or destroyed. It can thus afford to be more concise and must take advantage of this.

Discretion

Frequently written communication will be more discreet. Irrelevant stories and witty asides that hold the audience's attention in a talk and which may retain their sympathy have no place in written communication. These may be dangerous, or at least contentious, if they are not supported by the facial expression and gesture of the speaker to show that they are not to be taken entirely seriously. Indeed, the law of defamation allows things to be said that should not be written:

> . . . anything communicated in a form of permanent character *and* visible to the eye is libel,
> . . . anything temporary and merely audible is slander.[13]

It has been held for instance (*Osborne* v. *Thomas Boulter & Son, 1930*)[14] that dictating a letter to a typist is slander but onwards transmission of the same letter is libel.

Admissions will frequently be made in speech that would not lightly be committed to paper. Professional firms might readily discuss limitations of their performance in a conversation with the officers of their controlling body, but they would be reluctant to commit them to a report.

Accuracy

The limitations of human memory mean that impromptu telephone and spoken inquiries are often answered in round figures. The question 'How much money is involved?' may have to be satisfied by 'About £50,000'. If a written reply is required, the files and data storage systems will be consulted so that something like £47,650 can be given, or whatever rounding is appropriate in the circumstances.

As has been indicated, gesture is an essential part of everyday communication. In certain circumstances it may be more communicative than words. On a noisy railway station, the inquiry 'Is that seat taken?' will frequently be indistinguishable from its opposite 'Is this seat free?' Such an inaudible inquiry will usually best be answered by a gesture. However the generality of a gesture inevitably means that it is imprecise. The minute specificity of words which constitutes such an important characteristic of written communication is discussed at length in Chapter 6.

Even within the marvellous precision that words afford, a business report calls for greater accuracy than would be appropriate in a political tract, a novel or an academic paper. In these other forms the words must leave something to the imagination, so that every concept described can be more meaningful to each reader. As Quarles says in *Point Counter Point*, 'Real orgies are never so exciting as pornographic books'.[15] Regretably this kind of titillation is outside the scope of report writers.

Deliberation

Because written communication is more deliberate than the other two types, it invites careful planning, sequencing and honing of each document. There is likely to be some sort of research, albeit sometimes of a brief or trivial kind.

Feedback

In morse, semaphore and radio communication every word or phrase is acknowledged by the recipient. In the last-mentioned the proword 'Roger' is used for this purpose. In face-to-face communication, nods, smiles and words or grunts of acknowledgement perform the same function.

An explanation of how to get from Chancery Lane underground station to Farringdon Road will proceed in stages:

> You come out of the underground on the north side of Holborn. Then go round the corner past Woolworths into Gray's Inn Road . . .

The explainer will pause and read the expressions and signs which the listener is offering. If he looks puzzled or vacant he will repeat that stage of the route in slightly different words:

> You come out of the underground up the staircase marked 'Gray's Inn' then turn hard right and take the first turning left . . .

Then, when all is well and more receptive signals are offered, the itinerary will continue in easy stages up Gray's Inn Road, down Clerkenwell Road and all the way to Farringdon Road.

With a telephoned explanation, where no visual indications can be offered, the progression will be even more cautious.[16] However, with a written communication, these green lights of acknowledgement are not available. The report or letter goes in the post or internal mail and stands or falls in its entirety. To ensure that it is made as acceptable as possible:

1   It may have to enjoy one or more drafts.

2   It may have to be circulated for comments. If possible this should be amongst readers who are innocent of the subject matter, so that their comments will be unprejudiced.

Length of reports

So reports, like other forms of written communication, will be more deliberately prepared, more accurate, more discreet and more concise than comparable transmissions in speech. Yet two factors will over-ride all others in determining the length of all reports, whatever their purpose:
1   The time the reader wishes to spend on the document.
2   The time the writer has got to spend on it.
The reader's time may require a length anywhere on the continuum in Figure 1.

One-line decision
unsupported by   ◁ □ □ □ □ □ □ ▷
justification

Several hundreds of
pages for the reader's
own analysis

Figure 1

In some companies a decision on the purchase of new premises will call for 1,000 pages of typescript supported by maps and diagrams for minute scrutiny but the management committee. Elsewhere, exactly the same decision would go through on the nod with half the management committee out of the room. The discrepancy reflects, of course, the measure of faith in the report writer.

In the other dimension, the amount of time the writer has available may be an even more insuperable restriction. The simplest report at the upper end of the continuum in Figure 2 would be something like that shown in Figure 3.

△   A memorandum on top of the file
□

□

□
▽   A detailed analysis that will have compared
        many permutations of the available facts

Figure 2

```
From: Assistant General Manager
To: General Manager

NEW FORK LIFT

1   You wanted to know which I recommend. Here is the file.
2   Your requirement is at folio ④ . The only possibilities
    are at folios ⑦ , ⑨ and ⑩ .
3   The one at ⑨ looks best because of price, weight
    capacity and safety record. Fuel consumption is dodgy
    though.

1 April 1984                           F.Bacon
```

Figure 3

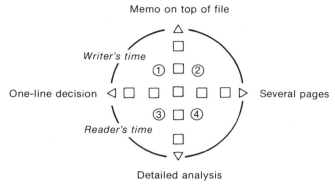

Figure 4

When the two factors ennumerated above are superimposed, see Figure 4, a conflict will therefore sometimes arise in quadrants 2 and 3.

Tone suggested by purpose

Not only will the length of a report vary according to its purpose and the time available to writer and reader, the purpose will also suggest the tone.

A report may be opinion, such as an analysis of an accident recommending ways to avoid recurrence. It may be a suggestion, such as unsolicited paper recommending organisational changes, or a Government Green Paper. It may be fact, e.g. a banker's clinical and impartial analysis of a company's robustness. It might equally take the form of explanation: a sales manager accounting for the unhappy performance of his sales force.

A report may make recommendations or it may eschew doing so. Sometimes the terms of reference will require recommendations to be made. On other occasions this will be totally inappropriate, as when the report is just descriptive, e.g. an archaeologist's report. Even a routine monthly or weekly report may contain recommendations, suggesting possible improvements which may have come to light.

The tone of the recommendations themselves will vary. They may be insistent as with a report on nuclear safety. They may be monitory, as in a surveyor's report. They may be advisory as in a broker's suggestion.

The range of report purposes

These principles of report writing apply to the whole gamut. Fourteen examples of report type will serve to show the diversity of ways in which reports vary in length and tone.

This cannot be a comprehensive catalogue of report types. It is not intended to be one. It is just an illustrated indication of the range of uses to which reports can be put.

The subsequent chapters of the book examine specific aspects of report writing in detail. These examples give overviews of various reports as complete individual entities, describing their purpose, their problems and – in general terms – their overall layout.

Shift reports

Shift reports are almost non-reports or reports by exception. These are reports where only the most simple variables need to be recorded and the routine of the shift – using that term in the loosest sense – can be presumed to have been in order and to have passed uneventfully. This type of reporting is best covered by a simple form such as the Cabin Staff Routine Flight Report of an airline shown in Figure 5. The relevant species of staffing and passengers can be set out at the top. Section 5 at the foot gives a flexible guide to such separate reports as it may be necessary to attach.

If quite such a simple form of reporting is not appropriate, yet the areas of interest are likely to be the same every week, a proforma is still likely to be a good idea. More room will be provided for comments on unusual occurrences. (The weekly change-over report of the supervisor of information services in a retailer at Figure 6 illustrates this. The comment space is somewhat compressed: the original report is spread over five sheets).

Motor manufacturers' inspection and test reports

Two further examples of the use of forms will illustrate the value of this type of report. A motor car manufacturer relies on a great deal of documentation to keep control of his product. To this end, a dealer report form, which will be consistently and regularly used throughout the distribution network, will be helpful. The Colt Car Company's report is shown in Figure 7. This has the following advantages:
1 It ensures consistent and similar reporting throughout the network.
2 It ensures that all points are covered.
3 It keeps the replies simple and ensures that the report does not ramble into unnecessary detail.
Conversely, it is important that the space 'General Comments' should be large enough for any observation likely to be helpful. In the design of such forms there is sometimes an inclination for the size of this box to be dictated by the coincidence of paper size.

The second report is a test report for use on particular trials. Cars of various manufacturers will be compared. The simple data specifications on this proforma (Figure 8), which is also from Colt, ensure that the comparisons are consistent. However, its simplicity and, in particular, the limitation of six categories whereby the features in the bottom half of the page can be compared, mean that this basic data is likely to be supplemented by prose reports.

Bank reports

Many routine bank reports are set out on forms. Reproduced below are two extensively used forms employed by a merchant bank.

The first, see Figure 9, is a straightforward two-sided Basic Information Report (known as a BIR). These details covering all aspects of a customer's operations are available for reference by the bank's officers at any time. It should be noted that provision is made (bottom right-hand corner foot of front side) for recording updating of the particulars. The report is useless and dangerous unless updated. It is also important that the revision and its date should be recorded.

More difficult, if only through pressure of time, is the Call Report (see Figure 10).

BRITISH CALEDONIAN AIRWAYS

Cabin staff routine flight report

THIS REPORT TO BE COMPLETED FOR ALL FLIGHTS/SECTORS AND SUBMITTED TO THE DUTY BRIEFING OFFICER IMMEDIATELY AFTER FLIGHT COMPLETION.

1. FLIGHT NO. BR.................... FROM.................... TO.................... DATE....................

   A/C Reg: G-............................ S.T.D............................ A.T.D............................

   CAUSE OF DELAY..

2. CAPTAIN....................................

CABIN STAFF	FIRST CLASS	ECONOMY
1		
2		
3		
4		
5		
6		

3. NO. PASSENGERS: 1st CLASS.............. ECON.............. UNAC. MINORS..............

4. DETAILS OF ENTRIES IN TECH. LOG

   I.F.E. TC 101E FORM NO. (IF APPLICABLE).

5. SEPARATE REPORT SUBMITTED ON THE FOLLOWING MATTERS

CATEGORY			CATEGORY		
☐	1	CATERING	☐	9	LOST PROPERTY
☐	2	CABIN AMENITIES	☐	10	BONDED STORE (DUTY FREE BAR)
☐	3	CUSTOMER RELATIONS	☐	11	SEAT DUPLICATION PROBLEMS
☐	4	TRAFFIC U.K. STATIONS INCLUDING LGW	☐	12	CABIN STAFF CREW LIAISON OFFICER
☐	5	TRAFFIC OVERSEAS	☐	13	OTHER CATEGORIES i.e.–
☐	6	RAMP SERVICES LGW			MEDICAL ☐
☐	7	LINE MAINTENANCE (CABIN INTERIORS, FITTINGS ETC.)			BRIEFING UNIT ☐ SAFETY & SURVIVAL ☐ ADVERTISING ☐
☐	8	FLIGHT COSTS–DRINKS WRITTEN OFF, FREE FOOD ETC.			CABIN STAFF ADMIN. ☐

S.C.S.M. SIGNATURE..   Form 5418A   MB

Figure 5 *British Caledonian routine flight report for cabin staff*

Such a report must be completed after every meeting between an officer of the bank and his customer. With perhaps half-a-dozen calls in the day and associated travelling, it calls for a lot of self-discipline to write up a detailed analysis of the day's business on return to the bank at 6 o'clock or so. Yet this must be done. What seems crystal clear on coming out of the customer's office will be shrouded in confusion by the next call in three months' time if a full record is not made. Further-

WEEKLY CHANGEOVER REPORT

DATE:

TO:

FROM:

NOTE:(i) Any additional information should be put on a separate
      sheet of paper and attached to this report.
    (ii) Other areas to be consulted:
          Incident reports
          Network incident reports
          Program amendment binders
          Fails/faults log

HARDWARE (Central Site)
Problem areas and machinery currently 'down'

People/manufacturers who need contacting, and for what reason

Pre-arranged maintenance/repair

SYSTEMS, SOFTWARE, LIBRARY
Problem areas

People with whom to liaise

Amendments done

Note: Please consult 'INCIDENT REPORTS' binder and 'PROG
AMENDS' binder

COMPUTER ROOM ADMINISTRATION AND QUALITY
Problem areas, i.e. ribbon usage, print quality, etc.

Problem areas currently being monitored

Unfinished reports, etc.

NETWORK CONTROL (including remote site hardware)
Problem areas

People/offices who need contacting, and for what reason

Areas requiring further attention

Note: Consult 'NETWORK INCIDENT LOG' binder

Figure 6   *Typical supervisor's changeover report*

COLT CAR COMPANY LTD.   N⁰ 0333

COLT

DEALER REPORT FORM

To : ....
Copy ....
....

Dealer..
Address ....

Proposed/Number......................................
Telephone No. ....

	Area Sq. Ft.	Appearance and Condition
Workshop		
Workshop Office		
Reception		
Bodyshop		
Paintshop		
Service Parking		

External Condition of Building...

Proposed Extension...

Number of Work Bays_____	Body Bays_____
Lifts_____Type_____	Spray Bays/Booth_____
Pits_____	Preparation Bays_____
Wash Bay_____	
Lubrication Bay_____	

Sub-Contractor Bodywork_____

Job Card System_____	Wheel Alignment_____
Warranty Record Book_____	Engine Dialnostic_____
Recovery Service_____	C.O. Meter_____
M.O.T. Facility_____	Battery Charger_____
Part Binning_____	Wheel Balance_____
Micro Fische Reader_____	Stock Control System_____

Service Manager_____	Skilled Mechanics_____	Training Courses_____	
Workshop Foreman _____	Semi-Skilled Mechanics_____	Name_____Date_____Course	
Parts Manager_____	Apprentices_____		
Warranty Clerk_____	Partsmen_____		

General Comments

Signature_____ Date_____

Parts and Service Area Manager

Figure 7 *Colt dealer report form*

more the call report helps to maintain a complete record of the bank's dealing with the customer against the account officer having the misfortune to fall under the proverbial bus or the good fortune to have a holiday.

The layout of the call report is important. Such a call (and the principles can be extrapolated to other types of visit) will yield three kinds of information:

1   The objectives (which will, of course, be known when the officer sets out on his visit).

```
T E S T   R E P O R T   (GERMANY)  M A Y   1 9 8 2
---------------------------------------------------

     MODEL : _____   DATE : _____


  GENERAL SPECIFICATIONS :
  ENGINE : _____   TRANSMISSION : _____
  CYLINDERS : _____   CLUTCH OPERATION : _____
  CAPACITY : _____   WHEELS/TYRES : _____
  FUEL SYSTEM : _____   TANK CAPACITY :_____ Lts.
  MAXIMUM POWER : _____   MAXIMUM SPEED : _____
  MAXIMUM TORQUE : _____
```

	EXCELLENT	VERY GOOD	GOOD	AVERAGE	FAIR	POOR
BODY CONSTRUCTION						
BODY FINISH						
PROTECTION						
INTERIOR FINISH						
SEAT BELTS - FRONT						
SEAT BELTS - REAR						
DRIVERS SEAT POSITION/S						
SEAT COVERING						
DRIVER COMPORT						
PASSENGER COMFORT						
LEGROOM - FRONT						
LEGROOM - REAR						
STEERING						
SUSPENSION - FRONT						
SUSPENSION - REAR						
BRAKES - FOOT						
BRAKES - HAND						

Figure 8 *Colt test report*

2   The results of the call, which must reflect all the objectives (however unsuccessful) and may incidentally throw up some more information.
3   The follow-up action. There is bound to be some more action, even if it is just that there will be a further visit in six months' time.
   Previously this bank used a more elaborate form of report which sub-divided the sheet into a number of boxes and, under 'Objectives' and various other headings, suggested answers which might be ticked. This is too restrictive and the open-plan form in Figure 10 is more satisfactory, provided that information is entered under the three essential headings.

Figure 9   *Basic information report*

Appraisal reports

Appraisal reports, which also make extensive use of proformas, are a very special responsibility. They represent, in an absurdly small number of words and symbols, an employee's performance over (usually) an entire year.

The appraisal report system will usually be closely involved with much wider aspects of an organisation's personnel policy: training, promotion and the whole pattern of appointment.

Because of the great importance and sensitivity of this type of document, it is discussed in detail in Chapter 13.

OPERATIONS	
Products	
Administrative And Manufacturing Facilities	
Where Applicable Distribution And Selling Terms— Domestic And Export	

AFFILIATED COMPANIES AND RELATED BUSINESS

SUBSIDIARIES	% owned	Account with FNCB			AFFILIATES	% owned	Account with FNCB		
		HO.	Br.	NO			HO.	Br.	NO

OTHER COMMENTS:—

Accident reports

Also covered in a separate chapter (Chapter 14) for similar reasons are accident reports. The significance of this type of report cannot be overstated. On the perception of the inspectors, the completeness of their investigation and the lucidity of their recommendations will depend the safety of equipment and the lives of its handlers in future.

In internal investigations they will usually be completed on a form which will ensure that various critical questions are answered. Inevitably these outlines will be supported by a number of statements: from the relevant line, production or traffic managers, from the drivers and operators, and from inspectors before and after the accidents.

TBP 166	CALL PLAN AND REPORT	

LOCAL COMPANY	BRANCH OR PRODUCT OFFICE	DATE
	CALLING OFFICER	

CALLING ON

1) OBJECTIVES, 2) RESULTS OF CALL, 3) FOLLOW-UP

Figure 10   *Call plan and report*

Health and Safety Executive reports

Akin to internal accident reports, but much more sophisticated, are the printed and published Health and Safety Executive reports. These are exemplary in their presentation and the clarity of their argument. They are most strongly recommended as models for companies which need to report the results of any complex investigations.

The assessment of the radiological hazards at Hartlepool/Heysham I Power Stations that could result from a dropped fuel stringer accident during on-load refuelling

Contents

Summary

1   Introduction

2   Event sequence

3   Calculation of activity released to coolant circuit

4   Fission product removal from the reactor coolant circuit

5   Fission product releases to atmosphere

6   Atmospheric dispersion of released fission products

7   The evaluation of resultant dose to the public

8   Discussion

9   Conclusions

10   References

11   List of tables and figures

     Distribution

Figure 11 *Outline structure technical contingency assessment*

The later chapters of this book are illustrated extensively from the report on *The Accident at Bentley Colliery, South Yorkshire, 21 November 1978* (published 1979)[17] to illustrate various points of sound layout. This 18-page document is a particularly good example.

A more recent but shorter, and perhaps less typical report of this kind, is that on *The Explosion at Cardowan Colliery, Stepps, Strathclyde Region, 27 January 1982.*[18] This report (published 1982) discusses the circumstances in which 40 men were seriously injured underground in the Cardowan Colliery near Glasgow. It starts with a description of the colliery, its output, its management, the geology and ventilation of the relevant Cloven Coal Seam and the specific V52 Face. The explosion and investigation are described. The report then covers the source of the firedamp which caused the explosion and moves on to the possible sources of ignition (shotfiring, electrical apparatus, etc.). Finally conclusions are drawn and recommendations are made.

More substantial examples are the Health and Safety Executive reports on the safety of pressurised water reactors[19] and the safety of the proposed pressurised water reactor station, Sizewell B, in Suffolk.[20]

Technical reports

This somewhat broadbrush heading covers all types of report that rely heavily on technical content. Three examples will show different approaches.

A Department of the Environment/National Water Council paper, *Copper in Potable Waters by Atomic Absorption Spectrophotometry*,[21] is a glossy-covered 10-page report. It is one of a series describing methods for determining water quality aimed at bodies responsible for handling water and sewage. The method, hazards, reagents, apparatus and sampling are described and the analytical procedure is spelt out in 14 detailed steps. The paper ends with checking procedures and sources of error. The above paper is entirely self-contained, which would be unusual in more complex technical reports. Most technical layouts would provide for extensive tables and figures. The layout of National Nuclear Corporation reports is demonstrated by the specimen structure of a hazard assessment in Figure 11. The logical development of the discussion through the chronology of the contingency to the evaluation is easy to see from the list of sections.

Many technical reports will record the progress of experimental work. A simple layout will suffice and will ensure consistency. Monthly reports at Johnson Matthey Chemicals follow the format shown in Figure 12.

Strategy documents

Strategies for the forthcoming years are frequently set out in the form of a report. Such plans were published by the Chemical & Allied Products Industry Training Board (ITB) for the period 1977–82.[22] An ITB was (and is, in such instances as are still in existence) a very good example of an organisation which had to put across its plans to a readership of widely differing sizes and, in some cases, questionable motivation. The Chemical & Allied Products ITB laid out their strategy centred on three interconnected aims:

1 Improved organisations.
2 Better use of manpower.
3 More effective training practices which it was hoped would follow from the first two.

```
                                          Period: March 1982
                                          Project No. WSJ/3/A

       EXPENSE:   Allocated budget complete
                  Cumulative to date (including this month)
                  Hours in financial form

       STATUS:    Active/closed/suspended

       PROGRESS:

       Distribution (not more than 12)
```

Figure 12 *Progress report format*

The report opened with a summary in suitably encouraging language.[23] The nine key areas, which were announced as 'Missions' in the summary were then explained in detail, such as:

> To secure an improvement in Health and Safety by ensuring that all managers, safety representatives and safety advisers are trained in the hazards likely to be encountered and that all firms have adequate training arrangements to meet the requirements of Health/Safety legislation for all employees.[24]

They were then plotted on a matrix as functions of the chemical firms' needs and the ITB's specific commitments (Figure 13). The tabulation could be made easier to read if the Missions were listed at the left end from which people start to read. However there is no ambiguity and the details in the matrix have not been too greatly over-simplified as is too often the case in such displays.

Financial predictions

Budgets and financial predictions may be put into report form. Certainly the comparison of performance against projected budgets will be presented in this way. This is likely to be analysed in financial and percentage terms. The headings will, of course, vary according to the industry. The outline shown in Figure 14 is taken from such a report by a water treatment consultancy and illustrates a helpful sequence.

Chartered accountants' report

Amongst the longer types of unpublished reports are chartered accountants' and management consultants' reports. These are of particular significance as they embody the whole of the professional advisers' work. The accountants' and consultants' reputations stand or fall by the advice contained in their reports. It is appropriate that they should be carefully structured.

The system of layout employed by Price Waterhouse's British firm is an excellent example of the sort of discipline that is appropriate to reports of this sort of complexity. Their reports will begin with a covering letter of maybe six or a dozen paragraphs explaining:
1   The reason for carrying out the investigation. The letter instructing them to do so may well be attached as an appendix.
2   The use of any particular techniques or methods during the investigation (such as statistical sampling).
3   Any records or audits to which reference is made. This enables the reader to have the documents to hand and highlights the authorship of such supporting papers.
After the covering letter the report will move on to a number of 'Parts' which are the chapters of the report. The first Part is likely to be a summary of the Salient Points to emerge from the investigation. The outline of the Parts depends, of course, on the particular company or topic being examined. However an outline of an examination of a company might be:

Part I   Salient features
Part II   History and activities
Part III   Trading results
Part IV   Net assets
Part V   Future prospects
Acknowledgement

Diagram 3: Key Targets for CAP ITB 1977 82 period

STRATEGIC AIMS	
Firms' Current Training Needs	**Firms' Longer Term Manpower Requirements**
All leviable firms have themselves prepared written Training Action Plans to meet their current needs. (1978)	90% of all leviable firms have implemented a form of Manpower Development Planning including Training Action Plans. (1982)
All leviable firms implementing planned basic training for all newly appointed managers/supervisors. (1978)	Assistance provided to firms on management of change (significant impact in a minimum of 100 firms by 1982).
Employee participation encouraged in all firms on the development of training policy and its implementation. (1982)	
All firms have health and safety training arrangements, including the training of managers and safety advisers, which enable them to meet legislative requirements. (1980)	
Assistance to firms on production productivity improvement through analysis and training (significant impact in a minimum of 100 firms). (1982)	Assistance provided to firms to help them respond to the shifting emphasis within R & D towards development projects (significant impact in a minimum of 50 firms). (1982)
Assistance provided to firms on identification of export marketing manpower requirements, including selection and recruitment. (1978)	Assistance provided to small/medium firms on development of long term marketing strategies (significant impact on minimum of 100 firms). (1982)
All leviable firms implementing planned induction, basic and development training for people entering Industry direct from the Education System. (1980)	
Individual development plans are available and being implemented —for all full time training staff —for the key part-time training staff in small/medium firms where they have no full time training staff. (1982)	

Figure 13 *Matrix used in strategy document*

```
     Introduction
     Selling expenses
     Net operating profit
     Selling expense/Gross margin ratio
     Manpower
     On-site availability, % sale time in hours
                          actual sales hours spent on site
     Sales hours spent per new client gained
     Number of new clients gained
     Average EAV (estimated annual value) per new client
     Total EAV of new clients gained
     Percentage EAV invoiced of new business in 1980
     New business invoiced
     Service hours
     GP (gross profit) per service hour
```

Figure 14 *Outline financial prediction*

Overall CAP Industry Training Needs	CAP Industry Long Term Manpower requirements	Note : target dates refer to 31st March of year stated. MISSIONS
Publication of developments on the management of change from in company work. (1982)	An Industry Manpower Model has been developed to provide trend data to firms and other interested bodies. (1980)	**Manpower Development Planning**
		Management of Organisational Change
Advice published to Industry on (a) Communicating understanding of business operations to employees. (1978) (b) Approaches to training for consultation/participation. (1978) (c) training implications of legislation. (1978)		**Relations at Work**
In conjunction with the Unions to provide advice on the training of safety representatives such that they all receive appropriate training on appointment. (1982)		**Health and Safety**
	Developed improved training facilities for the Industry for training laboratory/process staff in Instrumentation/Control. (1982)	**Productivity including Energy/Material utilisation**
	Adequate Marketing/Sales training facilities established to meet needs of small/medium firms. (1980)	**Export and Commercial Performance**
Output of Education System, in quality and quantity terms, more closely matches CAP Industry requirements. (1982)	Improved liaison achieved between Education, Careers/Employment Service and Industry. (1979)	**Transition from Education to Industry**
Compile and disseminate to Industry information illustrative of good training practice. (1980)		**Training Technology and Achievement**
	Adequate additional training facilities operating within and outside Industry to provide for supply of key skills for CAP Industry, i.e. maintenance personnel at all levels, development chemists, chemical engineers. (1982)	**Contribution to National Training System**

Either the report or the covering letter will always end with an acknowledgement of assistance. The exact form of words would depend on the extent and type of assistance given.

The reports are extremely detailed and the paragraphs of minutiae will be compiled in accordance with the laudably strict systems of layout the partnership lay down. These ensure uniformity of presentation and consistency of layout throughout the practice. Where there are general lessons to be learnt from these conventions, allusion is made to them in ensuing chapters of this book.[25]

Because their subject matter is so detailed, these reports rely extensively on appendices. These will include voluminous numerate tabulations of financial details and may include some graphs, bar charts and so on to indicate changing patterns. There will also probably be some appendices in prose describing products, remuneration policies and so on. It will not be uncommon for about half the pages of such a report to consist of appendices. It is important, though, in such cases where lavish appendices are customary, to avoid packing in every available piece of information. Relevance must be carefully evaluated.

Annual reports

Another field closely involving the accountancy profession is the preparation of annual reports. Strangely, there is very little statutory guidance as to the requirements for an annual report. Such as there is is set out in the various Companies Acts.[26] Companies are required to file accounts within six or nine months of the year end. Certain details have to be shown, such as the names of directors, details of their appointments and resignations, and nature of trade; these are specified in greater detail as from April 1983. An excellent short guide to the provisions of the Companies Acts is published by Gee & Co.[27]

Nationalised industries are subject to special provisions (the *Coal Industry Nationalisation Act 1946* in the case of the National Coal Board and the *Aircraft and Shipbuilding Industries Act 1977* in the case of British Shipbuilders). The Civil Service College has produced a useful booklet[28] which helps the reader to interpret the reports of nationalised industries.

The English Tourist Board report[29] places more emphasis on the record of their achievements in developing tourism. The accounts (dealing with gross expenditure of only £15 million) take up but 10 pages of the 73. The regions are reported in some detail. There is much space given to the Board's guide to tourism development opportunities. This itemises, by size and area, the opportunities available, along with the local government officer to be contacted.

Reports in the private sector are astonishingly varied, both in content and presentation. Some, such as Cement-Roadstone,[30] are copiously illustrated with photographs. Elsewhere the chairman's foreword and report of the directors are highly factual but without pictures, such as Guest Keen and Nettlefolds[31] or Westland Aircraft Ltd.[32] John Menzies[33] produce a slim report of 24 pages of which 15 pages are the accounts, one page each a list of the directors, a statement of their interests and the notice of the AGM. Small companies sometimes produce no more than the basic details of AGM, directors, and the basic statements and accounts.[34] In some instances, the audited accounts and the chairman's statement are presented as separate documents in the same folder, as in the case of the Midland Bank Plc.[35]

There has generally been a move towards more glamorous reports in recent years. This is well illustrated by the Cadbury Schweppes Ltd reports.[36] The 1981 report is a glossy 60-page publication with 16 pictures of the group's products and staff; 1976 saw an unillustrated report of about two-thirds the size.

Government Green and White Papers

Government policy is frequently expressed in Green Papers and White Papers. The former indicate proposed policy and the latter specific intentions. The difference is well demonstrated by the conclusion paragraph from a Green Paper on *The European Monetary System*:[37]

> The Government cannot yet reach their own conclusions on whether it would be in the best interests of the UK to join the exchange rate regime of the EMS as it finally emerges from the negotiations. However, the Government's basic objectives will remain unchanged whatever decision is taken. The Government will vigorously pursue the policies which are necessary for improving growth and reducing unemployment. The foundation for these policies must be an improvement in our industrial performance and victory in the battle against inflation. Only these can provide a lasting basis for the stability of the exchange rate.

Very often these Green Papers will invite comment. The *Report of the Inter-Departmental Working Party on Road Traffic Law*[38] was produced jointly by the Home Office and Department of Transport. It sought to simplify the law of penalties for road traffic offences. The points system, whereby different mis-demeanours are allocated various penalty points which tot up, was proposed and its benefits explained. However, clearly such a radical departure from precedent calls for comment from a wide range of informed and lay opinion. The Foreword, jointly signed by the Home Secretary and the Secretary of State for Transport, ends with this invitation:

Any comments should be sent in writing, *not later than* 22 June 1981, to:
Department of Transport, C16/16, 2 Marsham Street, London SW1P 3EB.[39]

The role of a White Paper in declaring specific intentions is demonstrated by the annual Defence White Paper. This is presented to Parliament by the Secretary of State for Defence generally every spring.[40] It covers, in considerable detail, the Government's defence priorities, its interpretation of the threat, the specifics of its deployment of the three services and its allocation of the budget.

Exceptionally other Defence White Papers may be issued during the year.[41] As might be expected, the form of the Defence White Paper has been greatly expanded – and, in the main, improved – by Margaret Thatcher's Conservative Government. The main report has been increased in size.[42] Illustrations are more prolific. Important new detail or change of policy is highlighted in blue. The whole has been supplemented by a second volume containing statistical data.

With most White Papers which are reissued in annual, or other, revised editions, the hand of the same civil servants can often be detected in regurgitated word forms, regardless of the Minister associated with it.

Religious reports

A few words are appropriate on major religious reports to identify the main distinc-tions separating them from the secular inquiries that are described next. Whereas, of course, evidence will be heard, the recommendations of reports dealing with spiritual affairs will be based more on the experience, values and moral judgements of the committee than would be the case in temporal affairs. Perhaps for the same reason the recommendations will often be expressed at greater length, and may be more equivocal – a cynic might say – to the point of being evasive.

A giant among these reports and one of which the effects are now most evident was *Putting Asunder*,[43] the report on divorce prepared under the Chairmanship of the Rt Rev. Robert Mortimer, then Bishop of Exeter. The committee, which consisted largely of churchmen of one kind or another and lawyers, was required by the Archbishop of Canterbury to suggest some system of reconciliation of lay and spiritual attitudes to the issue. The problem was a difficult one. The report had to suggest practical policies with legal implications without compromising moral principles and scriptural authority. The dilemma is typical and the dichotomy of the contradiction is evidenced throughout the report:

Divorce is a perilous theme for Churchmen. . . .[44]

We are acutely conscious that our terms of reference are capable of causing uneasiness in many minds, both in and outside the Church. . . .[45]

The conclusion we came to in the end was this. Divorce is a drastic piece of surgery, the unnatural severing of what should be one and indivisible. As such it is bound to cause pain and loss and leave lasting scars. To demand that a divorce law shall let no one be hurt is therefore to ask the impossible. . . .[46]

Whatever may happen to the law of divorce, it will always be necessary to provide protection and relief for a spouse who is being treated in a manner utterly inconsistent with matrimonial obligations.[47]

Their solution to this intellectual puzzle – whatever the theological wisdom of it – was certainly a very brave and imaginative achievement. Their argument is expounded in 77 pages of the report (the remainder of the 170-odd pages being relevant but not essential appendices). There are six chapters. The first two detail the terms of reference and the Church's involvement with secular divorce law. The thesis is then unfolded:

Chapter 3   The main drift of the argument.
Chapter 4   The existing law (based as it was then on the notion of matrimonial offence) and what was wrong with it.
Chapter 5   The detail of the new idea including rebuttal of various anticipated or actual objections.[48]
Chapter 6   Practical points of legal administration which would need to be altered.

Thus without losing the balance of their argument by appearing bigoted or one-sided the committee developed their proposal through most of their report. There were no sections headed 'Discussion', 'Conclusions', or 'Recommendations'. The need for reform, the suggested scheme and its problems were subtly developed throughout the paper. This is very difficult to do. It is not generally recommended unless the authors can be sure to avoid:

1   Appearing to prejudice the issue without considering both sides.
2   Appearing so ambivalent that the proposal loses all credibility.

Reports of committees of inquiry

Committees of inquiry are easily the most complex type of report considered here. Involving large numbers of contributors (of deliberately different persuasions) and even larger numbers of witnesses, they are required to examine, often in an almost impossibly tight time-frame, a subject that inevitably has wide-ranging philosophical and moral implications. Frequently their terms of reference are so general that the chairman has to spend some time restricting the vast area of his investigation.

Two reports with the same chairman will serve to demonstrate these problems. In 1972 Sir Alan (later Lord) Bullock was tasked by the Secretary of State for Education and Science (Margaret Thatcher) to investigate the teaching in schools of reading and other uses of English. At the end of 1975 he was invited (by Peter Shore) to advise on the matter of extending representation on boards in the private sector in the interests of industrial democracy. The reports, which were the subjects of inevitable controversy and, in the latter case, outrage, were called *A Language for Life*[49] and *Industrial Democracy*.[50] Both have been known by the nickname 'the Bullock Report', which is logical yet confusing.

Lord Bullock has emphasised that both reports are essentially highly political.[51] *A Language for Life* was prepared against a background of questioning the unconventional teaching methods of the late 1960s. This was a period when society's cheerfully liberal attitudes to mores and discipline reflected a general departure from received standards, in British cities and universities along with Paris and Berkeley, California. In Britain it was directly or indirectly associated with the first Socialist Government for 13 years.

The Conservative Government returned in 1970 sought to identify objective and, if possible, quantifiable measurements whereby standards of the use of English could be judged. This proved impossible. No criteria could be found against which trends could be judged with any accuracy. It was generally feasible by circulating a questionnaire to judge which schools employed progressive methods. However, anything more definitive was out of the question.

Nonetheless, although the report could not point Cassandra-like to general literary disaster, it yielded a wealth of invaluable information on highly diverse subjects. It subsequently became an important basis of discussion among educationalists. All levels of the teaching profession were represented.

The committee deliberately chose an extensive rather than an intensive approach to their formidable task. Therefore the report covers all the principal facets of English-language teaching: reading, oral performance, drama, writing, spelling. Its contents are so comprehensive that the chairman chose an unusual form of conclusion and recommendation, whereby every group of paragraphs was summarised in a sentence or two. There are 333 of these.[52]

The major problem the committee faced was the enormous volume of information and often contradictory evidence with which they were confronted (the list of organisations and individuals who gave evidence runs to 16 pages). In sorting this data and co-ordinating the processing of the drafts of such a report, the burden falls on the secretary. The powers of concentration and resilience required of the secretary are substantial. It is important that he should have no other responsibilities to distract him during the report's preparation. In this case the committee were particularly fortunate in Mr Ron Arnold who was unjustifiably harshly handled by the Press at the time of the inquiry. A former soldier who had become an HMI, his tireless efforts were crucial to the fluency of the 600-page document.

The *Industrial Democracy* report was even more directly political. The report was commissioned by one Labour Secretary of State and submitted to another. Six months after submission, the same Government produced a White Paper[53] which was generally supportive of the report's recommendations. Whereas the political controversy in *A Language for Life* raged nationally outside the committee between two ill-defined schools of thought arguing on vague premises, in *Industrial Democracy* the dispute extended into the committee itself.

However, given terms of reference which presumed the acceptability of 'the need for a radical extension of industrial democracy in the control of companies by means of representation on boards of directors' and a committee that comprised three chairmen of major industries, three senior union officials, two academics (one from the Industrial Relations unit at Warwick and one from the London School of Economics), the Director-General of Fair Trading and a solicitor, the preparation of the report was bound to be stormy. It was of vital importance that the chairman held the committee together and ensured a modicum of common ground. The question of the minority report which proved inevitable is discussed in Chapter 5.

Time was short. In one year they had to sift and read written evidence from about 350 individuals and organisations and to take as much evidence as time allowed.

They were somewhat handicapped by the absence of any model of their subject in the United Kingdom. Lord Bullock chose to investigate two Continental countries with experience in the field: one representative of a western-capitalist and the other of a socialist economy, West Germany and Sweden. The full committee met 29 times including a two-day session at the Civil Service College. The meetings largely took the form of 8-hour sessions of vigorous argument and latterly drafting and re-drafting. This imposed great strain on the committee, but the end product is a model of crisp, concise writing.

Summary

This chapter has described the whole range of uses to which reports can be put. The ungainly leviathan of the Royal Commission has been omitted. This is a slothful creature whose habits are of interest only to its own keepers and have no interest to the general report writer.

The examples have been discussed in varying lengths and amount of detail since the problems they represent differ so much. At one end of the spectrum are the moral and political wrestlings that faced Bishop Mortimer and Lord Bullock. At the other end are the simple confirmations ticked off by aircraft cabin crew in British Caledonian Airways. All are reports.

All must respect the principles of written communication: discretion, accuracy and conciseness. Yet each will do so in a different way. Every type of report calls for slightly different treatment. Every report must be as concise as possible but no more concise than enables the writer to do justice to the problem.

CHAPTER THREE

Making information more digestible

The previous chapter considered the enormous range of subjects that reports can cover and the variety of uses to which the craft of report writing can be applied. The examples discussed have given a preliminary indication of the ways in which the design, style and tone of the report will vary. The extent of these variations make it essential, before taking the matter any further, to define some limits and answer the question: when is a report not a report? In other words, what are the characteristics of a report that distinguish it from a letter or a memorandum?

Of course, these points are not clear cut. Every report and every organisation producing reports will differ slightly. In the main, however, a report is distinguished by differences in readership, personality, formality and layout.

Readership

In many cases a report will be addressed to a single individual. Frequently there will also be a substantial list of copy addresses. A chemist's report is probably likely to have copies for the company's accountants. An internal audit on stock-handling practices will have a distribution extending beyond the audit department. The inclusion of copy addressees raises many problems, e.g. the copy addressees' technical awareness and their knowledge of the particular subject.

Circular letters and general distribution memoranda may share some of the problems. However they are undoubtedly more pronounced, more frequent and more serious in reports.

The writer must strike a balance between giving so much detail that he patronises the knowledgeable reader and writing over the heads of the innocent. The latter is clearly more serious as the message will be lost. Both should be avoided, however.

The possibility of relegating specialised details to an appendix is discussed in Chapter 5. This is, however, an extreme and exceptional measure. Most internal reports should not be littered with appendices dealing with every possible level of readership. The writer must contrive the report so that it strikes a happy medium which can be understood by its whole readership.

Personality

A report is inevitably less personal than a letter. However, when the reader can be identified, either by name or even only by appointment, a communication can become more personal. Points of probable or likely interest to the reader can more easily be included if this sort of rapport is possible.

It must certainly be made clear where there is a division in the report between uncontrovertible fact and the writer's opinion, if the situation allows both to feature in the report. This should either be in a paragraph prefaced by the word *Comment* or just by clear wording as in the following paragraph from a Colt Car Company report. This is a first-class example of a report which remains a very personal communication without losing its impact. It is also made clear that one of the observations is the personal view of the writer. (The context is a trial in which vehicles of various manufacturers were being compared.)

> Appearance is really a matter of opinion, but the interior and exterior were highly rated. Some commented that with such substantial changes the car should have been made to look totally new. I disagreed, because it still retains its identity and that, with familiarisation, does in fact look a great deal better than the superceded model. The internally adjustable mirrors did little for the appearance and a lot less for the wind noise, which was otherwise outstandingly good.[1]

Formality

The combination of a general readership and a less personal approach will inevitably make a report more formal than a letter. This does not mean to say that it should become indigestible. The form of writing should never become pompous or stilted, arrogant or tedious to read.

Colloquialisms, which may colour and enliven a letter, are less suitable in a report. Some morbid cynics insist that humour has no place in a report. Certainly it is less likely that jokes – appropriate to the intimacy of a letter – will feature in a report. However, the 8-line quotation (on an otherwise blank page) from G.K. Chesterton's *Cautionary Tales* about John Vavasour de Quentin Jones, the celebrated stone-thrower, is harmless enough in a Central Policy Review Staff (Think Tank) paper on vandalism. It adds nothing to the main drift of the argument but it lightens a serious piece of writing without detracting in any way from its dignity or effect.[2]

The important topic of register and the need to pitch the report at the right level is given separate treatment in Chapter 7.

Layout

The most important and the most obvious difference between a report and a letter or memorandum is its layout. Paragraph headings, paragraph numbers and possibly a table of contents all help to make a report more digestible. In a longer document they are absolutely vital and may facilitate selective reading.

It would be a mistake to pretend that these things do not sometimes have an entirely proper place in a letter or memorandum. Many Civil Service layouts call for these refinements to both letters and memoranda.[3] The layout of a Ford Motor Company dc (departmental communication) is similarly disciplined. Both systems add greatly to the fluency of communication both within and outside departments.

However, such requirements undoubtedly have the effect of making a letter more formal. Headings and numbers in a letter will distance, or even antagonise, the reader. In a report they should only clarify the information and make it more digestible.

Headings

Headings are signposts to the reader to steer him through all the information. They are of particular importance in longer reports but can have a role in a simple one-page brief. The principles of use of headings are these:

1 There should be enough of them but not too many.
2 They should be to scale with the information. Just as on leaving London a signpost indicating 'The North' will suffice, when the driver passes Doncaster more detailed indicators such as 'Leeds', 'Hull' and 'Wakefield' are appropriate.
3 Headings should not employ general wording which does not provide precise pointers, e.g. 'Miscellaneous', 'General' or even 'Odds and Sods'. Nobody ever looks in a file called 'Miscellaneous' because they do not know what is in there, and they are not likely to be helped by such a vague paragraph heading.
4 Headings of the same rank should represent topics of roughly equal importance.

The next chapter investigates the closely related topic of the structure of the report. Here it is just necessary to contemplate the number of headings that it will be appropriate for a report to have. The number must reflect the extent to which the reader will wish to pick out and identify individual topics. The Cabinet Office paper *Industrial Innovation*, published by the Advisory Council for Applied Research and Development,[4] is a 20-page report divided into four sections with virtually no subdivisions: '1 Introduction', '2 Approaches to Introduction', '3 Strategy', '4 New Companies'. It is questionable whether these signposts give any worthwhile information. A more recent publication by the same body, *Information Technology*,[5] is more thoroughly broken down and thus more digestible. At the other extreme a report which enjoys lavish headings is the monthly report by the Project Director (near Kuala Lumpur) of the Malaysian operation of the Centre for British Teachers Ltd to headquarters in London. This organisation is a charity supplying teachers of English, in this case British and Australian teachers, to Malaysian schools. His report covers the entire gamut of problems and activities, professional difficulties and achievements, introduction of new teachers, their travel, accommodation and so on. An elaborate system of headings is, therefore, essential. Figure 15 shows the headings as they appeared on a typical monthly Project Director's report.[6] It also indicates the frequency and distribution of these headings by A4 sheet. (Petaling Jaya is the suburb of Kuala Lumpur in which the headquarters' offices are located. Phase One and Phase Two refer to the year-groups of teachers introduced into the system. *Collaboration* is a form of co-operation with Malaysian colleagues.)

The logic of the report's structure can be ignored as yet. However the detailed set of headings provides a precise and lucid guide through the jungle of highly diverse pieces of information.

Notice, in particular, that main headings are not divided up unless this would be helpful. 'Financial Matters' and 'Work in Hand' (Page 5 in Figure 15) are not so divided. Yet the 'January Workshop' division of 'Pedagogical' is a very complicated issue and deserves further breakdown (Page 2).

Of course, some hairs may be split and nits picked. It seems an unnecessary encumbrance to repeat 'Pedagogical' against each of the states (Johore and so on) when the whole group is headed 'Pedagogical' (Page 2). The heading 'General' (Page 2) could be more specific, particularly as it did, in fact, cover just two related aspects of Malaysian Government education policy. Similarly the general heading 'Miscellaneous' (Page 7) should be more specific. All the information grouped here relates to the opening and closing of the Petaling Jaya offices and availability of staff through public and other holidays.

A slight flaw in the otherwise outstanding Bentley Colliery report[7] is in the choice

```
              1                                      2

┌──────────────────────────┐      ┌──────────────────────────┐
│ PEDAGOGICAL              │      │ Pedagogical: Kelantan &   │
│    Settling In: Phase Two│      │              Trengganu    │
│    Postings              │      │                           │
│    Pedagogical: Johore   │      │ General                   │
│    Pedagogical: Perak &  │      │ January Workshop          │
│        Penang            │      │    Ministry of Education  │
│    Pedagogical: Kedah &  │      │    CFBT Headmasters       │
│        Perlis            │      │    Teachers               │
│                          │      │    Report                 │
└──────────────────────────┘      └──────────────────────────┘

              3                                      4

┌──────────────────────────┐      ┌──────────────────────────┐
│ Timetable for Workshop   │      │   Heavy Baggage           │
│   Report                 │      │                           │
│                          │      │ PETALING JAYA OFFICE      │
│ Phase One Timetables     │      │    Staff                  │
│                          │      │    Equipment              │
│ Collaboration: Phase One │      │    Space                  │
│ Teachers                 │      │    Telephones             │
│                          │      │                           │
│    Ministry              │      │                           │
└──────────────────────────┘      └──────────────────────────┘

              5                                      6

┌──────────────────────────┐      ┌──────────────────────────┐
│   Safe                   │      │ Area Secretaries          │
│                          │      │ Documentation Procedures  │
│ FINANCIAL MATTERS        │      │ Emergency Procedures      │
│                          │      │ Ministry of Health        │
│ WORK IN HAND             │      │                           │
│                          │      │                           │
│                          │      │                           │
└──────────────────────────┘      └──────────────────────────┘

              7

        ┌──────────────────────────┐
        │   EP Fund                 │
        │   Reports                 │
        │                           │
        │ MISCELLANEOUS             │
        │ Petaling Jaya Office Hours│
        │ Public Holidays in near   │
        │   future                  │
        │ Staff Holidays in near    │
        │   future                  │
        └──────────────────────────┘
```

Figure 15 *Headings in Centre for British Teachers' Monthly Project Director's Report (by A4 pages)* of headings. The report is itself entitled *The Accident at Bentley Colliery, South Yorkshire, 21 November 1978*. It is therefore surprising to find a heading within the report labelled 'The Accident'. Nevertheless this can probably be justified: the previous section deals with 'Description' and the following one 'The Investigation'. On the other hand it is not sensible for the section heading 'The Accident' to be repeated as a sub-section covering 6 of its 20 paragraphs, thus:

```
Description
    General
    The Manriding Installation

The Accident
    Events leading to the accident
    The accident
    The recovery

The Investigation
    Inspection of the site
    No 18 locomotive
    The carriages
    The couplings
    The Godwin Warren Arrestor
    Surface testing

Matters arising out of the Investigation
```

Table of contents

No guideline of length can be given as to whether a table of contents is required or not. It is a function of disparity. A 4-page report covering perhaps 20 widely diverse topics may merit a table of contents (by paragraph). An example is a chartered accountant's Internal Control Memorandum, a short report covering internal housekeeping improvements which have suggested themselves during audit. This might cover stock control, cash handling and arrangements for signature.

A 25-page report following one theme may be better off with none. Perhaps it has to be read straight through like a letter, and the reader should not be dissuaded from this approach.

If the headings are the signposts to the reader, the table of contents is the gazetteer. It is, therefore, important for the main levels of heading to be represented in it.

The table of contents (see Figure 16) of the Arts Council's *Report to the Arts Council of Great Britain and the Greater London Council on Lyric Theatres in London*[8] does not even attempt this. This is a pity since the report itself is well broken down with detailed headings covering capital costs, management costs, comparisons of Old Vic and Sadler's Wells, etc.

The National Trust *Annual Report*[9] takes it slightly further and certainly produces a useful list of appendices, as shown in Figure 17. It is still unfortunate that the content of the report is not itemised in further detail. The highly disparate activities of the Trust and the geographical distribution of their various properties are very well earmarked by elaborate headings in the report. This could usefully be reflected in the table of contents.

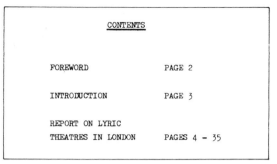

Figure 16   *Table of contents to report on Lyric Theatres*

On the other hand, the Central Policy Review Staff report, *Services for Young Children with Working Mothers*,[10] is clearly explained in its table of contents without being unduly complex (see Figure 18).

Two other good examples are shown in Figure 19 (Organisation for Economic Co-operation and Development)[11] and Figure 20 (page from a report by Communication Studies and Planning Ltd in conjunction with the Equal Opportunities Commission).[12]

Index

The amount of detail in the table of contents will depend, in part, on whether there is an index at the back of the report. An index is only suitable for longer reports or those dealing with extremely complex subjects, especially if the report is to be distributed to a wide membership of highly diverse interests.

If an index is included, the table of contents should be reduced to a fairly simple format. The index should never take the form of a slightly expanded version of the table of contents. A table of contents describes the main headings of the report in the order in which they occur. The index picks out every mention of significant topics and the length of time required to prepare an index and the attention to detail involved must not be underestimated.

Contents

Figure 17   *Table of contents to National Trust Annual Report*

SERVICES FOR YOUNG CHILDREN WITH WORKING MOTHERS

Report by the Central Policy Review Staff

TABLE OF CONTENTS

Figure 18   *Table of contents: Central Policy Review Staff report*

TABLE OF CONTENTS

Figure 19 *Table of contents of a traffic control report*

A good example of successful use of a table of contents (Figure 21) and index (Figure 22) is the National Coal Board's *Annual Report and Accounts*.[13]

Page numbering

Pages should be numbered in all but the briefest reports. This should be done centrally top or bottom or on one of the outside corners. Numbering on the inside corners means that the page number is in danger of being hidden by a staple or eaten

CONTENTS (continued)

Figure 20 *Table of contents of an information technology report*

Figure 21   *Table of contents: NCB Annual Report*

by the binding. It also gives the reader flicking through in search of a page greater difficulty.

It may be helpful to preface every page number with the chapter or section number. Thus the pages of Chapter 3 will be 3-1, 3-2, 3-3, etc., or 301, 302, 303, etc.

If the material is particularly sensitive the total number of pages can be given as '1 of 14' or '14 of 14', etc.

Paragraph numbering

Some readers are averse to paragraph numbering on the grounds that it is

Index

Figure 22 *Extract from index: NCB Annual Report*

unnecessarily rigid. This seems a very modest disadvantage compared with the precision a detailed system of paragraph numbering allows. It greatly eases discussion of the report at meetings, on the telephone and in informal conversations. It also simplifies amendment if the document is destined for a long life as in:

```
AMENDMENT

At Sub-paragraph 14(c)(3)
Delete: 153 skilled 166 semi-skilled
Insert: 281 skilled 210 semi-skilled
```

There are broadly two types of paragraph numbering system. Both have Arabic numbers for the paragraphs, chapters or sections: variation occurs with sub-paragraphs, etc.

1   *Decimal system*   This is sometimes known as the Continental System as it was almost ubiquitously used on the Continent before it became fashionable in the United Kingdom. Sub-paragraphs of Paragraph (or Section) 1 will be numbered 1.1, 1.2, 1.3; sub-sub-paragraphs 1.1.1, 1.1.2, 1.1.3, etc.[14] The example shown in Figure 20 uses this system.

2   *British system*   This arrangement may be informally called the old-fashioned British System. It was used throughout the British Civil Service, commerce and industry until the decimal system became popular in the late 1960s. It is now used by approximately one-third of British companies and is probably more popular than the decimal system in USA. It relies on arrangements of Arabic numbers, letters, Roman numerals and sometimes brackets. There is no generally accepted version of the system. Nonetheless any document must be consistent throughout all its paragraphs and it is accepted that any symbol in brackets such as (C) is essentially an inferior or subordinate paragraph to the same symbol without brackets, i.e. C.

The advantage of the Continental system is that at no place in the report will the reader have any doubt where he is. It is therefore particularly suitable for reports where sections are very long and perforce extended over many pages. An expression such as

```
143.7.18.2
```

leaves no doubt that it is part of Section (or Paragraph) 143, sub-section 7, sub-sub-section 18, sub-sub-sub-section 2. If the other system is used, all that may appear on the page is something like

```
f.
   (1)
   (2)
      (a)
```

so that the reader who is in search of Section 150 will have no idea whether to go backwards or forwards.

On the other hand, many companies feel that the very long expressions which are sometimes produced by decimal subordinate paragraph numbers are cumbersome and unwieldy. Some compromise by taking the decimal configuration only as far as the third level. Indeed if the numbering needs to be taken beyond that point, the writer should ask if the section or paragraph is not too long. Perhaps it should be redivided with the sub-paragraphs promoted to paragraphs.

Some French and Italian systems use capital Roman numbers as the first level of division (see Figure 19).

A selection of paragraph numbering systems is shown in Appendix B.

Non-numerate paragraph markings

Some writers are tempted to itemise paragraphs without actually giving them numbers. The usual expedients for this half-hearted endeavour are bullet points (●), dashes (—) and, sometimes, asterisks (*). A practical problem with bullet points is that they are not available on many typewriters and are then usually made, laboriously with a pen, by filling in a capital 'O'. Worse, apathy may reduce the typist to using a humble full-stop which stands out no more than any other stop on the page.

Dashes and hyphens are likewise insufficiently pronounced for this purpose. Like the other markings of this kind they offer no possibility of identifying the item by number for cross-reference or amendment purposes.

The use of asterisks in this way is perhaps even more mischievous. An asterisk is generally associated with a footnote and use in this way as a highlighter will only confuse.

Suitable use of bullet points

Whereas bullet points, and similar markings, are unsuitable as notations for paragraphs, they do have a legitimate use. Bullet points, in particular, can be used to advantage to stress recommendations. If they are also used at that point in the

```
We are experiencing difficulty in handling passengers who
require wheelchairs at Heathrow Airport. To assist us
resolve the problem I seek your support for this sub-
mission for a personnel carrier.

Background
Airlines at Terminal Three generally are having difficulty
coping with the demands for wheelchairs for both arriving/
departing flights. The reasons for this are:

● Distances that passengers need to travel within Terminal
  Three from the arrival gates to the immigration clear-
  ance area and vice-versa.
● Our VFR-type market means a level of elderly passengers
  who suffer ill-effects from long flights and on arrival
  find it difficult to walk the long distances in Terminal
  Three.
● Morning peak arrival patterns bring about a demand for
  wheelchairs that our agent is unable to cope with.
```

Figure 23 *A use of bullet points*

report they distinguish the separate recommendations. However they still deny the reader any way of referring to the items and are difficult to type.

Ford Motor Company uses them extensively in this sort of way. It can be extended to other parts of the report as in a QANTAS Airways example where they are used to spell out three separate important points of background; the report[15] begins as shown in Figure 23. However this should not be done to excess. The more bullet points used, the less powerful is the emphasis achieved by each point.

Summary

Although the distinction between a report and letters or memoranda is principally one of length, this difference extends into other more important forms. Because it is longer, it must be made more digestible. Because the readership will frequently be more general, a happy medium must be found between the highly technical and the absurdly patronising.

It must be less personal without being pompous. It will be more formal without being stilted.

Above all the greater volume of information must be arranged in a form of layout which makes it easy to absorb and easy to return to for particular and specific reference. It must also have a system of headings and numbers which enables detailed reference to be made to individual parts of it, both in other papers and in the report itself.

However well expressed and however lucidly described the subject matter of a report may be, it must be made digestible to the reader. Headings must be clear, unambiguous and precise. They are signposts to steer the reader through the report.

Paragraph and page numbers will facilitate cross-referencing. A table of contents and an index will make it easier to refer back to parts of a complex document.

The amount of heading necessary and the extent of cross-reference necessary must be gauged according to the length of the report, its purpose and its reader's attitude. The design of headings and numberings should never become stereotyped.

CHAPTER FOUR

How to lay out a report

'If you want something that's genuinely unstructured you have to plan it carefully.'

There is more than a grain of truth in Howard Kirk's apparently fatuous observation in *The History Man.*[1] For a report to read fluently and not appear stilted or brittle it must be planned very diligently.

Most reports fall simply, like Gaul, into three parts (see Figure 24). There will be an Introduction. There will be the meat of the report, in other words the main body of it. This will sometimes be called the discussion section, or may even be called the argument. It should not be labelled with either of these general tags, however. Finally there will be conclusions, to which may be added recommendations.

Title

However, before all this, every report must have a title. It must be set out in a way that makes it stand out clearly from the rest of the report. A title typed in lower case letters when a report has later headings in block capitals throughout is unlikely to stand out sufficiently. The title should be in a script which is at least as pronounced as any subordinate headings within it (see Figure 25).

Many organisations require all reports to be enclosed in a cover. If this is done, of course, the title will appear on it in whatever format suits the company's practices and the distribution of the paper. The subject of cover sheets and report presentation is treated in detail in Chapter 12 and some examples of cover sheets may be seen therein.

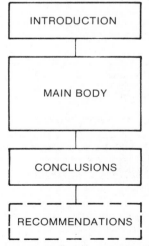

Figure 24 *Basic sequence of a report*

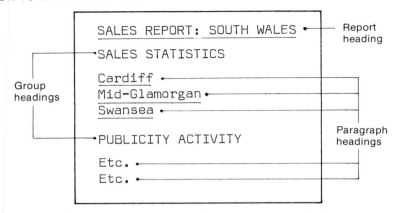

Figure 25 *Specimen sequence of headings and sub-headings*

The wording of a report title is a balance between the requirements of brevity and clarity. A regular routine report can get away with the title:[2]

```
MONTHLY REPORT JOHORE/TEMERLOH    JANUARY/FEBRUARY 1981
```

or:[3]

```
SIGNATURE VERIFICATION: POSITION PAPER
```

Extraordinary reports which do not follow an expected pattern may have to be more wordy:[4]

```
EMPLOYMENT AND TRAINING IN THE TELECOMMUNICATIONS
          EQUIPMENT MANUFACTURING INDUSTRY
```

In an academic or contemplative report a more cryptic title can be used provided that it is clarified by a sub-title:[5]

```
            PUTTING ASUNDER:
A DIVORCE LAW FOR CONTEMPORARY SOCIETY
```

or perhaps:[6]

```
ALCOHOLISM AND SOCIAL POLICY:
 ARE WE ON THE RIGHT LINES?
```

If there is the temptation to use more than about ten or a dozen words as in:

```
REPORT ON STAFFING LEVELS IN ALL DEPARTMENTS LESS
MARKETING AND RESEARCH AND DEVELOPMENT EXCLUDING
SITES IN SCOTLAND AND NORTH-EAST BUT INCLUDING
BELGIAN BRANCHES
```

then clearly some of these points must be eliminated from the title and relegated to the introduction.

The requirement for microscopic precision in choosing words in titles and all sorts of headings will be discussed later. The need for particular attention to this aspect results from the small number of words that are appropriate to a title. Every word must count for that much more than in a paragraph of the report where an ill chosen word can be corrected by other words in the paragraph.

The expression *Re* to introduce a heading is a foolish encumbrance which should be avoided. It adds nothing to a title which should be adequately pronounced if it is in block capitals or underlined. In any case, the *Re* does not stand for *Regarding*, as many of its users believe, but *In Rem* (Latin = in the matter of).[7]

Introduction

If the introduction of a report is poorly drafted, the writer will have difficulty in recovering the reader's attention, understanding or sympathy. In a poor opening to a lecture or oral briefing this shortcoming is perhaps more evident. A gimmicky introduction, a poorly told joke or a joke which – being recently borrowed from Morecambe and Wise – is already well known, can destroy any rapport with the audience. Similarly, if the speaker fails to state his objective or explain the rationale of his approach, he will lose his audience. It is exactly the same with a report. After a good introduction, the writer may still lose his reader. After a bad introduction he stands little hope of attracting him.

It is impossible to provide an all-purpose list of contents for an introduction. The criterion is that the introduction should include everything that the reader needs to know before he tackles the main argument of the report. It is highly likely that the following will feature (but not necessarily in that order):

1 Why the report is being written Who told the writer to produce the paper? When did he do so?

In your memorandum dated 1 April 1983 you asked me to investigate ways of improving delivery times.

Perhaps it is just a monthly return, as in:

Set out below are sales figures for the month of May 1982.

On the other hand, the report may have been compiled on the writer's own initiative. He may have noticed some shortcoming. Perhaps there has been excessive turnover of staff or there is some significant safety hazard.

The first paragraph of the Home Office Research Study *Alcoholism and Social Policy*[8] quoted above gives over the first paragraph of its introduction to the statement of reason. (Cross-references to other documents have been left out here.)

The prevention of alcoholism or alcoholic problems must be an important goal of public health policy for any government. A recent report suggests 'As a conservative estimate there are at least 300,000 people in this country with drinking problems of such severity as to merit the conventional label of "alcoholism".' The Office of Population Censuses and Surveys has produced a 'low' estimate of 235,000 alcoholics in England and Wales, and a 'high' estimate of 600,000, and since has revised this estimate to an even higher figure of 750,000. Many indicators show alcoholic problems to be many and growing. National Health Service admissions to psychiatric hospitals for treatment of alcoholism have increased twenty-five fold over the past twenty years. The Blennerhassett Committee on drinking and driving estimated the cost of road traffic accidents due to drinking must be about £100,000,000 each year. These are just some indications of the social costs of drinking. Any government must wish to lessen the incidence of alcoholic problems.

A QANTAS Airways manager,[9] wishing to justify recruitment of six extra staff for the summer months, set out his objectives and purpose as the first paragraph of his paper:

> This is a submission for the employment of up to six Summer Temporary Ticket Officers to work in the Sales Services Department, in either Piccadilly or Strand Ticket Offices, or in the Agency Servicing area, depending on need. These staff would work approximately $37\frac{1}{2}$ hours per week between 1 May and 31 October, which would work out at a total hours figure of 6,075. As in previous years, once an hours figure has been agreed, one has the flexibility to deploy staff to best effect, and again subject to demand.

2   What terms of reference have been given?   Any particular approach to the problem to be taken by the report must be stated at the outset. These are likely to have been given by the authority for whom the report has been prepared:

> . . . in the light of the proposed closure of the Birmingham offices. . . .

or

> . . . as modified by the Finance Act 1982. . . .

The Manpower Services Commission *Open Tech Task Group Report*[10] gives these terms of reference:

> The Task Group worked to the following terms of reference: Taking account of the responses to the Consultative Document and the consequent suggestions made to the Commission, the Group will complete its work on June 1982 and make detailed recommendations to the MSC on the management and direction of the Open Tech Programme for its first four years of operation.

3   What limitations there may have been on the treatment of the subject   If the treatment of the subject as described in the title is subject to any restrictions, these must be shown in the introduction. Not only should the limitations be given, but also the reasons:

> This report does not cover the current financial year, as figures are not yet available.

or

> . . . excluding our exports to Italy which are the subject of another report.

An Engineering ITB report explained a limitation on its treatment of its subject in these terms:

> The telecommunications equipment manufacturing industry is concerned particularly with the telephone system, including public and private switching equipment, transmission equipment and subscriber apparatus. It is important to note that this classification concerns the manufacture of telecommunications equipment and therefore does not include The Post Office itself or other aspects of telecommunication.[11]

This may be expressed more positively, as in the Cabinet Office's *Industrial Innovation:*

> In this report we have restricted ourselves essentially to an examination of the innovative process, and the manner in which it has operated in Britain compared to other countries.[12]

The limitations are essentially complementary to the terms of reference. Between them they will point out the approach taken by the report.

4   What sources have been used   It may be that the number of other reports and papers to which reference has been made are too numerous to describe in the introduction. It will then be appropriate to list them in an attachment. On the other hand, if the report makes continual reference to two or three other papers, Acts of

Parliament or sets of safety regulations these should be mentioned:

> Comparisons are made with the report for 1982.

This will enable the reader to have the specified report at hand to explore the comparisons in greater depth. Perhaps the report has been prepared in accordance with the specifications of some other document:

> The Health and Safety Commission directed the Health and Safety Executive to carry out an investigation and submit a special report in accordance with Section 14(2)(a) of the Health and Safety at Work etc. Act 1974.[13]

If any sampling has been done, this should be described:

> To gain an impression of the attitudes and experience of operators of the new office technologies we distributed one hundred self-completion questionnaires through management, trade union and independent contacts to word processing operators and other workers who used office computer terminals, e.g. data entry clerks. We did not restrict the distribution to women workers since we felt that the views of male operators in similar jobs were just as relevant. The questionnaire is shown at Annex A. We received 51 completed replies. Characteristics of the respondents are shown in Annex B.[14]

The questionnaires themselves would then be shown in attachments; or,

> The report covers a sample of 1 in 20.

A particularly clear and helpful statement of sources occurs in the' Trustee Savings Bank's *Economic Trends No. 4:*[15]

> The forecasts used in compiling this section include Phillips & Drew, de Zoete & Bevan (Stockbrokers) and the Treasury. The National Institute Review has not been included because it was published prior to the budget and although the London Business School figures are included in the tables, they arrived too late to be incorporated in the commentary.

5 Method of working In technical papers the method of working would be explained in a similar way. An outline of work done may suffice, with detailed work being laid out in an attachment.

In the Communications Studies and Planning Ltd/Equal Opportunities Commission report, *Information Technology in the Office: the Impact of Women's Jobs*, there is a sub-paragraph to the introduction:

> 1.4   Method
> The source material for this report was gathered by means of:
> - a literature review plus interviews with specialists in the electronic office field
> - self-completion questionnaires from 51 users of word processing and office computer terminals
> - case studies of ten organizations using new technology[16]

The *Open Tech Task Group Report* produces important information of this type under a heading 'Procedures' in its introduction:

> Between January and June 1982 we held six plenary meetings. To concentrate and progress our work and to utilise fully the knowledge, expertise and interests of all our members we also met regularly in three groups, which considered separate aspects of our remit.
>
> These sub-groups examined:
> a.   the identification of needs, initial priorities and criteria for selecting projects:
> b.   the management structure and operational and funding arrangements for the Programme;
> c.   criteria, systems and procedure required to secure quality, evaluation. . .[17]

and so on through their investigations with the help of submissions from here and there, advice from Government departments and the handling of the plenary sessions.

6 *Warning of recommendations* It is sometimes helpful to warn readers that a recommendation or two will be made at the end of the report. That is not to say the recommendations themselves should feature in the introduction. It could just be something such as:

> This paper will recommend ways of reducing this shortfall.

The authors of the *Open Tech Task Group Report* spell out their intentions more specifically. After they have explained their terms of reference, they go on:

> . . . To this end the Group will recommend
> 1. criteria in selecting, initiating and funding projects;
> 2. priority needs and opportunities;
> 3. initial projects, including any on which implementation can commence immediately;
> 4. guidelines for the management of the Programme as a whole;
> 5. means of:
>   — ensuring satisfactory objectives (including qualifications where appropriate) and standards of materials, delivery and support arrangements;
>   — effectively meeting publicity, information and teacher training requirements;
>   — securing an ongoing review and evaluation of the Programme.[18]

Sequence of introduction

The aspects discussed in the forgoing paragraphs are all included in the example, but they do not, of course, all fall out in the regimented sequence described above. Indeed there will be quite a lot of overlap. One or two other items, which are not usual and so have not been described above, may be relevant in particular cases (see the example below).

An overview of the introduction to the Health and Safety Executive report, PWR[19] on the generic safety issues of pressurised water reactors may be helpful. It is a straightforward 8-paragraph introduction to a 369-paragraph report and its analysis is shown in Figure 26.

In a very simple internal report, the introduction might just consist of four lines, such as that shown in Figure 27 from an Argos supervisor.[20] Section 2, however, of this report was a more detailed statement of objectives (see Figure 28). For consistency, Objective 5 should start with an infinitive: 'To provide a more compact . . .'. The split infinitive, which may have irritated a reader or two, will be discussed in Chapter 8. (Anyone who did not notice the split infinitive need not waste time hunting for it, as obviously it has not done any harm.)

Main body of the report

The main body, or meat, of the report will, of course, be divided up into easily digestible chunks. It is neither necessary or helpful to surmount it by a heading 'Discussion' or 'Argument'. It needs a series each of which will be the peer of the Introduction.

The QANTAS report in which the manager was justifying his six extra summer staff developed the argument in several short logically sequenced paragraphs. The headings were these (Piccadilly and Strand are QANTAS' principal points of sale in London):

HISTORY
PICCADILLY
STRAND
AGENCY-SERVING
WORKLOAD
TICKETS ISSUED
PASSENGERS SEEN (including refunds)
RETURNING PASSENGER SERVICING
TOTAL TRAVELLED
WEEKLY REPORTS
OTHER FACTORS
TRAVELLED REVENUE
ELIMINATION OR COMBINATION OF WORK
OVERTIME
ANALYSIS OF NEED
PENALTIES
ALTERNATIVES
PRODUCTIVITY IMPROVEMENTS
COSTS

Sometimes instead of just paragraphs, the report's main body can take the form of a number of formally numbered sections. For instance, the Argos report just discussed goes on into four sections:[21]

Section No.	Description
3	Remote Terminal Operations
4	The Office
5	Proposed Site
6	The Cost

The precise layout will be dictated by the subject. In a simple internal report dealing with stock adjustment, a very basic layout of the discussion such as that shown in Figure 29 from Warner-Lambert (Eastleigh)[22] may suffice. In more substantial reports the sections may be dignified by the title of 'Chapter' as in Lord Bullock's *Industrial Democracy*:[23]

Chapter 1: Introduction
Chapter 2: Size and shape of the private sector
Chapter 3: The pressures for change

and so on. A Building Research Establishment report, *Bracknell and Its Migrants*,[24] on the problems and achievements of a new town proceeds from its introduction into

Chapter 1: The development of Bracknell as a new town
Chapter 2: The nomination system and growth of new town firms
Chapter 3: Socio-Economic characteristics of inward migrants

There may be a need for further sub-division: *Industrial Democracy* is broken down as shown in Figure 30. Of course such sub-divisions need not be uniform. Some sections of the report may call for sub-division, while with others it is not necessary.

Paragraph	Actual (or outline) content of para	Function in introduction
1	The White Paper (Cmnd 5695) published in July, 1974, entitled 'Nuclear Installations Inspectorate' (NII) had been asked to bring to a conclusion their studies on the Generic Safety Issues of Light Water Reactors.	Reason for and background to report
2	Two basic concepts of Light Water Reactors are commercially available, the Boiling Water Reactor (BWR) and the Pressurised Water Reactor (PWR). This review has concentrated on the latter version, that is the PWR, since it is this type of reactor in which the CEGB has declared an interest.	Limitations
3	This report, which is a summary of a more detailed technical report, sets out the main considerations and conclusions arising from the study of the generic aspects of PWR safety conducted by the Nuclear Installations Inspectorate following publication of the 1974 White Paper.	Status

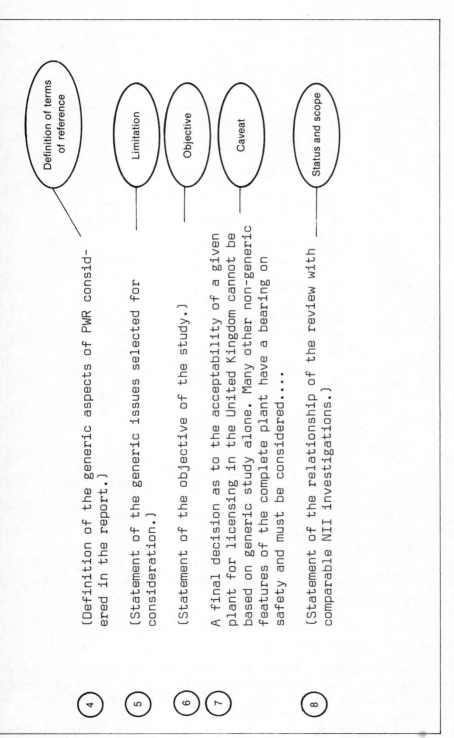

Figure 26 *Analysis of the introduction to a report*

```
Section 1: INTRODUCTION

This report is designed to emphasise the necessity for a
two-terminal remote operational office for the computerised
Stock Location System. To be sited in the Random Storage Area
for Green Shield Merchandise within the Daventry Warehouse
Complex.
```

Figure 27 *Example of a brief introduction*

```
Section 2: THE OBJECTIVES

The objects of the project can be summarised as follows:

1. To improve certain aspects of the system.
2. To improve the efficiency of the Random Store Operation.
3. To reduce the time and labour aspect of the auditing
   function in this area.
4. To vastly improve the environment in respect of working
   conditions for the operators and auditors within the
   area.
5. A more compact, efficient and manageable unit.
```

Figure 28 *Detailed statement of objectives*

```
1. PRESENT SITUATION AND BACKGROUND: BULK TABLETS

   (Problem is described in nine introductory lines)

   Alternative 1
   Comments
   Alternative 2
   Comments
   Alternative 3
   Comments

2. PRESENT SITUATION AND BACKGROUND: BULK BACKGROUND:
   PART-FINISHED STOCK

   (Problem and two solutions are described in six
   introductory lines)

   Solution 2
   Comments
```

Figure 29 *Basic layout of discussion*

Alternative arrangements of the main body

The mechanics for arranging the material in this way are covered in Chapter 10. One further facet of the design of the main body should, however, be considered here. The same information can be presented in several ways. A report on choice of a secure delivery system will serve as an example.

Suppose that a company with several London and a number of provincial offices is looking for a new contractor to deliver confidential papers to these establish-

Contents of the Main Report

	Page
Chapter 1: Introduction	1
Written and oral evidence	1
Terms of reference	1
Study of European experience	2
Organisation of our report	2
Chapter 2: Size and shape of the private sector	4
Enterprises and employment	4
Trade union membership	10
Unionisation in relation to size of establishments and enterprises	11
Number and size of unions	16
Chapter 3: The pressures for change	20
Industrial and economic changes	20
Social changes	22
Trade union and legislative developments	23
Developments in Europe	24
Conclusion	25
Chapter 4: The main proposals before the Committee	26
The TUC position	26
EEC policy	28
The CBI proposal	30

Figure 30 *Table of contents for Industrial Democracy (part)*

ments. Various companies submit proposals: Shaw Deliveries, WHA Parcels, Lamb Express, Marvell Ltd. Certain criteria must be applied to them: cost, speed of delivery, working hours, the size of parcels they can carry and (in as far as it can be disentangled from the semantic jungles of their propositions) the reliability of the contending firms.

Is it best to examine each company in turn or each criterion? The former is generally to be preferred – see Figure 31. It enables the reader to focus on one company at a time. The alternative, see Figure 32, focuses on one characteristic at a time. This is likely to be harder to follow. The reader can easily bear in mind the features of performance required, e.g. delivery must be next day and the company must have London offices open 24 hours a day. These will be related to everyday

```
SHAW DELIVERIES
  Cost
  Speed
  Working hours
  Size of parcels
  Reliability

WHA PARCELS
  Cost
  Speed
  Working hours
  Etc.
  Etc.

ETC.
```

Figure 31 *One company at a time*

```
COST
  Shaw Deliveries
  WHA Parcels
  Lamb Express
  Marvell Ltd

SPEED
  Shaw Deliveries
  WHA Parcels
  Lamb Express
  Marvell Ltd

ETC.
```

Figure 32 *One characteristic at a time*

	SHAW DELIVERIES	WHA PARCELS	LAMB EXPRESS	MARVELL LTD
COST				
SPEED				
WORKING HOURS				
SIZE OF PARCELS				
RELIABILITY				

Figure 33   *Tabulation to give comparative results*

practicalities which he understands. However, the names of the competing companies are new to him. If the information about them is spread under four or five headings he will have to make frequent cross-reference in order to clear his mind on the performance of one company.

It is easier, therefore, to deal with one company at a time and to pass the requirements in front of each. It may, if course, be suitable to set the whole thing out as a table (see Figure 33), provided accurate and precise wording is not sacrificed to symbolised generalisations. This type of presentation – and its limitations – is explored in detail as part of the treatment of tabulations in Chapter 9.

One more point should be made before leaving the parcel delivery example. If a fifth company, say Swift Packages, submitted information which showed it to be thoroughly unsatisfactory, should it be considered in the comparative process? Unless one of the competitors stands out as being absolutely ideal, all the possibilities should be included. The reader will need detailed comparisons in order to clear his mind. All feasible answers should therefore be shown. If there is no case whatsoever to be made for Swift Packages (perhaps because it is 50 per cent too expensive or it has failed to submit enough information) it could be eliminated at the very beginning. This should then be stated as a limitation in the introduction and no further mention be made of Swift Packages. However this will be an exceptional step. If there is even the remotest possibility of choosing an option it must be kept in the comparative process.

Layout of routine reports

If a report is submitted regularly and the content is likely to follow a similar pattern on every occasion, a standard format should be evolved for the main body of the report. This will ensure uniformity and enable comparisons to be made as a check on progress.

Direct supervision of the routine work and administration of the Centre for British Teachers in Malaysia is the responsibility of Regional Project Directors, former Centre teachers with experience of the peninsula. Their areas may cover several hundreds of square miles. The body of the reports which they submit monthly to their Director[25] in Kuala Lumpur is laid out under a heading of Duties, as a diary. The entries are of variable length. Days of travel are also included. Important, difficult or confidential visits are then supplemented by separate Visit Reports to which cross-reference is made in the main report.

The Middle East office of Sentipharm AG in Athens is responsible for promotion and sale of the group's pharmaceutical products throughout the East Mediterranean (Greece, Syria, Egypt, Saudi Arabia and elsewhere). The geographical diversity and size of the area makes consistency of reporting particularly important. The promotional cycles for their products are therefore reported under the headings shown in Figure 34.

Conclusions

The purpose of the conclusions of a report is to set out the answer to the question posed by the report. Conclusions may, of course, have special interpretation in recommendations.

The difference between the two is an important one. Conclusions draw the threads together from the foregoing argument. Recommendations suggest steps that should be taken to improve the situation. Any reader who does not completely understand this vital distinction must compare the examples given under this heading with those under 'Recommendations'.

In the main body of the report, the different facets of the problem will have been examined discretely in isolation. In a report on area sales staffs, North-West, North-East, Wales, etc., will all have been examined separately. No comparison will be made of one area with another. This ensures that the order in which the areas are treated does not prejudice the argument.

In the conclusions it is appropriate to make the comparisons which have been avoided up to that point. For instance the report might reveal a staffing shortfall at Bradford (covered in the section on the North-East region) and a surplus at Warrington (covered under the North-West). In the conclusion these two facts will be drawn together.

```
     I.   SALES REVIEW

    II.   CYCLE MEETING HIGHLIGHTS
          Previous cycle
          New cycle

   III.   MARKET INFORMATION

          always including a subordinate heading:
          New laws and regulations affecting business

    IV.   INSTITUTIONAL BUSINESS

     V.   HEALTH REGISTRATION

    VI.   OTHER COMMENTS
```

Figure 34 *Outline of Sentipharm AG cycle report*

No new information may be added at this stage. Comment is, however, quite in order.

The Health and Safety Executive Bentley Colliery Report[26] provides some good examples. The main body examined events leading up to the accident, the accident itself, the recovery and so on. Then 11 conclusions are drawn from these several sections. For example:

> Parts of the track were inclined at gradients steeper than 1 in 15 contrary to the requirements of the Coal and other Mines (Locomotives) Regulations 1956 which prohibits. . . .

and

> The Godwin Warren arrestor had been deliberately defeated and could not, therefore, arrest the runaway. There had been previous experience of this arrestor successfully arresting runaway vehicles and there is no doubt that it could have done so in this incident.

Further good examples in which even more diverse main bodies are drawn together into some comprehensive conclusions are the Price Commission reports, for instance, the last on Whitbread and Company Ltd.[27] The sections cover company background, operational structure, management structure, tied houses, take-home sales and many other relevant aspects. Among the conclusions were:

> We examined the distribution of the company's products and the operation of its transport fleet and found that both were efficiently organised. Indeed, the company has been an innovator in efficient trailer design.[28]

and

> The company's profitability increased substantially in 1978–79 and was planned to increase by a further significant amount in 1979–80.

It must be noted, of course, that the conclusions are not an opportunity to restate how the writer has gone about his business. This temptation does arise and must be resisted. The first 15 words of the first Price Commission conclusion above are just a helpful lead into the result of the investigation.

It may be desirable to sub-divide the conclusions. Figure 35 shows those of a report by a major retail chain entitled *Identification and Development of Potential Branch Management*.[29] The views of all and sundry have been solicited on their experiences of a centre for the assessment of potential branch managers. In drawing the conclusions it is important to keep the points separate so that the originators can be identified.

A very satisfactory example of an informal conclusion is the last sentence of an article by Alan Gibson in *The Spectator*.[30] Brearley's captaincy of the England cricket team had ended and a successor was being sought. In his article of about 1,000 words Gibson examines in turn the suitability of Rose, Fletcher, Botham, Boycott, Willis and every other conceivable candidate. Then he ends:

> If it is thought that Botham is not ready for the job yet, and that Fletcher is a little beyond it when the bowling is so fast, there is a case for Rose.

Recommendations

It is sometimes suggested that conclusions are in the past and recommendations are in the future. While this is dreadfully simplistic, it may provide a valuable touchstone. If any comment does not concern the future, then it has no place in a recommendation.

CONCLUSION

DISTRICT MANAGERS VIEW

Where possible I have obtained views of the District Managers
familiar with Assessment Centres, (see Appendix v).

The District Managers all acknowledge having benefited in terms
of increased knowledge of trainees and an increased awareness of
assessment methods.

TRAINEE MANAGERS VIEW

The trainees have indicated they enjoy the experience and
through exposure learn more about management.

PERSONNEL MANAGERS VIEW

The Assessment Centres in operation have worked successfully.
They provide an information system which up to now has not
been available in reviewing a trainees performance over a concentrated
period of time rather than for short occasions over a period of
several years.

Using these two processes Branches Control are now in a position
to identify and train development areas at the very earliest
opportunity.

Figure 35 *Sub-division of conclusions*

Recommendations must follow directly and obviously from the conclusions. They should never surprise the reader. They should be brief and to the point. Very frequently one or two lines will suffice.

It is sometimes a helpful expedient for the writer to discipline himself to start every recommendation 'It is recommended . . .' or 'We recommend. . .'. This has two important effects:

1   It gives the recommendation directness and emphasis.
2   It ensures that the writer does not fill the recommendation with woolly justification which should be properly placed in the conclusions.

In the case of the staffing discrepancy between Bradford and Warrington described above, the comparison between the two would be made in the conclusions and a recommendation might read: 'It is recommended that six sales representatives be reallocated from Warrington to Bradford'.

It will be helpful to quote examples of recommendations that fell out of the Health and Safety Executive and Price Commission reports quoted in consideration of conclusions. First, in the case of Bentley Colliery:

> Manriding trains should be provided with effective means of signalling between the conductor and driver preferably with direct means of speech communication.[31]

and

> Tests of locomotive brakes should be carried out on a selected length of track clearly identified and marked, equivalent to that of the most onerous braking condition.[32]

In the case of the examination of Whitbread:

> We recommend pursuant to section 6(5)(6)(i) of the Price Commission Act 1977 that there should be no restriction on the notified weighted average increases in Whitbread's prices.[33]

and

> We recommend . . . that those prices and charges so increased should not be further increased during the period of 12 months beginning. . . .[34]

Sometimes it will be appropriate to temper a report with pragmatism. In the Bentley Colliery instance, two less forthright recommendations bring up the rear of the 11:

> Efforts should be made to modernise or replace older types of locomotives so that they conform to. . . .

The second is even more mindful of the constraints of realism:

> Consideration should be given to the more widespread use of locomotives such as the 'rack' and 'captive rail' types.

The Price Commission add an observation. This is a dangerous practice if attempted too freely as it can lead to the writer avoiding the main issue. (An observation is essentially something outside the main terms of reference.) However observations can be justified in moderation:

> We feel that Whitbread should re-examine its methods of financing capital expenditure, particularly where this is designed to secure new, tied outlets. We recognise that this observation might extend to the brewing industry as a whole.

Sometimes a writer might find it expedient to set out his recommendations in a slightly different way. Bogdanor in his National Council for Educational Standards report, *Standards in Schools*,[35] calls them 'Summary of Proposals' and expresses them:

1. Strengthen HM Inspectorate and re-institute cyclical inspections.
2. Secure a concensus between teachers, industrialists and government upon the skills with which schools should equip young people.
3. Establish standardised national tests for all children at the ages 9 and 13.
4. Require all local authorities to publish CSE, 'O' and 'A' level results. . . .

Exceptional structures

The framework shown in Figure 24 is the most usual, the most simple and, in most cases, the most logical structure for a report. It is therefore the one that is encouraged here and described in detail. However it would be naive to pretend and foolish to suggest that variations on this general theme were not sometimes used. Here are six examples of instances in which such variations have been used to good effect:

1 A Language for Life[36]   The background to Sir Alan Bullock's masterpiece on standards of English teaching has been described in Chapter 2. After 510 pages of detailed discussion (divided into nine parts: 'Attitudes and Standards', 'Language in the Early Years', 'Reading', and so on) Part 10 is a 'Summary of Conclusions and Recommendations'. Almost all of this section is a summary of every part of every group of two or three paragraphs. Sometimes individual paragraphs are given a three-line summary in this way. For example, Paragraph 20.8[37] of the main paper (which goes on for almost a page) is summarised:

> Schools with pupils of West Indian origin should look for opportunities to draw upon the support that parents and community can give and should acquire a knowledge of the Caribbean and its culture.[38]

Before these 333 paragraphs of summary, 17 items are picked out as 'Principal Recommendations'. Bullock does this with great reluctance as is explained when he describes the logic of his approach:

> We have chosen to present our conclusions and recommendations in a manner which requires some explanation. The form in which they are set out constitutes a summary of the Report, and it was with reluctance that we singled out a smaller number as representing our principal recommendations. Our reason for this reluctance was that we have been opposed from the outset to the idea that reading and the use of English can be improved in any simple way. . . . We are anxious that the complete summary, and the Report it represents, should be read as a whole, for it would be altogether misleading to take these 17 (principal) recommendations) as a distillation of what we have to say.[39]

2 The Brixton Disorders, 10–12 April 1981[40]   Quite a common practice is to itemise recommendations as they arise during the argument. In Lord Scarman's report on Brixton the recommendations pop up all over the place during the discussion of his investigations, as:

> There is nevertheless a need for the development of more effective channels of communication between the Metropolitan Police and the various communities it serves. The urgent need, in my view, is at the level of the London Borough. I am aware that in recent years the Commissioner has been seeking to develop, with your encouragement, liaison machinery at Borough level on a voluntary basis. The difficulty about voluntary arrangements – as the experience of Brixton amply demonstrates – is that they depend too much on willingness of all parties to participate: if, for any reason, a local difficulty prompts one of the parties to withdraw, the arrangement collapses and discussion stops. I therefore

recommend that a statutory framework be developed to require local consultation between the Metropolitan Police and the community at Borough or Police District level.[41]

It is important to note that the word 'recommend' is italicised wherever it appears – so that the recommendations are remarkably easy to pick out – and the whole lot are pulled together in a 'Summary of Findings and Recommendations' at the end.[42]

3 Health and Safety Executive: The explosion at Cardowan Colliery The Cardowan Colliery report adds a step, 'Consideration of the Conclusions', between the very short conclusions:

> From the evidence obtained during the investigation and from witnesses it was concluded that a plug of firedamp was forced into the V52 main gate from the South West Main Mine when two sections of auxiliary ventilation duct were connected together for a short time. The gas was diluted in the V52 District air current to a concentration a little above the lower explosive limit and passed through the face as a plug of firedamp and air. It was ignited by frictional sparking from the pricks of the shearer loader as the drum cut in the sandstone floor and the resultant explosion spread through the face and into both gates.[43]

and the highly functional recommendations such as:

> It is recommended that:
> (1) during a period when the ventilation is cut off from a heading, and particularly in the period leading up to the dispersal of accumulations of firedamp, officials and workmen are fully briefed as to the need for care . . .

and so on. There are 17 paragraphs of 'Consideration or conclusions'. These act as stepping stones between the generalities of the conclusions and the specifics of the recommendations.

4 Manpower Services Commission Reports of the Training of Trainers Committee[44] These two reports (24 and 32 pages long, respectively) state their entire findings under the generic heading 'Conclusions and Recommendations'. These are then sub-divided into the various subject matters. Both reports have an introduction from the chairman of the Training of Trainers Committee. Background and approach are also described.

The extensive conclusions and recommendations are preceded by a one-page 'Summary of Recommendations' which is cross-referenced to the more detailed treatment in every case.

5 TSB Central Board (Computer Division): Unipay: Future Developments[45] This report prepared and circulated within TSB follows the layout shown in Figure 36. The report examines the Unipay data capture system which TSB Central Board used and explains in outline how data might be captured in future. The facts of the (10-page) report are so simple and the conclusions are so clear that they are quite legitimately tucked away as two sentences leading into the recommendations.

6 Johnson Matthey Chemicals technical report The author of a technical report may also be justified in telescoping the end of the report in a similar way. In this example (see Figure 37) from Johnson Matthey Chemicals the experimental work is logically and chronologically traced through Sections 2.0 to 5.0. The results are then discussed in Section 6.0 which means that conclusions and recommendations can be combined into one section.

The temptation to amalgamate conclusions and recommendations is widespread and in anything more complex than this 10-page technical report it is to be resisted.

UNIPAY - FUTURE DEVELOPMENTS

CONTENTS

Para	Title	Page
1	Introduction	1
2	Current System	2
3	Future Data Capture	4
4	Unipay Reports	10
5	Recommendations	11

Figure 36 *Simplified structure: TSB report*

```
1.0  Introduction
2.0  Sweeps examined
3.0  Sampling procedure
4.0  Observations on material handling characteristics, etc.
5.0  Statistical treatment of results
6.0  Results and discussion
7.0  Conclusions and recommendations
```

Figure 37 *Technical report contents*

Management consultants often do it. The logic of the argument, which is crystal clear to the writer, will be lost on the reader in this way.

It cannot be stressed too strongly that these are exceptional structures. They are included to illustrate reasonable departures from the conventional approach at Figure 24. Such structural adventures should only be undertaken with good reason and if the writer is confident that it is not going to disturb the flow of his argument.

Embellishments to the three parts of the report

So much for the three fundamental constituents of the report; but various trimmings are now necessary to make the basic report more presentable.

Signature

All reports must have some sort of signature. In many organisations initials will suffice for internal reports. The TSB report just discussed[46] bears the initials and reference:

```
3160/12
KL
```

at the bottom left-hand corner of the cover sheet.

External documents produced by a professional firm will be signed by the name of the practice thus indicating joint responsibility for the partnership:

```
Yours faithfully
PRICE WATERHOUSE
```

Precise authorship (for guidance within the issuing firm) will be denoted by the reference.

A document produced by a committee will frequently bear the names of the whole committee somewhere at the front.[47] Possibly this will be at the foot of the introductory section or possibly on a separate sheet.

Typewritten documents carry a manuscript signature. In such cases it is important that the author's name, and usually appointment, should be typed underneath.

```
David Guard
Project Director
```

Some companies may have special signature requirements, such as the need for countersignature. Companies that are part of non-British groups may be subject to the laws or commercial law of other countries, e.g. German requires two signatures.

A few companies permit, or encourage, the issue of anonymous reports. There seems to be little to be said for this mischievous and unhelpful practice.

Date

A date must appear somewhere on the report. This serves two essential purposes:
1   It is a means (in addition to the reference) of distinguishing the document from others of similar title.
2   It identifies the moment at which the report's comments are timed.

The time taken to prepare the report and the period it covers will suggest how precisely the date should be given. The great majority of reports will be timed to the day. Government Green and White Papers are usually dated to the month. A few documents, such as Civil Service College Occasional Papers[48] are dated to the year. On the other hand, shift reports, representing one of perhaps three shifts in a day, will be timed to the minute.

It would be dreary to catalogue all the different ways in which a date may be expressed. However a word of caution is appropriate about all-figure dates such as:

```
5. 1. 1984
```

which would be interpreted as 5 January by a British reader and 1 May by an

American. The month should be written in full if even one copy is being sent to an American addressee.

With reports dated to the day there may be merit in inserting the date in ink. The month and year would be typed and the date inserted when the report is signed. This is a particularly good idea if there is a delay between typing and signature, as when:
1 The typing is done elsewhere.
2 The author's work is peripatetic so that he may be away from his office for some days.

What matters is the day on which the writer authorises the document and associates himself formally with its contentions. The date on which the typist chanced to type the date block is of little consequence and of no interest to the reader.

Acknowledgements

Many reports involve assistance from outside the originating organisation. Acknowledgement must be made for this assistance. Sometimes it will appear as part of an introduction. Often, if the assistance has come from many different sources, it will be necessary to put aside a separate section to do justice to this.

In the Arts Council report on the Lyric Theatres,[49] a section was given to this at the front – see Figure 38.

In other cases such as the report of the Court of Inquiry into the Flixborough

In the compiling of this report I had the assistance of two Arts Council Officers – Angus Stirling, Deputy Secretary-General, and John Cruft, Music Director – and two Officers of the Greater London Council – CJA Whitehouse OBE, Controller of Operational Services, and DG Riggs, Treasurers' Department.

For the compilation and processing of the survey we are greatly indebted to Mrs. Christine Craig, Department of Economics, Cambridge.

I must express my gratitude to all the people who took the trouble to submit evidence, either in writing, or in person, and not all of whom are referred to by name though the benefit of what they had to say has strengthened the validity of the report.

Nicholas Payne of the Finance Department at the Arts Council has been most helpful in assembling financial tables and I must express my special thanks to Hilary Pugh, who acted throughout as Secretary of the Enquiry, and enabled us to put the report into its present state despite the ramifications suggested and the great pressure on her from her other work.

Wynne Godley

Figure 38 *Form of acknowledgements*

disaster[50] it appears at the end:

> We would finally like to acknowledge the assistance we received from a great number of people. It is not possible to list everybody but we would mention specially the following:
>
> 1. The parties represented before us together with their Counsel, Solicitors and expert advisers.
> 2. The witnesses both lay and expert.
> 3. Sir Frederick Warner, his staff and associates . . .

and so on for a list of 11 bodies, some described generally and some named specifically.

It is most important that the form of words should reflect in some measure the amount of help received. It should not become stereotyped and, thus, stale.

Summary

Even the simplest report will have three parts. An introduction will set the scene, state the need and whet the reader's appetite. The main body of the report will develop the arguments and explain any alternative courses of action. The conclusions will draw the threads together and recommendations will suggest future courses of action in as concise and direct language as possible.

A table of contents may help the reader to find his way around the report if it is disparate or complex. A logical system of headings and a sequence of paragraph numbers will assist him in referring to it.

The conclusions and recommendations are the end-product of the report-writing process. They must be lucid and as brief as is commensurate with accuracy. Nevertheless they must be supported by a logical discussion section and an introduction to set the scene.

CHAPTER FIVE

Forewords, summaries, appendices and other attachments

So, the construction and layout of the basic core of the report is simple and uncomplicated. However, various facts of life combine to make matters a bit more difficult. For example:

1 Someone who has commissioned or authorised the report may want to say something at the front. So a 'Foreword' is added.

2 If a committee has compiled the report, some writers may disagree with the findings. If the terms of reference allow it, a minority report is then included.

3 Not everyone who reads the report will have the time – or inclination – to read the whole thing. A summary may therefore be necessary. Indeed, the skills of abstract writing are discussed in a later chapter. Here it is just appropriate to think about the need.

4 In a large number of reports, some of the writer's findings or deliberations will not be essential to an understanding of his argument or to acceptance of his conclusions. Yet this information may be sufficiently relevant to be incorporated in the report. This is done in the form of attachments. Terminology varies as to their description: annexes, appendices and so on.

5 Detailed fieldwork will sometimes be included in the main body. However, very often the work will be so detailed that it will be impracticable to include more than the principal findings in the central part of the report. The minutiae will therefore be relegated to a separate section at the end.

6 Perhaps the reader will wish to pursue some aspects of the subject in greater detail than the author has done, using his sources. A bibliography or reference section will assist in this endeavour.

7 Some expressions may call for explanation by footnote.

In this way the mainstream of a report is supplemented by a number of adjuncts which may be weighted more or less heavily than the core report. This is shown diagrammatically in Figure 39. Any of the deviations from the main heavy horizontal line distract the reader and should be added only when essential.

Foreword

Like the rest, a foreword is a distraction. It should be as brief as possible. A foreword can be justified:

1 To add authority to a report as in the Secretary of State's Foreword to *A Language for Life*:[1]

This report deserves to be widely read. All our education depends on the understanding and effective use of English as does success in so many aspects of adult life.

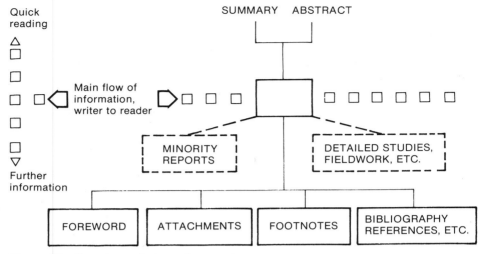

Figure 39 *Supplements to main report*

The Report concerns all who have responsibilities in education. Many recommendations are addressed to schools and teachers and call for a change of approach and redirection of effort rather than for additional resources. As the Committee acknowledges, recommendations with financial implications must be subject to current constraints; for the time being action on those which would involve additional resources must be postponed. Within this limitation I hope that local authorities and teachers at all levels will look carefully at the recommendations which concern them, as my Department will at those which concern the Government.

We are all greatly indebted to Sir Alan Bullock and his colleagues. They have given us an authoritative statement which will be of value as a basis for further discussion and development for many years to come.

DECEMBER 1974   REG PRENTICE

Indeed it has been a basis for such further discussion.

2   To clarify the terms of reference by allusion to the circumstances which prompted its commission. Figure 40 shows the Foreword to the Chemical & Allied Products ITB Strategy Document 1977/82[2] which achieves this purpose.

Minority reports

As will often be the case with forewords, minority reports will usually be confined to exceptionally detailed studies. Minority reports are likely to be confined to those subjects on which there is a disagreement on matters of principle. However, when they are included they are often very important to the balance of the report.

Authoritative commentators may have been asked to examine a subject. The fact that there are several members of the committee indicates the complexity of the subject. Therefore a minority view deserves preservation.

The *Report of the Committee of Inquiry on Industrial Democracy*[3] included a substantial self-contained minority report with its own table of contents and appendices. This minority report demonstrates a number of important points. After several meetings of the committee it became clear that the management members

Foreword

Each year the Board up-dates its
Strategy to respond to the needs of
the Industry it serves. The Industry
itself plays a major role in
development of this Strategy through
detailed and wide-ranging discussions
with Senior representatives from
Employers, Trade Unions and
Education.
   This booklet is about the future
manpower scene in the UK Chemical
Industry and the consequent Strategy
for the Board for 1977/82.
   It is more than a mere description of
what CAP/ITB intends to do
   ● it emphasises the way in which
     its activities relate to the needs
     of every firm
   ● it suggests how individual firms
     can use the booklet in helping to
     assess their own training needs.
   We hope, therefore, that the booklet
will be widely circulated and read by
firms and will also be of value to
Trade Unions, Education and other
bodies who each have a part to play
in ensuring that the UK Chemical
Industry continues its major role in
contributing to the National well-being.

[signature] Chairman

[signature] Director

Figure 40 *Example of a foreword*

(Mr N. P. Biggs of Williams & Glyn's Bank, Sir Jack Callard of ICI and Mr Barrie Heath of Guest, Keen & Nettlefolds) would never agree with the findings of the remainder. They took issue with the remit which required them 'to consider *how* such an extension (of the Board of Directors) can best be achieved' not *whether* 'a radical extension of industrial democracy'[4] should be achieved in this way. They considered their terms of reference 'far from satisfactory or even wise'.[5] Lord Bullock insisted that they produce a minority report within the covers of the majority's findings. If this had not been done, he would have failed in the task he had been given. Furthermore he held to the rules which do not permit a minority to read the majority report before writing their own document. A minority report must be:

1 Part of the main report.
2 Written within the same terms of reference as the majority view and not as a critique of the main report.

The report also contains a note of dissent by one member, Mr Nicholas Wilson. He was a member of the main committee who disagreed on a few – albeit to him – important matters.

   Minority reports and notes of dissent will be less common in internal management reports. However, the same important principles of discipline must be respected. The reports or notes must be presented as part of the main paper. They must be written in parallel with and at the same time as the majority view and within the same terms of reference. A minority report must never be a destructive criticism of the main document.

Summaries

Many companies have established the rule that all reports must be surmounted by a summary or even a 'reader's *(sic)* synopsis' (as though the rest of the report was written for the benefit of the writer). If the reader is not going to read the rest of the report, who is? This policy is based on the view that the reader is likely to be very busy. Indeed he may be so, although sometimes *busy* is a euphemism for a less charitable epithet.

Nevertheless, it must be accepted that in some cases not everyone who handles a report is going to have time to read every word. So companies who do use summary sheets will certainly ensure that the most important points are apparent to the superficial reader. Certain dangers must be noted:

1 Under no circumstances should the summary be drafted until every word of the report has been written. Otherwise the writer is in danger of justifying his summary in the report.
2 Not one jot of information or description which is not in the main body must be included in the summary.
3 Most important, the summary should not regurgitate the introduction, conclusions and recommendations. The reader could – or should be able to (if the report is well structured and clearly labelled) – find these for himself.

A very good summary appears at the front of the Chemical & Applied Products ITB Strategy paper discussed in the section on Forewords. It is one page long and is shown in Figure 41. This is indeed a helpful summary. It sets out both the rationale of the paper and also gives an idea of the structure and arrangement of the complicated information that follows.

Summary

The Board's Strategy 1977/82 to respond to the future needs of the Industry has been developed by an extensive review and consultative process involving some 300 senior representatives of Employers, Trade Unions and Education.

The future needs of the Industry are presented in the form of 'Trends influencing the Chemical Industry 1977/82' and a Scenario 1982, both of which incorporate data from Chemicals EDC.

The Strategy calls for a wider role for the Board than hitherto–concerned not only with training effectiveness but also such matters as the future requirements of skilled manpower within the Industry as part of the economy and helping firms in the Industry to cope with the changes in manpower policies arising from economic, social, legislative and technological pressures. This is reflected in a redefinition of the Board's Overall and Strategic Aims which confirm that the Board's main thrust will continue to be directed primarily to provide support to individual firms.

Nine key areas (MISSIONS) have been identified to which the Board should focus its activities over the 1977/82 period. Those of high priority include Manpower Development Planning, Relations at Work, Health and Safety, Export/Commercial Performance and Transition from Education to Industry.

There are many more opportunities open to the Board than could be pursued realistically within its resource levels which will not significantly change over the five year period.

The Strategy presented in matrix form, includes Key targėts and indicates the changing priorities of Key activities.

The Strategy for the 1977/82 period is comprehensive and demanding. Its successful implementation will depend on:-

i the Board having the ability to assess both its progress and the continuing relevance of its Strategies to prevailing conditions
ii the ability of the Board to develop and match its manpower resources to the changing demands of the Plan
iii working together with other external bodies, and in particular the Training Services Agency, all of whom are involved in pursuing various aspects of the strategies
iv securing the commitment of firms so that they accept responsibility for those aspects of the strategy relevant to their own needs.

The relevance of the Strategy to individual firms is described together with some suggestions to firms on how they might best take advantage of the Board services.

Figure 41 *Example of a summary*

Results at a Glance

£000	1981	1980
Turnover	91,869	88,697
Trading profit	5,648	5,789
Share of profit of associated companies	3,385	3,320
Profit before tax:		
United Kingdom and Europe	2,428	2,576
International	5,543	4,535
	7,971	7,111
Profit attributable to shareholders	3,811	4,281
Average capital employed	£45.4m	£38.4m
Return on capital employed	20%	24%
Earnings per share	16.5p	18.7p
Dividend per share	5.4p	5.2p
Assets per share	146p	133p
Number of shares in issue	26.8m	26.5m

Figure 42 *Example of results at a glance*

Other good examples of helpful and concise summaries can sometimes be found near the front of annual reports. Provided it is restricted to a modicum of salient information it will be a useful quick guide to the affairs of the reporting company. This will probably be about 12 lines and will comprise a simple comparison of the current and previous year's figures. For instance, Figure 42 shows 'Results at a Glance' from the British Vita annual report.[6]

With the more substantial reports, as of nationalised industries, greater detail would be acceptable. The figures in the NCB report[7] summary are supported by some 400 words of explanation. However such summaries should never exceed one page.

Organisations that make routine use of summaries often develop proformas for this purpose. These set out the salient points in a configuration to which the readers have become accustomed. Particularly excellent systems in this respect have been evolved by Shannon Free Airport Development Company. The company operates at Shannon in Co. Clare for the development of commerce in the area of Shannon Airport, the significance of which has diminished as aircraft ranges have increased.

Their precise structure will depend on the purpose of the report. However the blocked information at the head of the example which follows is common to all their

EXAMPLE III

MEETING:		AGENDA NO:
	INDUSTRIAL BUILDINGS & GRANTS COMMITTEE	4.2
		DATE OF MEETING:
		5/7/82
FROM:		REFERENCE:
	Small Industry Promotion Division	IH/416
		PREPARED BY:
		J. Fitzgerald
SUBJECT:		J Fitzgerald
	O'Leary Containers Ltd – Application for Grant and Accommodation Facilities	Project Officer
		DATE: 16/5/82

1. RECOMMENDATIONS

That the Committee approve the offer of the following facilities, subject to the conditions set out in Section 18:-

Buildings:

The lease of a 4,500 sq ft factory at Ballyfyne Industrial Estate for 25 years with rent reviews at 5 year intervals. The rent charged to be £1.80 per sq ft per annum for the existing 1,500 sq ft accommodation, and the remaining 3,000 sq ft building to be charged at the prevailing standard rental applying at the completion date of the additional 3,000 sq ft.

Grants:

(a)   A grant of 45% towards eligible expenditure on building modification, subject to a maximum grant of £900.

(b)   A grant of 45% towards the cost of eligible machinery and equipment, subject to a maximum grant of £31,500.

(c)   A rent reduction grant of 45% of the annual rental for the first three years of occupation of each factory unit.

(d)   A training grant in principle, the amounts to be determined in consultation with Anco.

RECOMMENDATION ENDORSED BY:-

F O'Loughlin   F O'LOUGHLIN, Section Manager.

Because of the particular location of this enterprise, I recommend the proposed support.

J Black   J BLACK, Division Manager.

Figure 43 *Summary sheet for a project appraisal report* reports for management committees. Figure 43 shows the layout suitable for the first page of one of their industrial project appraisal reports.[8] This page will be followed by a summary of the finances of the project concerned.

The report in Figure 43 makes definite recommendations. So these appear on the front sheet. All their reports over three pages long call for a synopsis at the front, whether they make recommendations or not. These may be up to half a page long, but sometimes it may be possible for it to be extremely brief.

A simple and very helpful form of this type of cover-sheet summary is found in the internal auditors' investigation reports of Coca-Cola Southern Bottlers. These are very thorough reports involving many detailed observations. The one-page summary sheet therefore sets out:

```
REASONS FOR INVESTIGATION
MAIN FINDINGS
MAIN RECOMMENDATIONS
ACTION:
        ALREADY TAKEN
        TO BE TAKEN
```

The semantics of this type of abbreviated description get a bit muddled. A summary of a different kind under the title 'Abstract' is found in the Communications Studies and Planning Ltd/Equal Opportunities Commission report, *Information Technology in the Office: The Impact on Women's Jobs.*[9] This just expands briefly on the table of contents to give a bit more guidance to the reader as to the content of the sections. This is helpful in the report in question, as it should be in Chapter 1 of this book.

Attachments

Attachments are a great deal more commonplace than the items described up to now. They are valuable ways of removing detail from a report. The more common terms for describing them are: Attachments; Appendices; Annexes; Enclosures; Exhibits (in American-controlled companies). These expressions are roughly synonymous and choice of term is largely a matter of house style. Enclosures, however, are generally taken to be documents which are complete in themselves, such as other reports or a section of an Act of Parliament. Quite possibly the letter or memorandum setting out the terms of reference might be added in this way.

Some systems use appendices as sub-divisions of annexes. Figure 44 shows an example of this. However, great care must be taken to ensure:
1 That such an elaborate system is justified before it is used.
2 That the appendices do stem from the annexes as is shown in this obvious geographical illustration.

Requirements for all attachments

With all attachments, however they may be described, four points must always be remembered;

1 Lettering or numbering They must be allocated letters (as in the case of the Communications Studies and Planning Ltd/Equal Opportunities Commission Ltd

```
Annex 1: Staff Strengths Scotland
         Appendix A: Glasgow staff by grade, sex and age
         Appendix B: Aberdeen staff by grade, sex and age
         Appendix C: Inverness staff by grade, sex and age

Annex 2: Staff Strengths Midlands
         Appendix A: Leicester staff by grade, sex and age
         Appendix B: Nottingham staff by grade, sex and age
         Etc.
         Etc.
```

Figure 44 *The use of appendices as sub-divisions of annexes*

report on women's employment discussed earlier[10]): Annex A, B, C, etc. Alternatively they may be given Arabic numbers as in the case of Health and Safety Executive reports or Manpower Services Commission reports. Some companies (such as Price Waterhouse, National Nuclear Corporation, Shannon Airport Development Company) use Roman Numbers.

Letters and Roman numerals have the advantage that they do not get muddled with paragraph numbers. However care should be taken with Roman numbering in reports with numerous attachments: many junior clerical staff are now unfamiliar with Roman numerals beyond those shown on a clock-face.

The letters (or numbers) must be allotted in the order in which they are mentioned in the text. This will enable the reader to keep moving his book-mark or thumb down through the attachments as he reads. The attempt which some writers make to allocate some spurious order of importance in the numbering of attachments is misleading and unhelpful.

2 Mentioning They must be mentioned in the report itself. They are essentially supplementary to the main core of the report. They may, perhaps, deal with specialist or esoteric matters. Thus as they sit on the fringe of affairs, if the reader's attention is not drawn to them, he may never get to see them.

This may be done by a note in brackets. A water-treatment consultancy report includes the sentence:

The tests we made (see appendix 1) indicate that more data is required, for it could be that the system is picking up hardness, from previously deposited scale.

It may be done by a complete sentence, as in the Communications Studies and Planning Ltd/Equal Opportunities Commission report:[11]

The questionnaire is shown in Annex A.

It may be somewhat more precise, as in the Flixborough disaster report:[12]

Many of the stainless steel pipes taken from the disaster site had suffered cracking due to a process of embrittlement caused by zinc. The zinc had come into contact with the steel whilst it was under stress and elevated temperature. The conditions under which such embrittlement can occur are described in Appendix II.

3 Listing They must be listed in or immediately after the table of contents. Figure 45 shows the list from an Organisation for Economic Co-operation and Development report on traffic control.[13]

If there is no list of contents they should be itemised at the foot of the report.

Figure 45 *Listing of appendices*

Apart from being a guide to the reader, such a list acts as an instruction to the functionary who staples or binds the report. Many report writers find this a tedious or tiresome measure. However, on many occasions, when this has not been done, the wrong bits and pieces have been appended to the report. In the list the attachments should be described minutely and precisely in their titles. This will include date and reference number where one exists, as in the Flixborough report:[14]

Appendix II Damage to the 8 inch pipe and related metallurgical investigations

or as in the Economic and Social Committee of the European Communities annual report:[15]

Annex B – List of Opinions drawn up by the Economic and Social Committee on its own initiative (1973–80)

It will also mention the scale and sheet title of a map or plan.

4 Independence of the report   The report must be able to stand on its own without the attachments. Figure 46 demonstrates this important point graphically. Consider Figure 46(a) as a schematic representation of the report and its attachments. It must be possible to start from the introduction, follow through the body, agree with the conclusions and accept the recommendations as in Figure 46(b) without reading the attachments as in Figure 46(c), unless the reader's whim or specialisation takes him there. For this purpose, it may be necessary to produce short two- or three-sentence summaries of the contents of the attachments. These summaries can then be insinuated into the main report so that it will stand on its own.

As attachments are so commonly used to remove detail it will be helpful to look at some information that two report producers have chosen to relegate to this position:

1 *Communication Studies and Planning Ltd/Equal Opportunities Commission report on Information Technology*[16]   This report, which has provided a number of useful examples for this chapter, has four annexes.
a A copy of a long (7-page) self-completion questionnaire, the results of which were an important part of the study.
b A numerical breakdown of those who completed the questionnaires into various categories.
c A basic factual description of 10 case studies.
d Prophesies on the labour force for the 1980s.

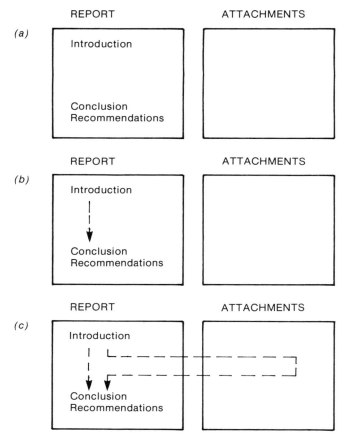

Figure 46 *Schematic representation of a report and its appendices*

2 *The Scarman Report*[17]   Lord Scarman has five appendices:
a A brief history of the inquiry, with particular reference to the visits to Brixton and other places, and the hearings.
b A detailed (13-page) description of Scarman's perigrinations around Brixton, Birmingham, Coventry, Liverpool and so on, and including the discussions which he had and the impressions made on him by social groups and individuals.
c A list of those giving evidence in various ways.
d A bibliography.
e A very detailed fold-out street map of Brixton showing every house.

Detailed fieldwork

In many cases detailed fieldwork will be set out as a series of attachments. The principal items will then be discussed in the main body of the report. The second of Lord Scarman's appendices is something along these lines. The point assumes greater significance in scientific reports.

In some reports the fine results of the research will be considered too important for relegation to the optional-extra status of an attachment. It may be considered absolutely germane to the argument.[18]

If there is any question of a series of reports, consistency is particularly important. Johnson Matthey Chemicals, the metallurgists, generally require all experimental work to appear in the main paper. They suggest the following material as suitable for appendices in this sort of work:

1 Results that are negative.
2 Unsatisfactory routes.
3 Side, or quasi-relevant, routes.
4 Associated relevant documents.
5 Duty specifications.

On the other hand, in non-scientific reports, a separate attachment explaining the method of working and sampling may be suitable. Such an example is the sole appendix, 'Method and tests of significance', to the 119-page Building Research Establishment report, *Bracknell and Its Migrants*.[19]

Bibliographies and reference lists

References may well take the form of one of the attachments, as has been demonstrated in the case of the Scarman report. However, their particular form of presentation calls for special mention.

References will be quoted in a report for two reasons:
1 As a courtesy to the source author.
2 To guide the reader in further investigation.

The amount of direction the reader needs must be borne in mind when the layout of the detail is devised. It may take the form of:

1 A list of books and reports just showing author/originator, date and publisher (if published) to which general reference has been made, thus:[20]

ENVIRONMENTAL POLLUTION, ROYAL COMMISSION ON. Firth report: air pollution control: an integrated approach. Cmnd 6371 [Chairman: Sir Brian Flowers] viii + 130 pp; HMSO (ISBN 0 10 163710 1)[20]

The page references here are just totals, i.e. 8 (viii) introductory pages and 130 proper pages.

Reference numbers are important:

(1) Department of the Environment, *File* WS/646/56 Paper SCA/4.41
(2) Hunt D T E, Filtration of Water Samples for Trace Metal Determinations, Water Research Centre *Technical Report* TR 104, 1979
(3) Department of the Environment, *File* WS/646/56, Paper SCA/4.4/2
(4) Standing Committee of Analysts, Atomic Absorption Spectrophotometry – an Essay Review, HMSO, London 1980[21]

Scarman[22] quoted 75 documents which had been 'available to the Inquiry', such as:

ALDERSON, John "Policing Freedom". McDonald and Evans, 1979.
ANDERTON, Bill "Police and Community: a review article" – in New Community, Vol. III, No 3, Summer 1974

2 A number of more detailed cross-references giving paragraph or even line:

Wright, P. Pointing the way to the ideal terminal. Computer Weekly, 20th September 1979, p. 24
AUEW (TASS) and National Computing Centre. Computer Technology and Employment. Manchester, 1979 p 105[23]

3 Sometimes the referencing may be taken a stage further, with the reference list including back references to the main paper

LAMBERT P (1976): Perinatal mortality: social and environmental trends $\underline{4}$ 4–8 (3.1.1)[24]

The 3.1.1 refers to the sub-sub-paragraph of the report alluding to the Lambert paper.

There are two ways of including mention of the referenced document in the main report.

(a) The name of the author and date is given in brackets in the text (the Harvard system), e.g.

> The test described here is essentially a modification of a technique described as applicable to the diagnosis of viral diseases (Bradstreet and Taylor 1962) and may be found particularly convenient in laboratories already undertaking viral complement fixation test.[25]

The full title is then shown in the reference list:

> Bradstreet & Taylor C.M.P. & Taylor CED (1962). Technique of complacent-fixation test applicable to the diagnosis of virus diseases. Monthly Bulletin of the Ministry of Health and the Public Health Laboratory $\underline{21}$, 96[26]

(b) Alternatively just a number can be inserted in the text, e.g.

> In the Metropolitan Police District the statutory provision for accountability is different. Very briefly, the Secretary of State is the Police Authority and the Commissioner, who is appointed by the Sovereign, is the Chief Officer of Police[1].[27]

The note ([1]) will be explained as a footnote:

> 1 Section 62 and Schedule 8 of the 1964 Act and Sections 1, 4 and 5 of the Metropolitan Police Act 1829 (as later amended.)[28]

or as a reference in a list at the end. The wider problems of footnotes are discussed later.

Provided the author's name (or, more difficult, authors' names or the name of a professional body) is reasonably short, the Harvard system is preferable. With such an arrangement it will often be unnecessary for the reader to turn to the bibliography. It is not used here because the references to source material are mixed with other note information.

The mechanics and specifics of both schemes are further explained (along with a lot of other useful things) in an admirable little booklet published by The Royal Society called *General Notes on the Preparation of Scientific Papers.*[29]

Footnotes

The need to avoid distraction from the main drift of the report is particularly relevant to footnotes. Sometimes they will be inevitable:

1 To show a reference.
2 To clarify a term.
3 To amplify a point with detail which is insufficient to justify an appendix.

The author should ask these questions:

a Is the information necessary?
b Could it be contained in the main script of the report?

c Is it best placed at the foot of the page or on an attachment at the back? Solution of the last problem is easier when a report is to be printed. The smaller print-sizes available enable the footnotes to take up less room and be less obtrusive.[30] With typewritten documents a note of more than four or five lines intrudes into the script and disturbs the flow of reading, thus defeating the object of relegating the detail to a footnote. Some of the novels of Sir Walter Scott are particularly irritating in this way. The need for speed of reference must be balanced with the distraction of massive notes on the same page.

Summary

The theme of this chapter has been the need to maintain the reader's flow and interest in the subject. The more attachments, footnotes and other encumbrances that there are, the greater the danger of distraction.

Yet it must be acknowledged that people receiving copies of the report have different levels of interest. As a practical fact of life they will read at varying speeds and in varying detail.

Summaries and abstracts can ensure that the glancing reader picks up what is important. The writer can highlight the points that are important for him to take away. It is not left to the risk of a chance scrutiny in which the reader might not happen to notice important points.

On the reverse of the coin, specialists and those who wish to work in detail must have the opportunity to pursue the topic in greater depth if they wish. The attachments and the signposts of the bibliography and footnotes will give them this opportunity, while leaving the main argument intact and comprehensible.

PART TWO

GETTING INSIDE THE REPORT

CHAPTER SIX

Choosing words

'Language is our most precious instrument' says Arnold Wesker.[1] He goes on to explain the wonderful and dreadful things that have been achieved by language. People can be encouraged, rebuked and seriously misled, either by accidental misuse or deliberate manipulation of the language.

In many societies competence in a particular language can lead to professional advancement. Lack of fluency can be disastrous.[2] Some cultures and religions place great importance on the minute accuracy of their holy works and guiding moral treatises. The Koran is the best example: Arabic as the language of God is the only vehicle for these divine pronouncements.[3] However, the obstacles that were encountered by early translations of the Bible into vernacular languages illustrate similar problems.[4] As late as 1903 riots in Greece accompanied a new translation of the Bible.[5]

It is impossible to pursue this study further without tackling the all-important and enthralling subject of words. It has proved unavoidable to allude to the subject already. This is not an optional sidetrack to the main theme of report writing. It is an absolutely vital component. Words are the basic raw material of a report. A report cannot exist without them. Even a report that consists largely of diagrams and tables must depend on words for its fluency. The illustrations must have headings. The axes must be marked. The variables must be labelled. All the illustrations must, indeed, be glued together with words.

It is words that elevate human communication above that of the animals.[6] Perhaps more important, it is words that limit human expression. There are many figures of speech which highlight this restriction: 'It defied description' or 'It was beyond words'. The third of Philip Howard's three-volume set of semantic essays is wisely named *Words Fail Me*.[7]

Language as a reflection of communicational needs

The form of language depends on what people want to say. It expands (and sometimes contracts) to reflect what people want to say.[8] Edward Sapir even went so far as to describe it as perfect.[9]

Various other languages show how their needs represent this. Ewe (an African language of Togoland) and certain Amerindian languages satisfy themselves with the same word for *yesterday* and *tomorrow*, i.e. not today.[10] The people of Lesu in the Pacific have at least 12 words for *pig* indicating different aspects such as colour, sex and so on, as pigs are particularly important in their society.[11]

To relate this principle to forms of English, Patrick Hanks (of whom more in a moment) makes interesting and important distinctions between the slightly precious, almost evasive, terminology of South African English and Australian. The latter is more direct, brash and, as Hanks puts it, full of 'cheerful relaxed vulgarity'.[12]

Borrowings of words from other languages indicate the relationship of the borrower and the lender. If relationships are friendly and intercourse is free, loans are likely to be numerous. Conversely, it came as a surprise to many at the time of the Argentinian invasion of the Falklands that the Falkland Islanders had borrowed so few words from Argentinian Spanish.[13]

To achieve the most accurate transmission of ideas, as rich a language, and within that language as rich a vocabulary, as possible is desirable. English has the richest vocabulary of any language using the Roman alphabet.[14]

Those who try to curtail word use by artificial rules perform a grave disservice. Language should be as natural as it can be. Professor Barbara Strang[15] said that the stock of words available had developed like a mature oak tree. It is therefore natural and uninhibited. Cardinal Newman[16] described the Church of England with the same metaphor. It may be argued that lack of discipline leads to weakness. However, an unrestricted oak-like form is nearer to nature and therefore nearer to human needs.

At the very beginning of *The King's English*, the Fowlers laid·down five simplistic rules of principle:

> Prefer the familiar word to the far-fetched. Prefer the concrete word to the abstract. Prefer the single word to the circumlocution. Prefer the short word to the long. Prefer the Saxon word to the Romance.[17]

Admirable as they may be as generalisations, they initiated a train of illogical and unwelcome inhibitions. Their principal disadvantage is that they take no account of context. These simplifications preclude the minute precision that a wide vocabulary allows as circumstances change from one occasion to another.[18]

The difference of every word

Guides to managerial communication sometimes produce lists of words and phrases that are desirable and undesirable, sometimes even dividing these into such titles as 'English' and 'Businessese'.[19] This is to avoid the issue. Every word has its uses.

One such guide[20] produces two columns: 'Business English' and 'Good English'. It is suggested that *letter* is to be prefered to *communication*, *want* or *wish* to *desire*, *clear* to *apparent*. There are undoubtedly many situations when this may be so. However, to suggest that they are totally interchangeable is surely misleading.

There are no true synonyms in English. If they do exist for a short time, as a result of an inrush of foreign vocabulary or through careless or thoughtless use for a number of years, their meanings are likely to separate. This happened extensively in the centuries after the Norman conquest.[21] French words had been imposed on a Saxon-speaking population. So in the short term the French *pastor* was synonymous with the Saxon *shepherd*. French *cordial* meant the same as the Saxon *hearty*.[22] *Folk* was indistinguishable from *people*[23]. The *sheep* which the Saxon peasant tended on the moor became *mutton* (*mouton*) when it reached the Norman's table. The temporary synonyms *perfume* and *stink* separated their meanings so that the Norman word described the more elegant smells and the Saxon term went to the less agreeable conditions of the villeins.

Alternatively if such duplication of words makes one redundant, one of them may die. This fate overtook:

witen	replaced by *obey*
inwit	replaced by *conscience*
schire	replaced by *pure*[24]
eam	replaced by *uncle*
oepele	replaced by *noble*
cypere	replaced by *witness*
scyldig	replaced by *guilty*[25]

and so on.

Perhaps *flammable* and *inflammable* are now indistinguishable in this way. Maybe the language would suffer no serious communicational loss if one of them died. Some distinctions are essentially worth preserving however.

The blending of words

A dichotomy appears now. It has become quite clear that it is churlish to resist changes to the language. To adopt a reactionary stance just means that words are being used that are either archaic or in some other way out of touch with real life. Yet at any particular moment, words, although they may be changing in meaning and perhaps drifting together, do mean different things. For the time being these distinctions must be maintained in the interests of clarity, even if in 20 years' time they have become indistinguishable.

It is not relevant to pass comment here on why these words appear to have been drifting together. It is not suitable to talk of misuse. It is important only to point out that at the moment they are still different and the differences must be respected.[26]

affect/effect

This is a particularly difficult pair. A careful reading of several dictionaries is recommended for anyone who is entirely confused. The following example will help to illustrate the importance.

> An improvement in the morale of bus staff will be affected/effected by vandalism.

Affected suggests, quite reasonably, that the morale improvement the transport authority have been trying to achieve will be damaged by an increase in vandalism. *Effected* suggests that the only way to improve the morale is to let loose a few vandals to sharpen up the bus crews.

authentication/authorisation

This represents the important distinction between checking that something is valid and permitting something to happen. The distinction seems elementary and vital, but it is remarkable how frequently they are interchanged, either deliberately or inadvertently.

continual/continuous

Some dictionaries allow no distinction here. A simplistic but helpful difference is that *continuous* allows for no breaks and *continual* suggests reasonable breaks. For example:

> This man lectures in industrial relations *continuously*

suggests that he has no breaks for meals, weekends or anything else. As a mnemonic, the concept of continuous stationery may help.[27]

disinterested/uninterested

This is another one where many lexicographers have given up the unequal struggle. The importance of the distinction is shown by the example:

> The Chairman was *disinterested/uninterested.*

In the former case the Chairman has no vested interest and therefore can chair in an impartial and unbiassed way. In the latter case, things are less satisfactory: the Chairman is bored, turned off and generally not giving his heart and soul to the business in hand. (A strange definition frequently offered by managers in conversation is that *disinterested* means that interest fell off after a bit. Where this fascinating distinction comes from is a mystery. It has no foundation in lexicography, fact or fiction.)

elicit/illicit

To *elicit* something is to draw it out, usually with a bit of difficulty. *Illicit* is an adjective that means unlawful, but generally in connection with an institution or a practice. Originally it was used of commerce (smuggling, in the 18th Century), then love[28] and more recently of an *illicit* still, or worse.

ensure/insure

A broad brush division that will get the writer into no trouble is that *ensure* makes something happen, while *insure* may be restricted to making arrangements for financial compensation.

extraterrestrial/extraterritorial

These two cognates (words of the same root or origin) are unlikely to be very seriously blended, although some internal low-level reports sometimes muddle them. *Extraterrestrial* refers to something outside the Earth. *Extraterritorial* refers to something outside some particular specified area. So the sales manager for Wales who has temporary responsibility for Merseyside for six months must refer to these duties as *extraterritorial* responsibilities (unless he is in the business of space invaders).

gambit/gamut

These two words are flung around with cheerful abandon. *Gambit* is originally a chess term referring to an opening move. It is now extensively and helpfully used to describe any move or manoeuvre, as in industrial relations. *Gamut*, on the other hand refers to a range of something.

> the whole *gambit* (of management styles) from democratic to autocratic[29]

must surely mean *gamut*.

industrious/industrial

Industrious means hard-working while *industrial* means having to do with industry.

imply/infer

Of all the pairs shown here, this one is the least clearly distinguished. The distinction is hanging on amongst careful users by the skin of its teeth. A writer or speaker can *imply* something by indicating in an oblique or indirect way. Anyone may infer something, from a set of circumstances, without opening his mouth, or his pen.[30]

militate/mitigate

Facts, events and situations have the effect of being in force against something when they *militate* against it:

   The continuation of this dispute will *militate* against the order being delivered on time.

Although cognate with *militant*, it has nothing much to do with it now. The verb *to mitigate* can best be understood by the concept of *mitigating* circumstances whereby the severity of a punishment may be reduced. Its etymology from the Latin *mitigare* (mild) is also helpful.

official/officious

An *official* is harmless, or should be; so is the adjective. Someone who is *officious* is a busybody, probably over-zealous and generally bad news.

perspective/prospective

Perspective is the art of seeing things in the correct relationship to each other. It was originally an artistic term. A two-storey building in the foreground will be larger than the Post Office Tower in the background. It has nothing to do with sequence. Discussing the company bridge tournament for ten minutes (as opposed to two hours) at a four-hour general management meeting is getting it in perspective. It has nothing to do with whether it is taken first, last or in the middle. *Prospective* is intended and (of an appointment) usually already appointed, so the 'prospective Personnel Manager' will probably have been nominated but has three months in which to pack up his house and last job. The concept of prospective parliamentary (or council) candidates is confusing: that title has a special legal significance relating to expenses.

principal/principle[31]

In the main, *principal* is an adjective (meaning main or chief) and *principle* a noun, describing moral guidelines. *Principal*, however, has a special function as a noun meaning the head of an institution of learning or the party represented by a professional adviser (such as an accountant at insolvency proceedings).

The value of every word

If every word means something slightly different, then every word must count for something. Cyril Connolly has pointed out:

> The perfect use of language is that in which every word carries the meaning that it is intended to, no more and no less.[32]

The padding described in Chapter 3 as a legitimate ploy of phatic communication – to alert, to amuse or just delay – is not appropriate in the razor-shape precision of a report.

Few managers treat their vocabulary – one of the most valuable assets available to an English-speaking executive – with the care that they would accord to their staff or their product. Report writing is not a necessary evil to a manager. It is his opportunity to express his decisions, attitudes, values and priorities to his colleagues, customers and others with whom he deals. This calls for precise use of words. Generalisation and inaccuracy have no place in word choice for reports. Philip Howard writes of the 'common and deplorable pattern of blunting the precision of a word by firing it from a blunderbuss instead of a rifle in the hope of hitting everything in sight'.[33]

Verbally, derived from Latin *verbum* (word), traditionally and etymologically means having to do with words. In recent years a secondary sense has developed, referring to the spoken as opposed to the written word. There can be no harm in this. It is an entirely proper drift in people's use of the language. However the reader may have a problem if faced with the following sentence in an auditor's report:

> No significant criticisms were noted during our review and minor items were verbally brought to the management's attention.[34]

Were the items expressed by use of words (as in the first sense) – perhaps, in this context, as opposed to numbers – or specifically by the spoken word (as in the second and more restricted sense)?

A first-class example of the value and use of every word occurs in this passage from a Colt Car Company report comparing vehicles of various makes:

> The tallest Importer Representatives naturally, complained about accommodation, although they agreed that there was an improvement. I felt that in the search for space, the seating padding was marginal and *may* lead to complaints of sagging.[35]

The tallest representatives have been commenting adversely on the inside of the car. The word *naturally*, which may seem insignificant, is absolutely essential to a proper appreciation of this paragraph of the report. The single word makes it quite clear that their comments – while not invalid – were very much the result of their great height. Those of more conventional build would be unlikely to be inconvenienced.

The directions of movement in the language

If a language, in which every word counts for so much, is to reflect the writer's needs so precisely, it must perforce develop and evolve to take account of things that he wants to describe. English, a magnificently dynamic and uninhibited language, developes in two directions, as shown in Figure 47.

Language is expanding all the time. Dr Robert Burchfield, Chief Editor of The Oxford Dictionaries, estimates that English adds 460 words a year, more than one a day. Some new words are the work of manufacturers, through the currency of the

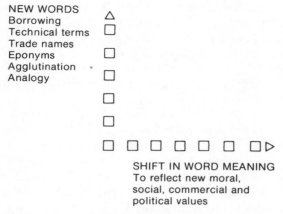

NEW WORDS
Borrowing
Technical terms
Trade names
Eponyms
Agglutination
Analogy

SHIFT IN WORD MEANING
To reflect new moral,
social, commercial and
political values

Figure 47   *Directions of development of English*

market names of their products or through technical expressions achieving widespread use. *Teleconferencing*[36] is now a well accepted function to which some space is given in Chapter 17. *Contraflow* has been born of the need to carry out extensive maintenance on motorways now that they are into their third decade. *Faction*, a straightforward agglutination of *fact* and *fiction*, describes an increasingly popular type of TV drama. The events, usually of a period of recent history, are amplified by fictitious episodes and putative conversations of the protagonists. The expression was described by Christopher Reid as 'necessarily pejorative'.[37] At Heathrow and other major airports a *travelator* is a welcome amenity for those with heavy luggage, or not much energy.

Analogy is a device that is productive of many useful new terms. The ending *-ise* (or *-ize*) enables report writers to describe the Thatcher Government's wish to *privatise* extensive parts of nationalised industries. Simeon Potter described the suffix as particularly useful.[38] Likewise *-ism* gives *entryism*, a technique of overt political infiltration by extremists (who are, of course, engaged in *extremism*). The terms are in good historical company. *Absentee* dates from the 16th Century, *refugee* from the revocation of the Edict of Nantes in 1685 and *evacuee* (in the sense of an individual being removed from some danger) equally precisely from the arrangements in 1939. At the time it prompted some mirth among the medical profession who had hitherto associated the term with those undergoing bowel evacuations.[39] Similarly a local transport executive preparing reports on *ridership* is following the pattern set by *horsemanship*, *statesmanship* and so on.[40]

Some such formations are humorous and many are not intended to stay the course. It seems unlikely that *jockette*, meaning a female jockey, popularised by Colonel Mad's greatly missed column in *Private Eye*, will ever feature in a Jockey Club or Wetherbys report; although it is remarkably widely used. After Watergate, the ending *-gate* produced a plethora of entertaining but ephemeral terms.[41] Among the latest is *Liffeygate*. The enthusiasm for the word *quango* when the Conservative party opened the quango-hunting season in the late 1970s gave rise to the more fanciful *quangocrat*,[42] *quangocracy*[43] and *quangology*.[44]

The introduction of eponymous words, frequently by accident, has always been entertaining.[45] A *mae west* was named after a film actress who was built in a way which suggested she was wearing a life jacket. The verb to *boycott* is derived from the wretched experiences of Captain Boycott, a land agent in Ireland, in 1880. His problems with the estate he managed were brief, but the impact was such that this unhappy term has survived and led a useful life.

Trade names and proprietary words have made an important contribution to the precision of the language, despite quite a lot of opposition. In 1978 Bernard Levin[46] drew attention to Burroughs Wellcome's defence of their product, Tabloid, and to Ansafone who took exception to a more general use in a *Times* feature entitled 'Gradual Acceptance of Answer Phones'.

The shift in word meaning is less obvious and therefore more dangerous to the report writer. The subtle creep of words is not so evident as the introduction of new expressions or new senses in media or in technology. A handful of examples will suffice to illustrate the principle. A quarter of a century ago, the adjective *imperial* was an epithet of splendour or magnificence. Even the word *colonial* was functional and neutral. Now all writers will reflect carefully before choosing either word. *Obscene* meant, in about 1960, sexually lewd or offensive to chastity. Since then it has become a popular term to describe attitudes that are widely different from the writer's. For example, it has almost become a cliché of CND and related lobbies in describing Trident and Cruise weapon systems. It was used at the annual conference of the National Association of Schoolmasters in April 1979 to describe the Assisted Places Scheme. *Censure*'s original meaning of opinion of any kind has tightened to mean an adverse (and now *censorious*) opinion.[47] *Orchestrate* is slowly achieving an unhappily derogatory meaning, which means that it must be employed with care.[48] Peter Jenkins recently expressed fears that the hitherto innocent *moderation* and *pragmatism* were going the same way.[49]

Some interesting developments in this field are to be seen in the area of racial terms. A more cautious approach to the use of racial terms has been evident lately. This reflects the urgency of the need for more tolerant attitudes in a highly multi-racial society. In South Africa, the term *kaffir* has become actionable in some areas.[50]

Hostility to change in language

Clearly reports must no more be written in Victorian English than they would be written in the Middle English of Chaucer.[51] The report writer, however conservative, cautious or staid his business, must keep abreast of developments. It is no more and no less than keeping up with fashion, without which his work – and thus his company – will appear dowdy, out-of-date[52] and reactionary.

Yet the enrichment of language has not been without its enemies. As long ago as 1712, Dean Swift wanted to call a halt, saying

> . . . some method should be thought on for ascertaining and fixing our language for ever, after such alterations are made in it as shall be thought requisite.[53]

This Luddite proposition antedates the railways, photography, socialism, trades unions, air travel and hosts of other complex subjects that Swift could never have described with any precision. Indeed he admitted

> . . . it is better a language should not be wholly perfect than that it should be perpetually changing.[54]

He has his heirs. They write almost daily in the broadsheet newspapers and frequently broadcast their misgivings.[55] Nowadays, in conversation, people frequently follow their use of a new word with the apology 'dreadful word' as if it were embarrassing in some way. In 1928, Logan Pearsall Smith in a paper for the Society for Pure English wrote:

> We all have new words; I myself hate them as much as anybody. And yet new words are often needed; not only names for new phenomena, but finer tools for the more delicate discrimination of our thoughts and feelings.[56]

(Indeed his paper is entitled 'Needed Words'.)

If the language is being devalued, it is only because it represents the subjects writers find it necessary to discuss and those writers' attitudes to them. Therefore the language is not debased: it is just that the attitudes have changed. The criticism must not be of the words but of the attitudes they represent.[57] Orwell said:

> When the general atmosphere is bad, language must suffer.[58]

The need for guidance

At this stage the reader may reasonably ask where all this is leading. The chapter appears to be engaged in a wild semantic adventure through uncharted and fantastic regions. Words are zapping about all over the place without any apparent control or discipline.

It is appropriate to take stock. Users of English for report writing are fortunate enough to enjoy an unequalled stock of the raw material for their trade. It is a stock that changes in quantity and context to meet the particular need of the subject and the time. This dynamic quality gives a splendid flexibility to communication. It is for this reason that many of the examples so far have been from the fringes of received language. This is where innovation is most evident and least inhibited – in the more flamboyant kinds of journalism and the emotive area of political commentary.

However, much of this vocabulary is not appropriate to the report writer. It is seldom open to him to indulge in the semantic whimsy of the more lively journalists or the fanciful usages of broadcasting, until the words or senses are better established.

If every one of this mobile population of words means something slightly different and every word must count for something in the report, two important problems are raised

1　How can the writer tell what words will be acceptable to his reader?
2　How can he tell precisely how the reader will interpret the words which he chooses?

The prescriptive approach to grasping words

The problem has long been acknowledged. Many of Swift's contemporaries shared his anxiety that the language was running away with them or getting out of control. To remedy this, a strong lobby attempted to set up an English Academy to regulate and control the development of words.[59]

This dogmatic and authoritarian approach has been adopted by the French since the establishment of the Académie française in 1635 and by the Italians with the Accademia della Crusca in 1582.[60] Not least this was needed to control vernacular dictionaries that were cropping up all over the place and lending a spurious respectability to regional variations.[61] Recently[62] the French Académie pronounced against *jumbo-jet* and *package tour*. They have also expressed a distaste for *bulldozer*, encouraging instead *bouter*, a more general and archaic word (meaning to push in Old French). Resistance to a lot of words, such as *weekend* and *parking*, has been considered unnecessarily reactionary by many Frenchmen. As one French manager put it, the expression *weekend* 'is not just two days: it is a concept'.[63]

The British approach to words

On the contrary, however, a more liberal tradition is now generally established in British writing. This produces more honesty, more directness and greater precision. The antithesis of this is the kind of communication straightjacket depicted by Orwell in *1984*,[64] and Burgess in *1985*.[65] These indeed became realities in the Germany of the 1930s and Stalin's Russia of the same period.

Of course, there must be a modicum of control. This must establish what words can generally be expected to be understood in non-technical reports. It must indicate as well as possible how readers will interpret those words. It must even go further and indicate received spelling so that the words in the rapidly expanding vocabulary can be distinguished without hesitation. Vallins writes nostalgically of the unregulated spelling of earlier centuries as 'the noble freedom of men of old'.[66] This would be impossible now. The speed at which it is necessary to read business reports would not tolerate individual variations in this respect.

Dictionaries as guides to word use

So in English-speaking countries the guide to word use is not a prescriptive academy but a descriptive dictionary. There are, of course, dictionaries of a more prescriptive kind which may even attempt to quantify usage in numerate terms.[67] There are dictionaries which are so descriptive as to be in danger of offering no guidance at all.

Much of this variation is the result of the fashionable attitudes of the moment. All dictionaries of the early part of this century – the era of the Fowlers and more rule-orientated teaching methods – were regarded as prescriptive and authoritative, whether their compilers intended it or not. This attitude is now certainly distasteful to most lexicographers.[68] Whereas the dictionary is certainly a guide to word use in reports, similes of the Bible are too strong and misleading. On the other hand the trendy thinking of the 1960s was not surprisingly represented in lexicography by a swing to progressive thinking. Tony Augarde, Senior Editor of the Oxford Dictionaries, describes the third edition of *Webster's Dictionary*[69] as 'the high spot of the descriptive mood'.[70]

Some management courses recommend that if the writer has to look a word up in the dictionary he should not use it. This seems most dangerous advice: it is suggestive of a spiral of increasing ignorance leading to increasingly poor communication. Vocabularies would get smaller and smaller and reports less and less precise as more and more general words were used. Dr Robert Burchfield, Chief Editor of the Oxford Dictionaries, has expressed his pleasure at his job 'rolling back curtains of ignorance'.[71]

It is important to remember that a dictionary is only a work of record. Ephraim Chambers,[72] the 18th Century encyclopaedist, said that the compiler of a dictionary was not supposed to effect improvements any more than a historian fought battles.

Barnhart has also used the analogy that it is not a mapmaker's job to move mountains and rivers.[73]

The development of British dictionaries

Dictionaries of a kind were produced in the late 16th and 17th Centuries. In 1582 Richard Mulcaster, a schoolmaster, produced one and in 1604, Robert Cawdrey of the same profession followed. In 1623 Henry Cockeram produced one dividing the vocabulary into three parts: hard words (a concept followed by Wesley in the next century), elegant equivalents of vulgar words and then, mythology. In 1721 Nathaniel Bailey produced a dictionary which was to be of great influence on Dr Johnson.[74]

These were more in the nature of selective word-lists or rambling essays than dictionaries, as they would be understood today. It was not until Johnson published his work in 1755 – in response to the need for linguistic discipline that Swift had indicated – that a dictionary in the 20th Century sense appeared.[75] It was, however, full of simplistic comments on matters that did not much interest Johnson, political comments and facetiousness.[76] Nevertheless it was a magnificent achievement for one man.

The Oxford English Dictionary

The great watershed in the development of dictionaries was the production of the *New English Dictionary*, later renamed the *Oxford English Dictionary (OED)*. In its original form this monumental task was completed in 1928, having started in about 1857.[77] The precise start point cannot be determined as the enterprise was beset by financial problems and disputes as to scope, before the Philological Society and the Oxford University Press reached a firm business arrangement. The protagonists were Frederick Furnival, a brilliant man of eccentric habits and a lack of tact which frequently jeopardised the whole undertaking,[78] and Dr (later Sir) James Murray, a Scotsman of enormous vision and dedication. His puritan way of life and great industry enabled him to work long hours in his scriptorium; a large garden shed stuffed with citations from diverse sources. By 1879 he had assembled $1\frac{3}{4}$ tons of material. By 1881 he had 800 readers, one of whom had submitted 100,000 quotations.[79] Murray's contribution to the use of words cannot be overstated. In particular he is responsible for the proper historical analysis of word meaning. His personal strength of character prevented the great dictionary being abbreviated into a shorter, less comprehensive work which would have been more to the immediate convenience of the financiers of the Oxford University Press.[80]

The size and depth of the *OED* is unparalleled in lexicography. Professor Randolph Quirk says: 'no one can form an adequate impression of the great Oxford Dictionary from a mere description'.[81] It stands at 12 volumes and the third of four volumes of the Supplement was published during the summer of 1982.[82] The length of time taken to prepare an entry both in the original and in the supplements is formidable. For instance, to prepare the entry on the suffix *-ing*, Murray took three weeks of research and two weeks of writing.[83]

So far as the report writer's scrutiny of the vocabulary available to him goes, one of Murray's greatest contributions is the diagram in Figure 48 and the philosophy associated with it.[84] It shows a hard core of English beyond which lie the

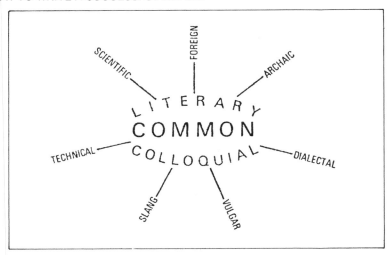

Figure 48   *Murray's diagram of the scope of English vocabulary*

vocabularies of an infinite number of specialisms. Regionalisms can be broken down into English regionalisms, few of which will be suitable for reports, and commonwealth regionalisms, many of which will be quite in order in certain documents. These can, of course, be further broken into such things as South African English, Canadian English, Australian English and all the others. Yet again, different parts of, say, Australia will produce different standard words. The diversity of American English, for instance between New England and Georgia, is even more pronounced.

A detailed dictionary of American slang[85] shows such a diagram covering slang variations. It has 13 petals to the diagram covering such areas as the cant of narcotic addicts, hobos and tramps and also more respectable jargons such as those of soldiers and railway workers.

Many further extensions of Murray's diagram can be drawn for all the professions involved in report writing. Architects, bankers, chartered accountants, chemists, lawyers, nuclear physicists all have their own special argots. Further subdivisions of, for example, accountants into the specialist parlance of auditors, insolvency accountants, taxmen and so on can be devised. Likewise there are constitutional lawyers, criminal lawyers and specialists in divorce and family law. The important need to deal carefully with these esoteric and sometimes arcane terms is covered in Chapter 7.

The dictionary however gives a clear – and indeed the only – guide as to what vocabulary can reasonably be used in a layman's report as at that dictionary's date of publication. There are three British dictionaries of the middle size and the first rank of scholarship. The middle size is suggested since the larger dictionaries such as the *OED* and the *Shorter Oxford English Dictionary*[86] are too large for office use. They also cast the net a bit too wide to constitute a very accurate criterion in the context of management reports. The very small dictionaries are admirable for checking spelling or rudimentary word differences. Yet, as they often have only room to define one word with another, this does not really provide the precision which is so essential to word distinction.

Concise Oxford Dictionary

It is appropriate to start with the *Concise Oxford Dictionary (COD)*[87] – the doyen of middle-sized dictionaries. It is based on the source material amassed for the OED and its supplement and the supporting work by its readers in the Bodleian Library and elsewhere. The first edition came out in 1911 when the *New English Dictionary* had only reached 'Sc'. In the earlier editions slight differences could be discerned between the style and presentation of the definitions up to Sc and those for the later letters. As the Fowler brothers who edited the first *COD* were working in Guernsey they did not have access to Dr Murray's source material in Oxford.[88]

There has been a total of seven editions of the *COD*, the most recent being in July 1982. Addenda are published between editions and, as with other dictionaries, the pages of addenda give an intriguing insight into social, commercial and technical developments of the relevant period. The addenda of 117 words added in November 1978[89] include *ACAS, chairperson, devolution* (in the political sense), *index-linked, MLR, mountain* (in the sense of butter mountain, etc.), *Ostpolitik*.

The word *quango* was an interestingly rapid assimilation. Its currency in the press dates from early 1978, although Oxford Dictionaries have citations from 1976 (and American references from as early as 1973). A slang introduction in the same addenda was *go bananas*. It is entertaining to speculate what this inclusion has to say about social trends of the period.

The seventh edition (1982) was produced rather more quickly after its predecessor (1976) than the intervals between any of the earlier ones. The staff of Oxford Dictionaries appreciate a greater interest in dictionaries and an increasing pace in supporting advertising.[90] A computer has been in use since 1980 and this obviously enables updating to be carried out more quickly. Extensive use is still made, however, of a fascinating card-index system which is the heir of Murray's scriptorium.

The editors do not see the dictionary as particularly conservative. It is, however, less bold than the other two in its extension into the outer reaches of Murray's diagram in Figure 48. It does not embrace the Miltonian, Shakesperian and Scottish usages of Chambers. It stops short of many of the more esoteric words in Collins.

Chambers' Twentieth Century Dictionary

Chambers[91] is produced in Edinburgh. It therefore, quite reasonably, includes more Scottish regionalisms than either of the other two. It also gives more archaic and defunct senses than either of the others. The report writer must make up his mind if he needs this kind of detail.

It is bulkier and physically more squat than the other two. Indeed it has the largest number of items; 180,000. Collins has 162,000. The *COD* has 40,000 headwords and 74,000 vocabulary items.

Although it may appear peripheral to the field of report writing, it is worth noting that the *Chambers' Twentieth Century* is the official reference dictionary for the National Scrabble Championship. Indeed, the editor personally adjudicates at the principal national and regional competitions. This is relevant as it indicates the character and scope of the book. In particular, words linger in Chambers. Betty Kirkpatrick, its editor, writes:

Removing words . . . is a perilous exercise, because it is a dictionary used by people who do crosswords and play Scrabble and they have a great love of recherché words. Also one of the strengths of the Twentieth Century Dictionary is that it covers a broad spectrum of the language covering a long period of time as well as many areas of interest. Thus one cannot simply remove obsolete words.[92]

It is a well established reference book and is frequently cited in court[93] by counsel and judges seeking definitions. This point may be remembered by those drafting reports with potential consequences in litigation.

Collins English Dictionary[94]

This is the only major dictionary to be produced in Britain since the war. It was well received on publication[95] and sold rapidly. It attempted to produce a global view of English, including some quite obscure usages of, for instance, Caribbean English.

Two main characteristics distinguish Collins from the other two described. Firstly, as the only new dictionary of standing for a quarter of a century, a more modern progressive approach was adopted. This is not to the taste of some people and may make the dictionary less suitable for those with whom a more conservative style of report is appropriate. To others this will be a refreshing and entirely welcome approach. Patrick Hanks, who edited the dictionary, says:

> . . . we did not deliberately set out to be modish. We did, however, deliberately set out to avoid being old-fashioned in phrasing and arrangement.[96]

By the same principle, in the ordering of the sense in a definition they 'did try . . . to start always with a sense that, by consensus, could be regarded as central, modern, and typical, and to work outwards from there'.[97] Hanks adds the essential point: 'Like so much else in lexicography, this called for a literary judgement rather than for statistical analysis'. It is worth remembering this point when the various numerate systems for analysing style are discussed (and dismissed) in Chapter 8.

Hanks' distinctive attitude to his dictionary is further demonstrated by his observation that he regards 'a citation file as a prompt or aide-memoire . . . rather than as the central point from which all else flows'.[98] He is quite happy to rely on the opinion of experts in particular fields once a citation or two has prompted his interest in a specialist word.

The second important difference is that Collins includes a selection of proper nouns. This is something that other dictionaries have avoided.[99] Johnson even avoided eponymous adjectives derived from nouns.[100] Artistic, political and other important personages are described in some detail; for instance, against the names of writers, their major works are listed. Countries and important towns are also included; even down to giving populations. The chosen geographical entries were included on a sliding scale, working away from the English-speaking world. The problems of including proper names are illustrated by their difficulty in producing a distinction between *Rhodesia* and *Zimbabwe*, for the position in that country had not been regularised at the time of publication. Both terms were sufficiently widely used to justify inclusion. Yet how was it possible to distinguish them without entering the political debate, however inadvertently, in the definition?

The limitations of dictionaries

For all its value as a guide to report writers, a dictionary can never be beyond criticism. Because of the time taken to compile and publish a doctionary, it is now a truism that it is out of date as soon as it is published. Because it is compiled by ordinary men and women it is necessarily subject to all human fallibilities. Johnson said that dictionaries were like watches: '. . . the worst is better than none, and the best cannot be expected to go quite true'.[101] Although his metaphor antedates the quartz era its point may still be appreciated.

Probably the smaller the dictionary the less it is evident that it is not up to date. However the bigger the dictionary the less frequently it will be possible to produce editions.

A lexicographer's work is restricted by two limitations: one as to scope and the other as to definition. Introducing his diagram shown in Figure 48, Murray used the metaphor of astronomy.[102] At the centre the Earth is generally well-known, like the hard core of English words. Knowledge becomes more obscure and acceptability more and more debatable in the outer reaches. A lexicographer must exercise some discrimination as to what words to include. Dr Burchfield was faced, in the case of the sixth *COD*, with such a decision on *monetarism*. He decided against it. Three years later the results of the 1979 General Election gave an unexpected significance to the term.[103] Dr Murray faced a similar decision with the medical sense of *appendix*.[104] He omitted it to find that the word achieved a sudden importance when the coronation of Edward VII had to be postponed through the King's illness. Collins just missed including *ayatollah* in 1979, to be flooded by citations shortly after publication.[105]

The inclusion of technical terms must be even more tricky. Cyril Connolly complained that the Penguin (paperback) Dictionary[106] did not contain the terminology of cribbage. Yet Collins did not find it a suitable inclusion in their dictionary $3\frac{1}{2}$ times the size.[107]

As regards the phrasing of definitions, lexicographers can only pass judgements in the light of what happens to be their experience. Hanks has expressed the view that definitions are part use, part memory and part hunch.[108] Anyone wishing to explore this riveting aspect further is recommended to read the essay, 'The Boundaries of Words and their Meanings', by William Labov of the University of Pennsylvania.[109] The article examines among other things the problem of deciding when a cup is not a cup. What are the qualities of cuplikeness that make it a cup as opposed to a mug? (It is not as simple as it sounds, as is demonstrated by one of its illustrations[110] showing 19 cup-like objects.) It is a fascinating insight into the lexicographer's dilemma.

Thesauri

Many people find thesauri helpful. The word is derived from the Greek word θησαυρὸς meaning a treasury.[111] It is therefore aptly named. It is a storehouse of words (without definitions) arranged by association. A thesaurus has the advantage over a dictionary that the words are arranged by meaning rather than in alphabetical order.

The principal British thesaurus is Roget's.[112] The first edition was produced in 1852 by Peter Mark Roget, whose father was a French refugee. The French pronunciation of the name has therefore, quite properly, been retained.

A new edition was published in spring 1982. The editor, Susan Lloyd, was criticised in the press,[113] albeit in a light-hearted way, for allegedly removing sexist terms such as *countryman* and *mankind* and replacing them with *countrydweller* and *humankind.* Clearly *countryman,* with its associations of rural expertise, is not comparable with *countrydweller* which merely specifies where someone happens to live. She was obliged to correct the misrepresentation in a letter to *The Times.*[114] The changes which had been misdescribed reflect only a change in the headwords of the groups of quasi-synonyms.

The current edition has retained the spirit and structure of its predecessors. It has expanded and developed to take account of changes in the language and values.

A word of caution about the use of thesauri is essential. A thesaurus is not a substitute for a dictionary and should never be treated as such. It must be used to jog the memory. A different word may be lurking at the back of the memory and needs to be teased out.

All words selected from the thesaurus in this way must have been seen in use. C.S. Lewis' remark that 'one understands a word much better if one has met it alive in its native habitat'[115] seems an understatement. The shades of distinction will be very fine. The precise suitability of a word can only be perceived if it has been seen doing the job for which it was intended.

Rules of thumb

The fundamental guideline is therefore that, faced with the great wealth of the corpus of English, word currency and meaning should be guided by:
1   A dictionary of the first rank.
2   The most recent edition of it.

Criteria of word choice

Some more guidelines will be helpful to the report writer:

(a) He must choose enough words to be clear. Ambiguity is almost always caused by inadequate wording.

(b) He must not use too many. If every word counts for something, then every word in the sentence must be there for a purpose. This chapter closes with a list of words that are frequently overused, being employed as padding words and adding nothing to a sentence, except confusion.

(c) He must choose words which most precisely convey his meaning. The need for this kind of precision is demonstrated by the microscopic scrutiny to which words of contracts and other documents are subjected in court.[116]

(d) Coyness and euphemism must be avoided. The elevation of the most basic functionaries to the title of *officer, manager* or *executive,* is harmless. In political handbills and journalism a kind of evasive writing may be appropriate.[117] However a more direct style is appropriate to reports. American companies have a wonderfully disparaging expression: a motherhood statement. The term is derived from 'all motherhood and apple-pie' and beautifully describes a facile type of report full of cosy sounding explanations but, in fact, saying nothing.

(e) Exaggeration devalues the words and thus devalues the whole report. If superlatives and extreme forms of description are used too widely, the report and its words will become devalued; just as a currency is devalued. These kinds of slack

usages are another infection from journalism. In that more spectacular arena they have their proper place. Just a few examples are:

Incredibly – has become an understudy word. It is summoned when a more specific word is not available.

Interesting – has become a very loose word. Copes in *Girl 20*[118] describes it as a 'postcard word': 'Interesting. That's a terrific postcard word, isn't it? Today we saw all round the folk museum; it was very interesting.'

Both words have their use. However they, among many others, have been grossly overused and exaggerated. Another example is *unique*, which was originally faithful to its etymology, Latin *unicus* (one and only), but has now achieved recognition in a wider sense.[119] Resisting this kind of change, at least for the time being, is not reactionary. For as usages are understood at present, it tends towards imprecision.

Padding words

There are many words which tend to be used as padding words. It cannot be stressed too strongly that all these words have their uses. If they did not, they would have disappeared from the language through the natural process of extinction. However they are overused to pad out sentences, distort the meaning of the sentence and have themselves become imprecise. The writer must ask himself if that is what he really means to say:

Of course It probably is *of course*, but does the *of course* need to be said? Indeed if it is that obvious, it may sometimes be possible to omit the whole sentence.

Further – to what?

In fact Is it *in fact* or is it just a matter of opinion?

Relatively *Relative* to what?

Respectively Does it relate to two or more things in that order? For instance, an independent television company says in its annual report that it has established news and information centres. If it continues that they are in Nottingham and Oxford *respectively*[120] that means news in Nottingham and information in Oxford.

Specific – or just general? The same goes for *particular*.

Intrigued This is a particularly dangerous word suggesting great surprise, disbelief and, in some contexts, a suspicion of dishonesty. It must be used with care in commercial contexts.

Viability/viable Is something capable of living? It can be used effectively of plans, schemes and proposals but is sometimes used where the metaphor of life is entirely unappropriate.

Terminal Is it really the end? The word must be used carefully because of its medical associations.

Penultimate Is there a last? *Penultimate* cannot accurately be used to describe something that is the last for the time being.

Tenders Are they tenders or just advertisements, proposals and general publicity material?

While Were the two things really happening at the same time? Is it helpful and relevant to say that they were? Vallins says 'an unnecessary and otiose *while* can do dreadful things to a sentence'.[121] Cottle[122] counts its careless use among his 'four wickedest idioms'.

Summary

The great wealth of English vocabulary is available to report writers to express their thoughts and recommendations. It is through these words that everyone manifests himself to other people. 'In a sense, each of us is his language: how, for example, can a person be witty, intelligent, charming – or stupid, nasty, boring – unless he so expressed himself in language?', says one lexicographer.[123]

The same commentator makes the point: '. . . language is infinitely plastic'. Language is changing the whole time to allow for new subject matter and changes in attitude. For this reason, it has proved so important to see word choice in historical perspective. What may be brilliantly clear and apposite at one moment will seem archaic, at best, and unclear, at worst, 20 years later.

The best guides through this perpetually changing stock of words are the most recent editions of the three principal dictionaries, augmented by a thesaurus as an *aide-memoire*. As every word means something slightly different, every word in a report must count for something. It must therefore be chosen deliberately with care and precision. Words must never be used as meaningless vacuous padding.

CHAPTER SEVEN

Pitching the report at the right level

Edward Sapir has described words as a form of privacy marking.[1] So they are. They are a form of code. It is therefore essential that both communicators use the same code. Certainly all report writers have the whole range of the language in which to express themselves, as described in the previous chapter. However this only goes part of the way.

A general level of competence in English and a norm of industrial, commercial and sociological awareness can be presumed for most readers. With widely circulated reports with substantial distribution lists this has to be presumed. However, there are wide variations in readership which will make different vocabularies and different forms of presentation suitable for different readerships. For instance:

1 *Wording:*
   a   More/less formal wording.
   b   More/less technical vocabulary.
   c   More/less authoritarian words.
2 *Presentation:*
   a   More/less supporting numerate detail.
   b   More/fewer illustrations.

In reports with possible legal consequences, well proven legal forms of words may be necessary. Crystal and Davy[2] have explained that legal language is 'perhaps the least communicative of all uses of language'. However there will be occasions when this type of code, taken from precedent, is appropriate.[3]

There will be occasions when highly technical – for instance medical – vocabulary is suitable, between those understanding that particular code. In other cases such use will prompt amusement or contempt, for example:

> A doctor may be offended or amused for instance, when a layman uses medical terminology too freely. It is interpreted as an unwanted claim to be treated as a member of the community.[4]

Register as a barrier to communication

Indeed, not only will the argot and register of a report seem out of place and even comical when used by those who are not entirely familiar with it, it may be incomprehensible to those outside the trade. A report by chemists, or by soldiers, or by data processing technicians will seem to lay readers like a message in a foreign language. The division of vocabularies and registers is not new. Old English had a separate vocabulary for poetry.[5]

Nor is the restriction found only in the field of written communication. A former *Guinness Book of Records* shows this charming and bizarre illustration of the problem:

> Some Rhodesian (*sic* 1965 edition) tobacco auctioneers speak at over 400 'words' (their inverted commas) per minute but no one outside the trade can understand what they are saying.[6]

Raymond Glendenning is alleged to have uttered 176 words in 30 seconds in commentary on a greyhound race.[7]

Some communicational tasks defy the problems of register. In *Ending Up*, Kingsley Amis describes the difficulty which Trevor (an advertising executive) has in finding any register appropriate to describing his job to his grandmother:

> Trevor had been telling his grandmother, on urgent request, about the work he had been doing recently. He simplified everything as much as he could short of downright falsification, a vain scruple, he knew, for the simplified version was still about as difficult for someone like her as say, fast colloquial French in a strong Norman accent, or would have been were she listening.[8]

Professor David Crystal of Reading University describes register as:

> . . . a variety of language defined according to its use in social situations, e.g. a register of scientific, religious, formal English.[9]

It is important to note that the register of a report is not just related to the amount of technical jargon in it, but also the formality of it and the language with which the reader feels at home. It is, then, relevant to bear in mind the reader's background.[10] The level of a report is then a fine balance between the jargon appropriate in the interests of precision and the limitations of the likely reader's vocabulary. Jargon only develops if it can describe something that commonplace language cannot describe. It therefore calls for very particular understanding of its code.[11] It is no good if communication fails when it is used.

Differences in register

The background

The register required for a report is going to be the product of the writer's and the reader's experience and knowledge. It is significant that Esperanto has no register. It has not been out into the real world, been used in reports and conversation and picked up any registers by association.

Bloomfield said that linguistics define meaning in terms of the speaker's (writer's) situation and the hearer's (reader's).[12] Allerton explained that communication could be seen in terms of the participant's knowledge. He identified three types of relevant knowledge:

1   Knowledge of the language.
2   Knowledge of the world in general.
3   Knowledge of the particular facts.[13]

With the preparation of a report, this is essential in order to get the right register, the right level, the right pitch. Allerton's 'could' becomes 'must'.

Knowledge of the language is probably the most difficult to identify. Only a few decades ago this was easier. It was easier in two respects: fewer levels of vocabulary were acceptable in reports and the number of specialist argots was fewer. In the first respect, commercial and managerial report writing was in the hands of a class that agreed on certain highly dogmatic linguistic usages. Standards of correctness, usually based on Johnson and Chesterfield's interpretations of classical style, were enforced unquestioned in schools. A received form of English, demonstrated by the work of Professor A. C. Ross [14] and commercialised by Nancy Mitford and others [15] was dominant over regional and less conventional forms. Since then (a period which coincided with the social and educational liberalism of the late 1960s) the accepted word forms have been questioned more frequently. Likewise wording, hitherto regarded as technological, has been accepted more quickly and more readily.

So received and acceptable vocabulary has widened, particularly in the last two decades. This makes the choice of register more difficult and more important.

Narrowing the field

The problem of register in any written document is simpler than with the spoken word because certain word forms are unlikely to be appropriate. Some types of wording can be pruned out straight away. They are not suitable for a managerial report. It is important to discuss them briefly so that they can be eliminated.

(a) Regionalisms and local vernacular   The phenomenon of diglossia, whereby a speaker uses one form of the language in one place (usually at home) and another elsewhere (usually at work), should not be apparent in a report. However, it is important to ensure that expressions which are only comprehensible in a particular region or by a particular subcommittee are not used in a report. The problem is described by Hardy, [16] by Bernard Shaw [17] and recently allusions are found in Margaret Drabble [18] and David Lodge. [19]

(b) Vulgarisms, slang and colloquialisms   Slang generates a lot of emotive chat as to its suitability. No definition has yet surpassed that of the Americans Greenough and Kittredge in 1901:

> . . . a peculiar kind of vagabond language always hanging on the outskirts of legitimate speech, but continually straying or forcing its way into the most respectable company. [20]

Colloquialism may have use in memoranda and even quite formal business letters, but none of these can be used in reports. Some slang words will become respectable: perhaps *jazz* and maybe *foxy* are examples. [21]

A dictionary, as described in Chapter 6, will be a reasonable guide as to what words can be eliminated altogether on grounds of being regional, vulgar, slang or in some other way peripheral.

The precise pitch of words

So far, certain words have been evicted from the report writer's vocabulary as being unsuitable to any report's register. The writer is now in a position to choose his level more precisely.

He must gauge the appropriate technical vocabulary. There is much of the mystique of the King's new clothes about technical jargon. Readers are too often afraid to admit their ignorance of the meanings. Some people learning the craft of report writing seek a vocabulary of technical words. If the vocabulary is not understood, the report message is certain to fail. However, a single technical vocabulary to cover the whole range of technical disciplines is neither possible nor sensible.

The various technical disciplines have perpetually expanding vocabularies (including such wide-ranging areas as nuclear energy, printing, and the theatre for instance). They provide – if they are understood – invaluable economies. A word of technical jargon may often represent a whole phrase of layman's language.

However it is important to remember the 'danger of accidental ambiguity' as Empson[22] called it. The field of report writing is particularly prone to this, as non-technical words may assume secondary technical meanings, e.g. *bootstrap* which has a computer sense as well as a sartorial one. Another type of ambiguity is pointed out by Bloomfield[23] where words have different meanings. A *house* in a local authority report is likely to mean a council house (or other dwelling forming a source of rate revenue). In a brewer's report it will – without further comment or explanation – mean a public house. In a police report it is quite likely to mean a brothel.[24] If so much as a single copy of the report is going outside the specific professional group described an explanation must be included.

The level of words must be taken a stage further. It has been shown that certain words can be eliminated on the grounds of being regional or slang. Now the scope has been further restricted by choosing a technical vocabulary within the reader's technical or professional range (the range of all the readers). However, even within generally received non-technical words, there will be differences of suitability for reports of various readerships.

Consider a report (on any subject) in which the writer wishes to express disapproval. He may say that he was *sorry* about the results on which he is reporting. In most contexts, however, this will be too neutral a register and in some it may even seem apologetic.

Consider further these alternatives which he might choose to replace *sorry*. Not only is the meaning slightly different in every instance, but in many cases the words will be suitable only for some readerships. He might say he was:

upset	*disgusted*	*aghast*
concerned	*appalled*	*mortified*
alarmed	*dumbfounded*	*surprised*
worried	*crestfallen*	*disappointed*

The reader of this chapter will be able to make up his own mind to which readers he would use these words and in what context. There is an opportunity for all of them, albeit fairly remote in some cases. For example, many readers will feel that *upset* is too domestic a word for most reports. ('The cat has died, she is very *upset*.') *Disgusted* is extremely strong and probably only suitable for a highly critical report on the performance of subordinates. *Aghast* and *mortified* are somewhat theatrical words, but could have their applications in a report where the writer's personal reactions are important and relevant to the subject matter. *Concerned* is a very feeble word, not really suitable to any register. It has become enfeebled by excessive overuse.[25]

Guides to simple English

Lord Robens has written 'Communications should be swift enough for decisions to be taken and implemented quickly. They must be accurate and simple enough to survive their passage through the organisation, i.e. they must be so designed that they cannot be misused.'[26] In pursuance of the philosophy set out by Robens and many other people a number of guides to simple English have been published.

However it is important not to forget the last part of what Robens says: '. . . they cannot be misused'. There must be no ambiguity or misunderstanding. In many cases if a word is simplified, some fine shade of meaning is lost.

One of the most notable of these guides is *Gobbledegook* published by the National Consumer Council in 1980.[27] The authors follow in Gowers' tradition[28] of urging the simplest possible form of writing to achieve maximum possible acceptance. Likewise, the Plain English Campaign[29] does sterling work trying to get Government departments and local authorities to simplify many of their publications which are aimed at a general readership. In that endeavour its protagonists do a first-class job. Indeed the term 'gobbledegook' is derived from American Congressman Maury Maverick who was thoroughly irritated by the obscurity of Government reports.[30] Gowers was himself writing for civil servants who were guilty of writing in an archaic register.

The danger arises[31] if these restrictive principles are extended beyond simple universally read handouts, such as Income Tax returns and national Census forms. (A case in the American courts, *New York State* v. *Lincoln Savings Bank* showed that the English used in a business document could be actionable by reason of its obscurity.[32])

Some ranges of publications (not strictly reports) are particularly successful in this way. ACAS Advisory Booklets, e.g. *Job Evaluation* (No. 1) and *Introduction to Payment Systems* (No. 2), are very good. Their codes of practice are generally satisfactory as well, when they manage to steer clear of legal terminology, which is difficult. The Health and Safety Executive booklets, e.g. *Noise and the Worker* (No. 25) and *First Aid in Offices, Shops and Railway Premises* (No. 48), are successful in point of vocabulary. However, some of their sentence structures are somewhat tortuous for a general readership.

These simplistic principles must be applied very warily to reports. It is more relevant to consider what Swift called 'proper words in proper places'.[33] Nevertheless there must be ways of presenting complex issues in a comprehensible way for the less informed. This function of changing gear is the second facet of the register problem, on which the rest of the chapter concentrates.

The issue of two levels of report

Where the information contained in a report is likely to be of interest to various types of readership, it may be easier to issue two levels of report. This is frequently appropriate with annual reports. The principles are well illustrated by two of them.

British Gas

British Gas Corporation[34] produce a detailed annual report (78 pages for 1980–81) setting out all the information which they are required to produce under the *Gas Act 1972*. The report is well illustrated with photographs, graphs and bar charts. About half consists of the audited accounts and a review of the year is supplemented by ample statistical data. This data compared the corporation's performance since 1971/72 in respect of turnover, operating costs, cost structure, cash flow, performance ratios and so on.

For employees an 18-page (for 1980–81 and the same length for 1981–82) simplification is produced. The length and the price (free to every applicant, as opposed to £2 for the full report) are the most obvious differences. It is most relevant to this discussion on register to identify the other principal differences of the employee report:

1   Cartoons and simple drawings, as opposed to photographs.
2   Simple three-dimensional representations replace compound bar charts and numerate tabulations. These are to create a general impression rather than to enable the reader to make his own calculations. (See Chapter 9 for further comment on this important distinction.)
3   No terminology is used which could not be understood by the general reader. (Accountancy and technical expressions are avoided entirely.)
4   Simple, unencumbered diagrams are used to explain those technical phenomena which have to be mentioned in the report, e.g. the British Gas/Lurgi slagging gasifier, the fluidised-bed hydrogenator, absorption heat pump and even a braille oven thermostat. This last is not a complicated control but it is difficult to imagine for someone who may not have come across such a thing.
5   Diagrams are, in the main, restricted to seven or eight labels to keep them simple.
6   Most sentences are limited to a maximum of one subordinate phrase.
7   The balance of the information is rearranged so that the proportions reflect the interest of the readers. Only four pages (two pages in 1980–81) are given to finance. This represents about 8 per cent (4 per cent in 1980–81) as opposed to 50 per cent in the main report. The workforce, their recruitment and benefits are given appropriately detailed treatment, as are the prospects for the industry and (in the particular year in question) the likely implications on gas showrooms of the relevant Monopolies Commission report.
8   The section 'Regional Highlights' is appropriately employee-orientated, with the achievements of several members of staff being identified by name.

Church Commissioners

The (Church of England) Church Commissioners provide another example of this type of reporting. Their readership is even broader-based than that of the British Gas Corporation, who at least have their industry in common.

The affairs of the Church Commissioners are highly complicated and somewhat mysterious. They are closely involved with the complexities of land ownership and are steeped in both lore and law. Yet churchgoers of all social groups, all means and all intellectual levels contribute to their funds.

The full report[35] gives a detailed explanation of the management of the Commissioners' estates and Stock Exchange portfolio. It explains the disposal of the income through stipends, pensions and the spectacularly increased cost of buying and maintaining property. The report also undertakes an explanation of their policy on the contentious issues of pastoral reorganisation and secularisation of redundant churches. The politics and legal technicalities of these arrangements are beyond the interest, and sometimes comprehension, of the lay congregations.

The Commissioners therefore produce a simple one-page A2 sheet which can be posted on church notice boards. (It is printed on both sides, so two are needed for the purpose.) The 1980 sheet is entitled *A Brief Report to Church Members*. The 1981 version is called *The Year in Brief*.

In the 1980 case, which is slightly clearer in design, one side consists of two simple pie charts showing income and expenditure, both totalling £53 million. The reverse shows as a simple diagram the six bodies who make decisions. It also gives a bit more detail on the sources of income in property and on the Stock Exchange, levels of clergy pay and pensions; in other words all that the general reader wants to know.

Annual Reports Ltd

The British Gas employees report is designed by Annual Reports Ltd,[36] a firm of communications consultants who believe themselves to be the only company in Europe specialising in annual reports to employees. Their Cadbury Schweppes UK employees report[37] won the 1982 'Accountancy Age' award. (Their British Gas report was second.)

This Cadbury Schweppes report is an eight-page publication composed almost entirely of diagrams and covering a range of topics comparable to the Gas report. Other of their products demonstrate different but successful approaches. The Granada Group[38] report to staff is largely illustrated by photographs, but they and their captions are highly personally orientated. Most illustrations show only two or three people and many staff are named. The Black & Decker[39] employee report is also highly personal with photographs of sample employees demonstrating various tasks in the company. This simple single-sheet (twice folded) report is more product-based than many and much space is given to depicting and explaining new items in the Black & Decker range.

Annual Reports Ltd's employee communications strategy, embodied in ten key factors,[40] emphasises the importance of what the employee wants to hear rather than what management wants to tell them. Their reports also illustrate their belief that while not denigrating employees' interest in their companies' affairs, information must be sold to them. They will not dig for it. Their products balance this point cleverly with their overriding acknowledgement that an employee report must never patronise the reader. Come to that, what report should?

Glossaries

It may not be practicable to issue two levels of report in this way:
1   Because of cost.
2   Because of time.
3   Because it is essential for all the intended readers to study the whole paper.
Yet various levels of technical awareness will exist and must be recognised. In this case a Glossary should be added. A Glossary will serve two functions:
1   It will explain the meaning of terms to the totally uninitiated.
2   It will sharpen definitions where it is necessary to give a general or household term a more acute meaning, e.g. *Draught beer* or *Lager*. Most British readers will be familiar with these as consumers but in a report a more precise meaning may be necessary.[41]

This type of sharpening will be particularly appropriate in documents with a very direct legal significance. For example these definitions in the glossary of a Stock Exchange Revised Draft Service Agreement.

Business day   Any day The Stock Exchange is open for business unless otherwise stated;

Cash benefit   Any benefit entitlement relating to money arising by way of any dividend, interest payment, capital distribution, premium distribution or such other benefit of a similar nature;

Certificate Any document of title issued by, or on behalf of, the issuing company which evidences the Account Holder's or, as the case may be, a Nominee's legal title to the securities comprised therein.

Foreign currency Any currency other than sterling

There are two pitfalls awaiting the compilers of glossaries:

1 Providing so much information that the description becomes an encyclopaedic item with details well beyond the need of the reader.

2 Defining the word in technical terms which still keep the meaning well beyond the lay reader's understanding.

The following selected examples from a Council for British Shipping paper on marine fuel oil terminology clearly demand a knowledge or, at least, understanding of petrol by the reader:

API gravity An arbitrary scale adopted by the American Petroleum Institute for expressing the relative density of oils. Its relation to relative density is:

$$\text{Degrees API} = \frac{141.5}{\text{Relative density at } 60°\text{F } (15.6°\text{C})} - 131.5$$

Asphaltenes Those components of asphalt that are insoluble in petroleum naphtha but are soluble in carbon disulphide. They are hard and brittle and are made up largely of high molecular weight polynuclear hydrocarbon derivatives containing carbon, hydrogen, sulphur, nitrogen, oxygen, and usually, the three heavy metals – nickel, iron and vanadium.

In this case the likely readership justifies this level of explanation. Such technical explanations would not work if any laymen were to read the paper.

The same paper illustrates the occasional need to distinguish between the same word as it occurs in two different contexts:

Base (Chemistry context) One of a broad class of compounds that react with acid to form salts plus water. This includes alkalies as well as other chemicals that have similar chemical behaviour. Water-soluble hydroxides ionise in solution and form hydroxyl ions (OH^-), which result in characteristic chemical properties of bases.

Base (Petroleum context) Term relating to the chemical nature of crude petroleum. Crude oil may be paraffinic, asphaltic or mixed base, according to the paraffin wax and bitumen in the residue after distillation. Naphthenic base is approximately synonymous with ashphaltic base.

Two good examples of glossary are shown below. A Waste Management Advisory Council report on returnable and non-returnable bottles includes these items[42] (of course the definitions refer only to that particular report):

Container mix The relative market shares, at a given time, of the different types and sizes of container used for packaging beverages.

Return rate The proportion of returnable containers (also defined in the Glossary) returned empty in relation to the number sold.

Trippage The number of times on average that a refillable container is used to deliver a product.

An Organisation for Economic Co-operation and Development report on traffic control[43] includes these:

Gap The time or space interval between individual vehicles measured from the rear of one vehicle to the front of the following one.

Progression, signal A signal system in which the successive signal phases controlling a given street give "go" indications in accordance with a time schedule to permit (as nearly as possible) continuous operation of groups of vehicles along the street at a planned rate of speed, which may vary in different parts of the system, or according to time of day.

It is usually preferable that the glossary should be kept separate in an easily identifiable section. In the Waste Management Advisory Council Report, it is at the front after the cover sheet, table of contents and acknowledgements. In the second case it is an Appendix (the first of six). In this way everyone knows where to find them. However, there may be just one or two special terms, perhaps borrowed from another document. For example, in an Esso internal report on signature verification,[44] it was appropriate to add two notes at the foot of the introductory section explaining what was meant by *False reject* and *False accept.*

NOTES
1   False reject is a valid signature which is rejected for some reason.
2   False accept is a forged signature which is accepted.

Summary

There are two aspects to attaining the appropriate register, to pitching the report at the right level for the reader. The vocabulary must be culled as far as possible so that it is apposite for that particular reader. It may also be necessary to change gear so that the reader is neither confused or patronised.

In trimming the vocabulary to a target readership, regionalisms, vulgarisms, slang and (usually) colloquialisms may be eliminated. Then technical terms a specific reader will not understand may be removed. Finally the range of vocabulary left must be used bearing in mind the reader's relationship with the writer and his likely reaction to each word.

In changing gear, it may sometimes be possible to issue two levels of report. In others, it will be adequate to produce a glossary. The glossary will translate technical terms and define general wording more sharply.

CHAPTER EIGHT

Style - and how to improve it

A singer, a politician or a hotel may be said to have style (presumably meaning – when judged against some indeterminate criteria – good style). Many companies and individuals quite understandably and properly seek to improve the style of their reports. This must, however, be seen as a matter of choosing the appropriate style rather than as one idealistic quest for some universal perfection.

Reports are frequently returned to the writer surmounted by the all-embracing condemnation 'Poor style' or, perhaps slightly more constructively, 'Improve your style'. Usually little or no attempt is made to specify the stylistic improvements being encouraged.

Another comment often seen is 'This not in this company's style'. Sometimes companies produce helpful rule books covering aspects such as paragraph numbering and section heading, but they seldom extend further.

Newspaper style books do often take the matter much further. On the same lines Keith Waterhouse has produced a most entertaining analysis of the *Daily Mirror*'s style.[1] This is not a style book in the conventional sense. It does not lay down precepts whereby *Daily Mirror* contributors must produce their scripts. It is a descriptive analysis of the style of the *Daily Mirror* over a set period. Not only is the book amusing, but it indicates the trends of tabloid journalism, which in turn affect the style of the tabloid readers.

In the case of management reports guidance of this kind is seldom available. The answer to the report writer's question 'Well, what is this company's style?' is usually 'Not this sort of thing anyway'.

It is scarcely surprising that replies are so evasive and definitions so elusive. Style is indeed the most nebulous area of report writing. It is best dealt with initially in negative terms.

Analogies of dress are sometimes helpful. Certain forms are definitely unsuitable for a dinner party. Others are definitely unsuitable for the ski-slopes or the football field.[2]

Style as personal manoeuvrability

Style is all the manoeuvrability that exists between any set of undisputed conventions. Such a set of conventions may be virtually universal within English usage such as the requirement for every sentence to contain a finite verb and to end with a full-stop.[3] It may be a national convention such as the American love of compound words, one-sentence paragraphs and heavy punctuation. It may just be a set of company conventions such as those in Ford Motor Company[4] favouring the use of bullet points and capital initial C for company, and in Price Waterhouse[5] for lower case initial letters for appointment titles. Everything else within such understandings is a matter of individual style.[6]

The restrictions on style should be as few as possible. In this way there will be as few restrictions on the individual writer's choice and his expression will be more natural and therefore more accurate. Michael Stubbs of the Department of Linguistics, University of Nottingham goes so far in this direction as to say:

> The style has no value *per se* and is not deliberately patterned beyond what is required to write grammatical and meaningful English.

The reference to 'grammatical' could be disputed. Grammar is itself a matter of style. The criterion 'meaningful' must be the touchstone.

This complex and highly personal aspect of report writing can best be examined in three stages. First, as implied earlier, there must be the inevitable eliminating round, to glance at some things that the right style is not. Second, it is important to consider the various ways in which the style of a report may be identified and measured. Third, some passages will be scrutinised for style.

What the right style is not

The style of a report must not be imitative. Legal documents are essentially imitative and justifiably so. Set passages which have proved themselves by precedent are copied from form books.[7] This second-hand approach can very seldom be justified in a report. Every situation on which a report is prepared will vary slightly. If this were not so, there would be no need for the report to be prepared. The expression of every point must therefore be drafted with the new situation in mind.

Very occasionally, such items as acknowledgement paragraphs can be copied from earlier examples. However the acknowledgement is there to express appreciation for help received. Was it absolutely and precisely the same assistance as on the previous occasion? Indeed if exactly the same wording is repeated the thanks become trite and meaningless, thus defeating their own purpose.

If patriotism is the refuge of scoundrels, so orthodoxy (for its own sake) is the refuge of not just the idle and the unimaginative but of the bad report writer. Because it is imitative, an orthodox style removes the text from the truth. It is describing the situation which is imitated. It therefore gives a false and inaccurate account.

Clichés

While massive blocks cribbed from other reports are – because they are second-hand and therefore not quite appropriate – bad style; so individually clichéd words are to be avoided for the same reasons. Clichés are forms of words that have become gummed together. The affiliation of a *church* or a *vicar* with the adjective *local* has reached absurd depths. It reached its nadir on a Press Association (taped) news report, describing a gunman as '. . . holed-up in a *local* church in Malton'. If the church was in Malton, how could it be anything else but local?

The scene of disasters, such as motorway accidents, are often described as 'like a battlefield' by eye witnesses. The fatuity of these comments is shown by the likelihood that most of the speakers who use the simile have almost certainly never seen a battlefield. It is just a traditional form of words which automatically goes with that sort of catastrophe. Because it does so, it adds nothing to the description.

Pressure is too often *tremendous*. A *search* by police is usually *massive*. These are the obvious expected communicational couplings. Because they are obvious and unoriginal, they can be anticipated and contribute nothing to the report. Longer clichés will also 'have a hypnotic and final effect, the sound of revealed truth'.[8] They take on an undeserved authority.

Cliché is a French technical term from the printing trade meaning a print block.[9] In other words it is a block of information which goes about the place together, indivisible. Whole forms of behaviour, replies to questions can become clichéd. There are various dangers to clichéd communication. It will be vacuous. In *The Realms of Gold*[10] Margaret Drabble describes a masculine after-dinner conversation about sex 'making predictable jokes' and trotting out all the old predictable lines of discussion.

It will also be uncommunicative. Alan Grey in Piers Paul Read's *The Professor's Daughter*[11] believed that a scandal is a worn-out cliché of bourgeois politics. In other words it had become so conventional that it caused no sensation and aroused no interest. Richard Ingrams illustrates the point well in one of his television reviews in the *Spectator*. Of Angela Rippon's interviewing technique he writes: 'Her smile is frosty and her comments clumsy and predictable – and in this case the usual clichés about how tough it is at the top and how few people make it up there in the first place'.[12]

More seriously, a cliché may actually be misleading. An Arab woman journalist writing in *The Listener*[13] described with feeling the ludicrous outdated and typified cliché of Arab women, belly-dancers, houris and so on. Because it is not representative, such a cliché becomes dangerous.

A set form of words can be used out of force of habit even when it is not appropriate. When a British Airways pilot announces to his passengers on what is supposed to be a through-flight from Athens to Heathrow that 'Our next *port-of-call* is Stuttgart', his precise navigational intentions are called into question. Ending a report with a set form such as 'Do not hesitate to let us know if we can be of further assistance' should not be used if the writer hopes that he has heard the end of the matter.

Clichés tend to be used more lavishly when times are hard or when there is something to hide. The report that is thick with them must be treated with suspicion.

The definitive work on clichés is Zijderveld *On Clichés*.[14] This merits study by anyone interested in this serious malaise in modern communications. He makes much of the important distinction between a cliché and a slogan: a slogan has a mobilising role.[15] A cliché has lost its mobilising power. The principal vocabulary of these iniquities is Partridge's *A Dictionary of Clichés*.[16]

Numerate rules

Numbers have a natural appeal to those seeking guidance on almost any subject. They are definitive and precise. They are not encumbered by what many people see as the woolly vagueness of semantic interpretation. To this end many have sought at least to analyse and frequently to regulate style by numerate rule.

In the second half of the 19th Century, Professor Augustus de Morgan (1851), Furnival (one of the fathers of the New English Dictionary) and the American Professor T. C. Mendenhall made various analyses independently of each other. Certainly their investigations identified, in classifiable ways, changes in style by various writers.[17] They did not set out to provide rules however.

Many of those who look for clear-cut classifications in this way are often surprised or disappointed that the results are not more pronounced. Sprent[18] analysed the transcript of two consecutive presidential addresses to the Royal Statistical Society. They were those of Sir Harold Wilson and D. J. Finney, Professor of Statistics at Edinburgh University. The average sentence length was almost the same, although the range of Wilson's sentences extended further in both directions.

Other concepts, however, aspire to provide more prescriptive guidance. Of these Gunning's Fog Index is the best known.[19] This investigates the fog and, conversely, clarity of a piece of writing by analysing the number of words per sentence and the number of syllables per word. It was first widely published in the 1940s and after a while Gunning recognised that the system was more complicated than it need be.[20] At about the same time Flesch was developing his Reading Ease Score which relied on similar arrangements. This led to the establishment of a readability laboratory in the US Department of Agriculture.[21]

North American commentators have been more prolific in this type of innovation than British. One of the most elaborate devices of this kind is Fry's Readability Graph, produced at Rutgers University Reading Center, New Brunswick.[22]

More recently J. O. Morris popularised the Clear River Test which uses the analogy of a boat's passage down a river. Various literary excesses[23] are measured numerically and as the numbers increase they take the form of barriers across the river, obstructing clear communications. The analogy is a good one, but the guidelines can only be general.

This is true of all these gimmicky systems. They are only intended to offer the most general guidance. Gunning makes it clear that this was always the intention. Morris says[24] that the Clear River Test is 'not a precise mathematical test'. He goes on: 'In measuring readability such a test would be burdensome to use and probably pointless'. However these concepts often fall into the wrong hands. To take their numerical generalisations as literally as many report writers and, more often, training managers – do is unrealistic and restrictive.

Such rules have their appeal in a kind of simplistic magic. However style is not measured or improved by magic tricks. As Lupton said in a different context: 'There are no rabbits to be pulled out of hats'.[25] However comfortably they may fit glib training objectives, they are far too crude to offer guidance for routine report writing.

The characteristics of style

To analyse the style appropriate to a particular reader or a particular company or a specific report, it is necessary to identify the characteristics of the style, or style-markers as Nils Erik Enkvist calls them.[26]

A traveller journeying from Didcot to Reading may look out of a train window and feel that the countryside looks like that of north Germany. This simple judgement is the equivalent of saying that a report is in the wrong (or the right) style. For more constructive comments, it is necessary to consider what makes it seem like German landscape. What items would have to be changed to make it seem less Germanic? He then identifies well defined woods on the hill-tops, isolated farms in small clumps of trees and roads with no hedges.

Words have already been described as the basic raw material of written communication. So they are the fundamental feature of style. It is appropriate to begin with some brief points on them.

Words

The style implications of word choice have already been discussed in the two preceding chapters and, indirectly, in the discussion of clichés earlier in this chapter. Apart from the actual choice of words, the following points of style are important in this connection.

1 *Repetition of words* is annoying and confusing. It irritates the reader like recurrence of blocked letters a or e on an ill-maintained typewriter.

2 *Statements of the obvious*, such as prefacing Conclusions with words such as 'After considering all the various possibilities'. The Conclusions would be a poor thing indeed if they were prepared without having considered the possibilities.

3 *Inclusion of redundant words.* Everyone has his own overused words. *Obviously, of course, however* and *on the other hand* recurred with embarrassing frequency in the earlier drafts of these pages. Each writer must identify his own vogue-words – be they the favourites of a moment or the habits of a lifetime – and trim their use so that they do not irritate his readers.

4 *Contradiction* is also irritating, as when an introductory line reads: 'The companies that have submitted quotes are . . .', to be followed by '. . . declined to quote'.

Sentence length

There are two extremes:

1 The Victorian length which was favoured by a generation reared on Latin structures rich in subordinate phrases and clauses, as in:

> The talk to-day, as the brown brandy, which the paler cognac has not yet superseded, is consumed and the fumes of coarse tobacco and the smell of spilt beer and the faint sickly odour of evaporating spirits overpower the flowers, is of horses.[27]

It is a style that Cyril Connolly called 'Mandarin English' and which presumes that the reader has a classical education, a private income and unlimited time.[28]

2 At the other end of the scale there is a Peter and Jane style appropriate to the authors of children's reading primers.[29]

Both extremes are represented in reports. For example this sentence length is rather uncomfortable:

> Together with a sustained growth in female participation rates, the admission to the EEC of the new countries with cheap excess labour, and the fact that British manufacturing industry is looking to a hard core of employees in order to increase productivity, with the tendency not to replace those who leave or retire – all these trends will act towards increasing the level of unemployment.[30]

The answer lies somewhere between the two extremes. The following paragraph from an Argos Distributors Ltd report shows suitable sentence lengths in an internal report on supervisor training:

> When the trainee supervisors have been selected they will receive a training scheme on supervisory techniques at present carried out by the Warehouse Training Department. On the completion of their training course they will enter into a department which has an established supervisor leading it. The trainee will then work alongside the supervisor,

learning about the department and how supervision works. This 'in the field' training will be carried out for approximately one month. When the month is completed the established supervisor is then trained in another department for a period of time. This training is carried out by the supervisor of the department he is entering. The supervisor trains the supervisor with the assistance of the line trainer, who helps in explaining individual operative functions. Whilst his training is going on his department is covered by the trainee. Also in the event of promotion the company would have trained supervisors ready to supervise departments. If a supervisor were promoted to a manager a replacement is quickly found.[31]

This paragraph is complete and it is taken, warts and all, from a supervisor's project report. There are several aspects of the style which the reader may have found not to his taste. Perhaps the word *supervisor* and forms of the word *train* come up more frequently than is strictly necessary or conducive to clarity. Perhaps it sounds a bit strange *entering into* a department, rather as one might *enter into* an agreement. Perhaps another comma or two here and there would add to the sense of it. However, notwithstanding anything which may suggest itself on these lines, the passage is extremely easy to read. This is because its sentence length is absolutely ideal for that sort of subject matter in an internal report.

It is most important to judge sentence length in relationship to paragraph length. What may have to be rather a long sentence when it is part of a complex paragraph in order to provide continuity of thought, can afford to be more thoroughly divided if those words are in a paragraph on their own.[32]

Sentence structure

Turner[33] admits that 'it would be difficult to exaggerate the importance of sentence structure in the European literary tradition'. This principle can certainly be extended to reports. Here is a sentence from the report of a water treatment consultancy:

The purpose of this programme is not only to ensure protection and conditioning of both oil and the whole of the oil holding/handling/distribution systems, but to maintain the fuel oil in peak atomising condition by implementing regular and frequent service visits to optimise the excess air levels thus ensuring that the boilers run at as high a level of efficiency as possible, and to further protect the fireside of the boilers from deposition, high and low temperature corrosion, acid smutting, etc.

Not only is this sentence too long for its subject matter, but many aspects of its structure make it most ungainly:

1 It starts clearly enough. 'The purpose of this programme is. . . .'
2 However, the 'not only . . . but to' construction is difficult to read when there is so much information.
3 The 'not only' section is complicated by including 'both oil and the whole of the oil holding. . .', etc.
4 Oblique strokes as in 'holding/handling' can sometimes be an economical form of expression. However three or more will often make part of the sentence rather top-heavy.
5 The 'but to' section leads into three separate functions ('to maintain . . . to optimise . . . to protect'). These separate infinitives could either be changed to three separate sentences, or three sub-paragraphs if the report structure was suited to sub-paragraphs.
6 The last of these infinitives is, of course, a split infinitive, 'to further protect'. This will annoy many. It does not actually seem to detract from the clarity here.

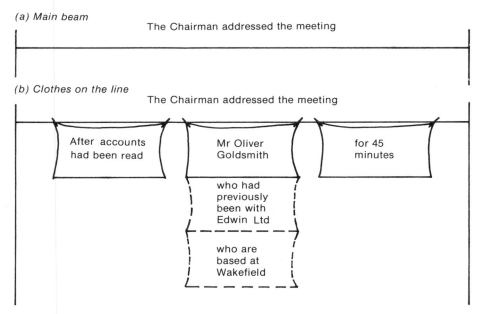

Figure 49   *The clothes line analogy*

Report writers seeking a simple method for analysing their sentence structure may find the analogy of a clothes line in Figure 49 helpful. The main beam of the sentence (subject, verb and any part of the predicate necessary to make sense of the whole) lies along the washing line. (In the Victorian example quoted earlier, the main beam is 'The talk . . . is of horses'.) The subordinate phrases and clauses are the linen on the line as shown in Figure 49(b):

1   There is no precise number of pieces of linen which may be hung on the line. The writer must judge that for himself. That is why the report is written by an intelligent human being rather than a monkey or a machine. There should be enough to enhance the main beam without making the sentence too cumbersome for its particular reader.

2   Every piece of linen must be affixed by a clothes peg in the form of a preposition (*in, upon, from*), a conjunction (*while, since, but*) or a present participle (ending in *ing*). If there is no such peg, the sentence should probably be broken into two (or, most exceptionally, joined by *and*). A simple example is found in the Argos Distributors report:[34] 'It is also a fact that we have no Trainee-Supervisors at Daventry Warehouse, this could be the link'. The comma could more conventionally be replaced by a full stop. Possibly the context might justify replacement by *and* to link the two thoughts together or a colon to suggest that, although they are two thoughts, one is the corollary of the other.

3   The writer should watch out for the danger of having too many bits of linen tacked one to another as is shown by the dotted appendages in Figure 49(b).

Paragraph length and structure

As with sentence length, two unhappy extremes occur with paragraphs. Some writers feel that a new paragraph is justified at the end of every sentence. The result is an ennervating form of mental stepping stones without any sort of grouping of ideas.

The other malaise tends towards grouping the whole document into one gargantuan paragraph. This problem is particularly apparent among writers who work from legal or other similar reference books such as tax handbooks.[35] It is difficult to shrug off a style that may well be justified in the source book on the grounds of legal precedent. Nor are the spectacular descriptive passages in Margaret Drabble's novels[36] or those of Edna O'Brien[37] appropriate for imitation in a report.

Whatever style of paragraph length and structure is chosen, the writer must also consider whether to give the paragraphs headings or not. Even if he decides that headings are not appropriate, the character and cohesion of each paragraph should be such that it could be given one. If there is no particular theme to the paragraph and it covers a ragbag of assorted topics, it has been badly structured.

Punctuation

There are really very few rules of punctuation, as such. There will, by everyone's acceptance, be a full stop at the end of every sentence. Yet what about a colon or semi-colon, or even the use of stops in abbreviations and acronyms? All these are likely to be a question of style. It may be national, house, or just individual style.

Punctuation has been described as the handmaid of prose. It should be just that. It has been suggested[38] that it was in danger of becoming a stiff-faced chaperone. To use another analogy, there is a danger of the punctuation marks overwhelming the words. Just as in the French legend, Gribouille jumped into the river to avoid the rain. Punctuation must always be kept to a minimum commensurate with clarity. It must always be subservient to the words.

This is not the place to provide a comprehensive schedule of possibilities in punctuation. Some excellent general guides are described in Appendix 3. Nonetheless it is a good idea to stress some overuses in punctuation style of which report writers should remain keenly aware.

(a) Inverted commas   Use of inverted commas should be minimised. The Press have shown an unhappy extravagance with them.[39] Some reports are so heavily laced with them that it is impossible, at first glance, to tell which words are inside and which words are outside the inverted commas. It should usually be possible to restrict their use to:

1 Directly quoted speech as

> The Committee concluded that 'the interests of the customer are best serviced by giving absolute and continuing priority to keeping costs under the tightest possible control', and went on to recommend ways in which the monitoring of economic efficiency and service to customers could be improved.[40]

2 Nicknames of individuals in an informal report, or the names of products, promotional campaigns and so on. The principle can also be extended to a rather more formal kind of terminology:

> The five members of the Board of Management of Royal Dutch and the three Managing Directors of Shell Transport are also members of the Presidium of the Board of Directors of Shell Petroleum NV and Managing Directors of The Shell Petroleum Company Limited. . . ; as such, they are generally known as 'Group Managing Directors'.[41]

3   The titles of other reports, books or even, as shown in this example, exhibitions:

> A new exhibition 'Cottages, Villages, Barns and Farms – the smaller buildings cared for by the National Trust', has been made and added to the existing exhibitions, 'About the National Trust', 'The National Trust Today' and 'The National Trust and Young People'.[42]

(b) Exclamation marks   There is no place for exclamation marks in a report. They are a cliché of house journals to indicate a joke (as in the old pantomime boom-boom). It is sometimes argued that they can give emphasis to a sentence. Indeed they may do so, but they are a slapdash and careless form of emphasis. (It was originally known as an admiration mark.[43]) Greater precision would be achieved by word choice or, if appropriate, commas. If it should ever be suitable to use an exclamation mark in extremis, single marks thus ! should be employed. When the exclamation mark was fashionable in private correspondence, multiples of !! and !!! occurred, as in this example from a letter of Wilfred Owen[44] in 1911:

> He is a sixth cousin of the great William Morris! has heard Ruskin lecture!! was introduced to Holman Hunt!!!

This rough type of communication is not suitable to a report (or indeed anything in the last quarter of the 20th Century).

(c) Dashes   Dashes were also in vogue in the private correspondence of earlier decades. John Simon[45] recalls that they are associated with 'schoolgirl correspondence of a bygone era'. Sir Ernest Gowers describes them as 'seductive'. This is most apposite. If they are used too loosely they will appear when a more specific form of mark should be used. In reports they should be used only as a form of parentheses stronger than a pair of commas less powerful than brackets. In this way they are particularly useful when the sentence is already awash with commas and other marks:

> Propaganda – films, posters, leaflets, etc. – is the most superficial approach to safety; whereas propaganda seeks to persuade, only training provides information and skill.[46]

(d) Hyphens   Hyphens have become increasingly popular in recent years. Geoffrey Wheatcroft has written of 'the advance of otiose hyphens'. On some occasions they have added clarity: on other occasions they have added nothing. The long-standing convention established by Bernard Shaw[47] and others, is that as few should be used as possible and then only to remove ambiguity. Various expressions are shown in, for instance, the *Concise Oxford Dictionary*, with hyphens:

> *hair-line*, but *hair shirt* and *hairspring*
> *long-range*, but *long haul* and *longhand*
> *red-handed*, but *red pepper* and *redhead*

However Tony Augarde, Senior Editor of the Oxford Dictionaries, explains that this is only a guide to received practice.[48] It can only be that. The old law applies: as few as possible should be used and then only to remove ambiguity.

There are areas where reduced usage is to be encouraged in the interests of fluent unhesitating style. There is one punctuation mark where the extended colloquial use is not only mischievous but actually wrong. Many are the corner post office shops displaying signs

IDENTIFICATION REQUIRED FOR ENCASHMENT OF GIRO'S

or

```
BANANA'S 15p EACH
```

Nothing is omitted from the *Giro's* or the *Banana's*. There is no possessive. They are straightforward plurals. It is most important that this infectious and misleading aberration should stop finding its way into reports.

Beyond these simple restrictions to avoid overuse of these marks, it is desirable that the report writer should make full, imaginative and unabashed use of the entire gamut of English punctuation. The whole range of parentheses should be applied from the heaviest ( ), through the intermediate – –, to a simple pair of commas , , . Likewise the range of stops should be employed from full-stop, through colon and semi-colon, to a comma. A gin advertisement appeared on the London Transport Underground during the summer of 1978 which suggested that there was something unpleasant about semi-colons. Nothing could be further from the truth.[49] Each of these weightings represents a slightly different level of weighting: a different level of pressure which may be important.

Grammar and idiom

Likewise, grammar is largely a matter of personal choice and highly individual style. As Philip Howard says in *New Words for Old*, 'English is not a drill yard for grammarians'.[50] Enkvist sees it as a framework of rules. Grammar defines the possible and impossible. Style is a choice of possibles.[51] Some writers[52] may find the analogy of a game of chess to be helpful. Perhaps the most colourful metaphor is that of John Simon[53] who sees style within grammatical convention as the actor's right to interpret Hamlet in the way he pleases but not going as far as 'a woman, a flaming homosexual or a one-eyed hunchback'.

In the 18th Century many classically based shibboleths were devised by Chesterfield and his friends and contemporaries. In particular the rhetoricians, Campbell, Kanes and Blair who lectured at Scottish universities on the arts of rhetoric and English composition took general principles to unsatisfactory extremes of dogma.[54] These have now sunk back to their more proper position of broad guidelines. In particular, these are noteworthy:

(a) Litotes   Of course, *not unpleasant* is a perfectly valid expression. A not unpleasant experience may be far removed from a *pleasant* one. When the Chairman of Taylor Woodrow was quoted[55] as describing the year's performance, in view of the different economic situation, as 'almost not unsatisfactory' he may have been giving a more precise and more accurate description of his company's position than he could have done with a more straightforward expression. Such convolutions should be used sparingly however.

George Orwell required users of this figure of speech to memorise 'A not unblack dog was chasing a not unsmall rabbit across a not ungreen field'.[56] Clearly in that quantity it is an irritating habit. In any case, each individual phrase in that example would be difficult to justify. In isolation, it can be a wholesome and harmless form of description.

(b) Split infinitive   The mystique of the split infinitive has also largely been dispelled. It is based on the impossibility of splitting an infinitive in Latin because it was all one word, e.g. *amare* (to love), *audire* (to hear). Its almost superstitious

preservation into 20th Century English was ludicrous. Many reputable writers have cheerfully split infinitives.[57] Shaw puts this strangely sensitive phenomenon into perspective. He wrote to *The Times* in 1907:

> There is a busybody on your staff who devotes a lot of time to chasing split infinitives. Every good literary craftsman splits his infinitives when the sense demands it. I call for the immediate dismissal of this pedant. It is of no consequence whether he decides to go quickly, or quickly to go, or to quickly go. The important thing is that he should go at once.[58]

However, notwithstanding the general fall from fashion of this particular form of nitpick, there are many people around who will still be irritated by it. That is sufficient reason for exercising particular caution.

(c) Active or passive mood　The question of active or passive mood has been less definitively resolved. Some insist on the active, 'Three departments have not submitted monthly returns', as opposed to the passive, 'Monthly returns have not been submitted by three departments'. There is a substantial difference of emphasis.

If no particular emphasis is required, the active generally reads more naturally. However the passive can be a very convenient alternative to an irritating repetition of the first person *I* at the beginning of every sentence.

The passive mood will often lead to uncomfortable constructions such as 'This matter is to be arbitrated on by . . . (such-and-such a) Court'.[59] The juxtaposition of *on* and *by* is unsatisfactory. It would read better: '. . . Court will arbitrate on this matter'.

(d) Dangling participle　Various dangling participles have entertained students of English for years, such as 'Coming round the corner, the police station came into view'.[60] These have been obviously and blatantly ludicrous. Nobody really believes that the police station was mounted on a trolley. In most reports the danger is more subtle as in 'Having considered and itemised our requirements, tenders were examined'.[61] Here the suggestion that the tenders did the considering is more dangerous, as the ambiguity to which it gives rise is less obvious to the writer.

Person

A separate question of style which may not be considered as strictly part of grammar and idiom, but is closely related to them, is the person in which the report is written.

In a business letter, the person may legitimately be varied within the same document as in: 'It is our practice to offer 10% off all orders over £10,000' but later 'I shall arrive on the 6.15 train from King's Cross'.

With a report, the person should be consistent. The writer must make two choices. The first, as shown in Figure 50(a), is whether first or third person is appropriate. The third person is clearly very impersonal. However, it gives the report (and more especially the recommendations) a formality that may make it more forceful.

> Finally it should be noted that . . . System X will begin to turn down the TXE series ordering programme, i.e. the semi-electronic TXE series ordering programme, i.e. the semi-electronic TXE 2, TXE 4 and TXE 4a exchanges. For some years, then, the British telephone system will be running with a new and obsolescent system running in harness.
> [*Engineering Industry Training Board report*[62]]

First or third person?

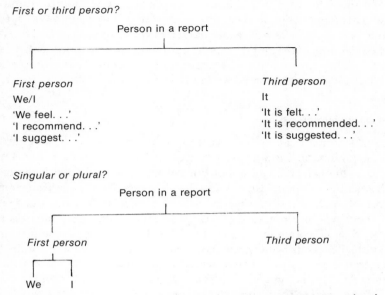

Figure 50   *Choice of first or third person and singular or plural*

If the first person is chosen, the writer must go on to consider the question in Figure 50(b) of *we* or *I*. He must consider whether the report is written on behalf of a committee or an individual. A panel of doctors considering the prescription and distribution of oral contraceptives reported:

> We recommend that no distinction should be made between progestogen only and combined oestrogen/progestogen oral contraceptives with regard to availability. [*Report of the Joint Working Group on Oral Contraceptives*[63]]

The report may be representing and commenting on the experiences of the world in general (or the experiences of a particular profession):

> In recent months, we have unfortunately witnessed a series of accidents involving the loss of lives and pollution damage. [*Draft Report by General Council of British Shipping*[64]]

Here the report is speaking on behalf of all seafaring folk.

Most internal reports will find the first person singular more suitable. Lord Scarman's report on the disorders in Brixton[65] quoted extensively in earlier chapters, was written entirely in the first person singular. In it, Scarman was reporting to William Whitelaw, The Home Secretary, and he was reporting his highly personal experiences in Brixton and other places.

Here is a paragraph from a perfectly respectable internal report. It is easy to imagine the writer addressing a senior manager in this way in conversation. Yet a written report in this vein does not lose dignity or clarity:

> Peak caps and shopping bags are being re-ordered through Regional Headquarters. Personalized book matches will be ordered and I would appreciate sample calling cards for this exercise. With regard to the matches, you may not be aware that the initial order was only on a limited basis at the request of UK/I (United Kingdom/Ireland) management to gauge the effectiveness of the idea.[66]

In all cases the writer must consider the tone in which he would address the recipient orally. At all costs the ludicrous Victorian pomposity 'the writer' must be avoided. At the same time, if an informal personal style is adopted, it must not become so matey and colloquial that it loses precision. Two centuries ago, Hazlitt pointed out 'It is not easy to write a familiar style'. He went on: 'You do not assume, indeed, the solemnity of the pulpit, or the tone of stage-declamation; neither are you at liberty to gabble on at a venture, without emphasis or discretion, or to resort to vulgar dialect . . . You must steer a middle course.'[67]

American style characteristics

Mention must be made of the peculiarities of American style. It is of particular relevance to multinationals who may be expected to write in American English. Some (such as the British operation of Ford Motor Company) may be required to write in British English in the United Kingdom but American English if the report is also addressed to Detroit. This practice calls for particular diligence and dexterity. Even for those who are not so intimately concerned, American practices are an inescapable fact of communicational life. The United States' commercial and technical influence is one of the principal reasons for the pre-eminence of English as the managerial *lingua franca*. It is essential to be aware of the idiosyncracies of American style. This commercial influence therefore makes this digression both relevant and important for virtually every reader.

Attitudes to American English

Most unhappily, ever since it was first detectable, American style has attracted widespread opprobrium. Initially this criticism was restricted to the spoken form, as when Doctor Johnson commented adversely on 'American dialect' and Wordworth's sister mentioned 'such a speech'.[68] Later, of course, the differences were discernible in the written form also. A Conservative Member of Parliament about 1930 actually went so far as to describe it as an 'evil influence'. Parliament was at the time being asked to impose a Board of Trade embargo on American films to 'protect the English language'.[69] It is difficult to know exactly what prompts this unwelcome hostility. Cynicism towards Australianisms as the cant of criminals or South Africanisms as the language of an enemy at the turn of the century might be comprehensible. There has been less adverse comment in these directions, however, probably because of the much smaller influence of those cultures. In the mid-1940s mild anti-American feeling was stimulated by jealousy. (American forces were said to be 'overpaid, oversexed and over here'.) Some of this may have lingered. It has probably now been extended to a suspicion of American innovation and managerial methods.

   Fortunately not every attitude has been so bigoted. Robert Bridges (1844–1930) wrote that when he 'was a boy there was a foolish prejudice against "Americanisms"' which he adds was 'indeed not only foolish but ill-mannered and offensively contemptuous'.[70] Philip Howard discusses the prejudices as those of 'Little Englishers, stick-in-the-muds and snobs'.[71]

Reasons for difference

There are four main reasons for the difference: time, influences in the north American continent, political aspects and the whim of Noah Webster. About 350 years have passed since the first settlers in New England established the language. Many terms such as *I guess* used by Chaucer[72] and *apartment* (meaning *flat*) have lingered in United States' use. Middle English *poke* (meaning *sack*) is still in use in south and mid-USA.

Many people fear that American English will depart so far from British English that the two forms will be almost mutually unintelligible. They cite as an analogy the diversion of Portuguese and Spanish from Roumanian and other east European languages of Latin base. However the unceasing intercourse of the two civilisations through cinema, television and the other arts – as well as commerce and technology – make this unlikely or impossible.

There have been many influences other than English or American communication since the 17th Century. The most notable have been French, Spanish, Dutch, German, American Indian and various African languages. Indeed about 1780 there were considerable lobbies which favoured adopting German or Hebrew as the national language of USA.[73]

Immediately after Independence, there was a conscious effort to establish a national identity in the United States, in the same way as this sort of feeling expressed itself in revolutionary France and the newly independent African nations of the 1960s. This sentiment was sharpened by strong anti-British feeling. Attitudes towards Britain around 1780 in USA were comparable to those now in many parts of County Fermanagh. The deliberate dissociation from things British was thus given an added poignancy.

Impetus was given to this thinking by the work of Noah Webster (1758–1843).[74] He wanted the American variation to be 'a band of national union'. He was, in a remarkably overt and direct way, the architect of the American style. Much of his work is enshrined in his dictionary, which, published in 1828, was completed exactly 100 years before the New (later Oxford) English Dictionary. While these two works are not comparable in any direct way, it is often overlooked by those who believe American English to be somehow less formal or less accountable than British English that the USA have had a complete major dictionary for exactly a century longer than Great Britain.[75]

Webster largely based his prescriptions on the need for simplicity. He wished to bring the written form nearer to the general accepted pronunciation. Astonishingly, he also believed that his briefer spellings would reduce the length of books and so have the advantage of making them cheaper.[76] This is doubtless true but the measure of difference must be microscopic. He attempted to introduce even more sweeping changes to spellings than those found in American English today but they were not able to achieve widespread acceptance; for instance, *bred* (for *bread*), *tuf*, *tung*, *thum*, inland and *wimmin*.[77] The main differences of which users of American style must be mindful fall under the heads: words, spelling, punctuation and grammar/idiom.

Words

Americans, probably because of the diversity of their national origins, are much more innovative than British speakers and writers.[78] Frequently these innovations survive any very evident need.[79]

Some American words are just not used in British English. For example:

American	British
commercial bank	clearing bank
custom-made	made-to-measure
faucet	tap
mutual funds	unit trust

Various others, such as *mail* (as a verb), are now commonplace on both sides of the Atlantic.

More significantly, there are a lot of words which appear in both forms but with differing (sometimes widely differing) meanings. Many are slang such as:

Word	British meaning	American meaning
broad	wide	woman
fag	cigarette	homosexual
knock-up	wake up	get pregnant
rubber	eraser	contraceptive

However they call for no less caution for all that.

Other words have a most direct bearing on managerial writing:

Word	British meaning	American meaning
flack	criticism (or anti-aircraft fire)	public-relations man (flack in this sense being described by Christopher Wain as an unappropriately ugly word;[80] a very subjective judgement presumably based on the British sense)
second floor	two floors above ground	one floor above ground
table (of a paper at a meeting)	placed before meeting	put aside until next time

In writing, Americans make a more direct and obvious attempt to choose different expressions where a danger of repetition suggests itself.[81]

Spelling

The most common variations to note are:

behavior	(British: *behaviour*)
catalog	(*catalogue*)
center, theater	(*centre, theatre*)
check	(*cheque*)
enuf	(*enough*)
instal	(*install*)
labor, etc.	(*labour*)
license	(as a noun and verb: British only as a verb, while the noun is *licence*)
pajamas	(*pyjamas*)
program	(in senses other than computer)
publicize	(*publicise*)
specialty	(*speciality*)
tire (of a wheel)	(*tyre*)

Punctuation

There are four principal differences in American practice:[82]

1   Americans generally punctuate more heavily than the British and use commas very freely. Particularly irritating to many British employees of American companies is the habit of invariably using a comma next to *and* in a list. To a British reader these commas suggest an emphasis which the American habit does not necessarily wish to convey.
2   Americans place commas and other stops[83] before quotation marks regardless of logic.
3   American writers use the double inverted commas as the primary set and the single inverted commas internally. (The division of British opinion on this topic is described in Chapter 11.)
4   American use of hyphens is a stage more advanced than British in that phrases such as 'sixth-most-popular country'[84] will be hyphenated and *submachinegun* will have lost its hyphens and been jammed together.

Grammar and idiom

Many of the differences of idiom are more evident in conversation than in writing; such as the opposite interpretation of the telephone operator's question 'Are you through?' However, some characteristics are generally evident in American writing:

1   Excessive, by British standards, use of prepositions. This produces slightly uncomfortable juxtapositions such as *meet up with* and *miss out on*.
2   Strangely, however, the preposition *on* is omitted before dates. A comma usually separates the date from the year, however; as in December 25, 1983.
3   The difference between use of *will* and *shall* which is preciously preserved by English and Welsh conservatives is unknown in America. The English convention is reversed in Scotland and Ireland.[85] Presumably because of the great influx of Scottish and Irish immigrants, no consistent pattern appeared in USA.[86]
4   Some verb forms are different: *dove* generally replaces *dived*.
5   A number of minor differences exist frequently concerning use of singular and plural as in 'I decided I didn't like women on general principles'.[87]

However, many features of American style may be regionalised. Differing uses may characterise the writing of a New Englander, a Californian or a Georgian. The divergence of regionalisms in the United States is extended to the written form of communication in British English where regional variations are really evident only in speech. This is the result of the enormous distances and is exacerbated by the absence of any national press in USA. Even the comments on grammar and so on, above, are generalisations. For instance one linguist has a map which shows some division of the *dove* (*dived*) usage in northern Illinois.[88]

American dictionaries

For guidance on American word use and style, the authority must be any of the Webster family of dictionaries. Regrettably Webster did not patent his name so that many pirate dictionaries exist.[89] Dictionaries bearing the name of the publisher *Merriam*, as in *Merriam-Webster*, should be used. In particular *Webster's New Collegiate Dictionary* is recommended for business use. Not only does it contain definitions of a suitable level, but also a 'Handbook of Style' covering punctuation, italicisation, capitalisation, plurals, use of footnotes and a section on forms of address like an abbreviated Debrett's.[90] This is even supplemented by a simple guide on the layout of business correspondence. In addition Merriam-Webster have published a most illuminating supplement to Webster III entitled *6,000 Words*. This incorporates new words accepted into American use between 1961 and 1976. It constitutes a very valuable guide to new American expressions and an intriguing insight into sociological and technical change in that country.

Demonstration of style

The whole nebulous and elusive problem is best demonstrated by scrutinising a selection of passages and considering to what sort of document the style is suitable. The passages are offered in no particular order and, at this stage, without comment. They come from the whole gamut of written communication. Eliminate from the mind any consideration of the subject matter. Identify the characteristics of the style (word choice, sentence structure, punctuation and so on). List them and then consider to what form of written communication the style is suitable. It is most important to forget the message. It is possible to say the same thing:

'It would be expedient to terminate this practice forthwith.'

'This should be ended at once.'

'Stop it now.'

in a number of different ways. In the same way, in speech, it would, on different occasions be appropriate to say:

'Sir, would you be so good as to withdraw.'

'Please will you leave the room.'

'Get the Hell out of it.'

Answers – as it were – follow Example Seven.

Example One

Some of the recommendations seem to be overdue. For instance, the priority in insolvency given to debts owing to the government should, Sir Kenneth Cork's committee recommend, be substantially diluted. The position of the small-time consumer who runs up hire-purchase debts which can't be met should be dealt with in a much more practical and humane manner than is the case now. Practical steps should be taken to help companies actually avoid insolvency and here Sir Kenneth's committee recommend the creation of a new figure, the administrator, who could be brought in to sort matters out before the final crisis. . . . The fact is that the state of the corporation sector is very poor indeed. Business is lousy. Unemployment, as we know, is over three million. The propensity to import is rising all the time.

Example Two

Despite advising you of a change of address much mail still finds its way to my old abode, much to the chagrin of the new occupier.

Many so-called head hunters use your lists. I regularly get calls in respect of jobs on completely the wrong responsibility levels. Obviously, a head hunter with his ear to the ground can isolate top quality material without recourse to your lists. Also I receive a considerable amount of redundant material through the post from other sources and I am confident that they use your lists for this purpose.

Example Three

Management should leave no doubt in the minds of personnel that it is particularly concerned about safety. A programme should be developed within each company to interest and educate all seafarers and to secure their active co-operation. Such a programme must be based on the full assumption by management of its responsibilities. The programme must supply leadership and executive drive.

Example Four
We all of us compromise in our private lives. No family man or woman can possibly for one moment exist in a family without giving as well as taking; without holding a view and finding it needs to be changed; without bending to the collective view of the family. That is the reality behind family life. And yet, somehow, we do find it rather harder to judge the compromises that we make in private, and accept as everyday and natural and reasonable, by the same standards as those compromises we see exposed to the public gaze.

Example Five
No doubt the French will break even this agreement (the friend, ally, supporter, hunting-partner, sustainer, dining-companion and ultimately betrayer of the mass murderer, torturer and infanticide Bokassa will hardly shrink from helping the Russians if it will help his own farmers, particularly since any geologist will tell you that the soil of Afghanistan is wholly deficient in diamonds), just as the Japanese will break any similar agreement on technology; but even if an absolutely united and unbroken front could be organized, it would still be inadequate – and, more to the point, seen to be inadequate – unless it actually involved a reduction, and more than a token reduction, too, in the amount America's allies are willing to supply to America's, and their own, enemies.

Example Six
Appearance, is really a matter of opinion, but the interior and exterior were highly rated. Some commented that with such substantial changes the car should have been made to look totally new. I disagreed, because it still retains its identity and that, with familiarisation, does in fact look a great deal better than the superceded model. The internally adjustable mirrors did little for the appearance and a lot less for the wind noise, which was otherwise outstandingly good.

Example Seven
As you know, action has already been taken to introduce a cargo sales accounting system onto the system 32 at Chiswick. The consideration of this introduction has been ongoing for some time and a decision has finally been taken to introduce it. It appears, however, that no capital expenditure applications have been lodged for this work. Marketing Systems are asking that this is done without delay.

Sources of examples

Example One   An article by Tony Rudd in the *Spectator*[91] on the Cork Report. The article is beautifully readable and informative. The colloquial vocabulary of the last four sentences: 'Business is lousy', '. . . as we know . . .' and so on indicate a journalistic style, however.

Example Two   A British Vice-President of an American company resigning from a British professional body, in a fit of pique. This is a thoroughly ludicrous piece of writing; as he admits in the cold light of day. The old-fashioned English 'abode', 'chagrin', which might be entirely suitable in many contexts and add charm and colour is quite unsuitable to this letter of complaint. It is unnecessarily wordy. Note also the meaningless use of the word *so-called*.[92]

Example Three   A draft report from the General Council of British Shipping. A good direct piece of authoritative writing. It is forceful without being pompous. It goes on: 'In the meantime, it is emphasised that the shipping industry has a very important and responsible role to play'.[93]

Example Four An address by Dr David Owen in Saint Andrew's Church, Plymouth; as transcribed in *The Times*.[94] This should be instantly recognised as oratory written down. Two semi-colons in one sentence, the 'without . . . without . . . without . . . structure', and the sentence starting 'And yet . . .', all indicate that this passage needs to be spoken for its full effect.

Example Five A magnificent Bernard Levin sentence.[95] Need more be said? (Such a structure should not find its way into a report however.)

Example Six A Colt Car Company internal report commenting on a vehicle (during comparison of various makes).[96] Its personal chatty style is absolutely appropriate to personal comments on matters of drive convenience, individual impression and similar matters.

Example Seven QANTAS internal report by a senior manager on UK Cargo Sales Accounting System.[97] The short simple sentences make it easy to follow and forceful. *As you know*, provided it is not overdone, is a useful and polite way of making sure that the reader remembers something which he should do. (However, the more it is used, the less powerful it is.) The adjective *ongoing* is properly used here, but it should be minimised because of heavy and well deserved lampooning by *Private Eye*.

Models of style

Those who feel that their style is getting stereotyped, stale or just plain tedious would do well to read contemporary (and conventional) novelists. They will then find, subconsciously, that their style is refreshed. For report-writing purposes the following prolific and readily available novelists are particularly recommended: Iris Murdoch, Graham Greene, H. E. Bates, Piers Paul Read and, for those with a taste for the Antipodean setting, Patrick White.

Patrick Hanks has particularly helpful views on this aspect:

> It's often overlooked that much of the process of developing a good prose style goes on in the *subconscious* mind – as it must, if any kind of fluency is to be achieved. I never met a good stylist yet who was not widely read in the best of our literature.[98]

He goes on to exhort 'all those chaps writing ghastly unreadable reports in pretentious language' to read widely. It is his clause 'if any kind of fluency is to be achieved' that is particularly significant. Fluency is not achieved by numerate ratings or slick rules. It must be 'subconscious' which he actually underlines in his letter.

Indeed Iris Murdoch has explained on several occasions that she recharges her batteries from Shakespeare:

> I read the plays again and again, hoping something will rub off.[99]

Summary

John Middleton Murray[100] has commented that a discussion of the meaning of style would be impossible in six books, much less six lectures. Style is something of a contradiction. It has no rules, yet it can be performed badly. Style is all the personal choice within the conventions of communication. It is something personal which gets the message on the right wavelength between writer and reader.

Perhaps the most apt of all the many analogies, some of which have been mentioned in this chapter and its notes, on style is one by Vallins.[101] He sees a bad stylist as a golfer who knows so many rules that he cannot even hit the ball.

Probably the best criterion of style is the test of ambiguity. If the reader has to hesitate – even momentarily – in understanding the sentence, the style is wrong for that reader.

CHAPTER NINE

Using visual illustrations

'A minute of maths is worth an inch in *The Guardian*' explained Kingsley Amis in *I Want It Now*.[1] Graphic and sometimes numerate presentations can add enormous clarity and great precision to a report. On the other hand very often it is a spurious enlightenment. The picture looks good at first glance, but adds nothing on closer scrutiny.

Numerate displays are a convenience. They are an immense convenience without which commercial life today would be ponderous, or impossible, to follow and control. However, numbers for numbers' sake may lead to an impersonal and therefore an inaccurate oversimplification. The journalist and broadcaster Mary Kenny has suggested:

> Modern society with its crushing materialism and emphasis on numbers robs us of our individuality.[2]

It is easy to ignore individual differences and distinctions in order to produce an attractive simplistic display. A few years ago the Soviet Union expressed an enthusiasm for quantifying everything: steel, petrol, shoe production and the rest. It was a convenient way of comparing pre- and post-revolutionary performance. Thus the Tula region could be shown to boast 42 writers, as opposed to one previously. No mention was made that the one was Tolstoy.[3]

Purposes for illustrations

There are three distinct purposes for including a table, figure or other illustration in a report. It is vital that the writer recognises the purpose of his illustration and chooses an appropriate medium:

1 It may be to create a general impression, such as a pie chart, a caricatured bar chart or a pictogram.
2 It may be to present complex (usually numerate) information in a compact form that is more easily digestible by the reader than a straight statement of figures. Examples include histograms and graphs. From these the reader may be expected not just to form a general impression but to be able to take detailed readings.
3 It may be to provide a diagram or other representation of a system from which the reader may learn its workings. This type covers not only mechanical systems but also the functioning of an organisation.

When choosing the form, it must also be borne in mind that although a diagram will make a message more obvious to the reader, it is seldom likely to be more economical on space.

Other preliminary considerations

Not only must the medium of the illustration – the type of picture – be chosen at the outset. Certain other decisions must be made.

Continuous or discrete displays

A discrete display is appropriate if the variables are separate distinct packages. Where there are an infinite quantity of variables which may be plotted, a continuous display is needed.

Placing of illustrations

In deciding whether to place pictures in the body of the report or as an attachment at the back, the writer should ask himself these questions:

1   Is it too large to fit in the main body?
2   Is it likely to cover more than one (or at most two) pages of the report and therefore likely to break the flow of reading?
3   Is it in danger of distracting the reader?
4   Above all, is it germane to the argument or just supplementary – perhaps specialist – information?

If it is decided to relegate the detail to the back of the report, it may be necessary to

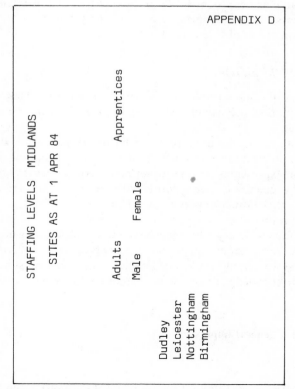

Figure 51   *Alignment of titles in a table in an appendix*

take some information from the tabulation, e.g. totals from the bottom, and to set them out in the main report, so that the report can stand on its own. In its most simplified form this is shown in the *Report of the Inter-departmental Working Party on Road Traffic Law*. Its Annex B, which is a 2-page matrix of offences and police force areas showing issue of fixed penalty notices, is summarised in the main body of the report:

> The table in the Annex B shows the category of offences to which the fixed penalty system is applied by the various forces; as may be seen, only six forces use the system for all the categories of offences.[4]

Wherever possible, tables should be the same way up as the text. However, if it is expedient to lay a table on its side so that it can take advantage of the shape of the paper, the titles and key must all be the same way up. The appendix number should be the same way up as the main paper so that it can be found easily (see Figure 51).

Although an illustration is supportive of the report, it must stand on its own. It must be comprehensible without reference to the text.

Introduction of an illustration

When an illustration is shown as an appendix, it can usually be allocated a page of its own. No problems arise. Insinuation of an illustration into the text calls for more care. The following aspects should be considered:
1   Avoid a table running from one page to another.
2   Place the table as near as possible to the text to which it relates.
These two points may sometimes be contradictory but a compromise must be reached in the interests of fluent reading.

The semantics of illustrations

No illustration will stand without words. They are an essential complement to line diagrams and numbers. Particular shortcomings in the wording associated with illustrations are:
1   Using a technical or obscure term in a table or diagram which the writer would never dream of using in the report itself without explanation.
2   Using vague expressions such as 'other major companies' to label graph lines. This sort of vagueness consorts poorly with the kind of numerate precision that a graph or other tabulation seeks to convey.
Particularly clear unambiguous word choice is essential for titling the illustrations and labelling the axes. Every table must have a title. The wording must be specific in stating the range of the table, e.g. period, geographical area covered. Likewise axes of graphs and so on should always be labelled. The writer must never rely on the reader's general knowledge or on the probability of him having read the preceding text.

Tables creating a general impression

Pie charts

Among the most popular (and, by some, the most derided) of the types of picture which create a general impression are pie charts. They are greatly enhanced by use

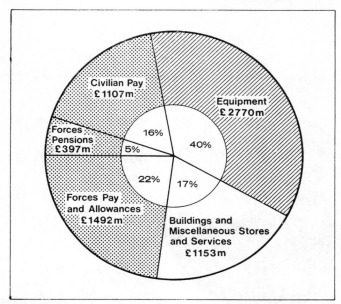

Figure 52   *Clear pie chart which could be improved by more distinctive shading*

of colours. If colours are not available the styles of shading used must be sufficiently distinguished. The pie chart in Figure 52[5] has much merit. However at first glance the segments on 'Forces Pay and Allowances', 'Forces Pensions', 'Civilian Pay' and 'Equipment' appear to be of a similar kind. Yet 'Buildings and Miscellaneous Stores and Services' appears to be entirely different and indeed to have something in common with the percentages which are also on whiter fields. Three distinct shadings for the sectors are required.

A good example of clear, distinct shading is shown in Figure 53.[6]

A pie chart should have at least three segments. The nine segments (or in extremis perhaps 12) shown in Figure 54[7] are probably a reasonable maximum.

If two adjacent pies are displayed to demonstrate a total increase from, say, £2.5 million to £4.9 million (in other words about double), the area of the pies must only double. If the diameter of the pie is doubled, the area of the diagram will increase as a function of π and will become disproportionately large and thus misleading.

The inclusion of a spurious third dimension to many diagrams is becoming increasingly fashionable. This vogue adds no precision to the picture but is generally quite harmless. Two such instances are shown in Figures 55 and 56. Both are from annual reports. Figure 55 shows the division of an insurance group's premiums.[8] Figure 56 shows the outline distribution of a property company's[9] investments. Although neither is misleading, Figure 56 points the way to two allied difficulties. If the segments were nearer the same size, it would be quite essential to label them, instead of writing the percentages in the margin. In the bottom pie, if the small slice was extended any more from pie it would be seriously misleading. It only represents 1.5 per cent of the whole. There is a danger of the side of the slice giving the impression of a much greater proportion.

Fanciful attempts to show pie charts with crusts, knives poised about them and,

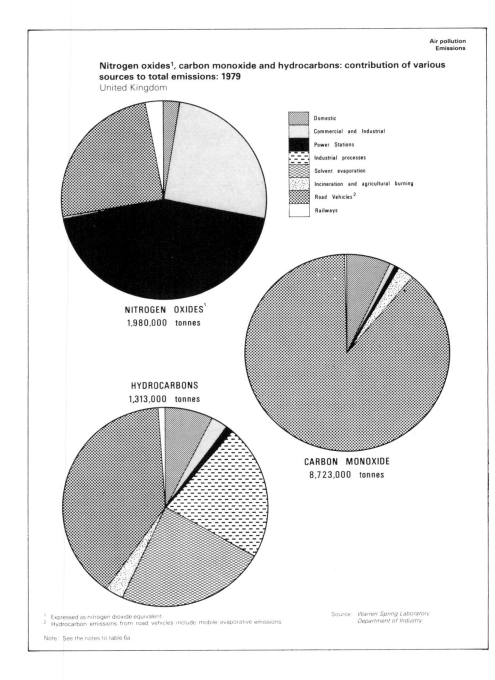

Figure 53 *Clear, distinct shading in pie chart*

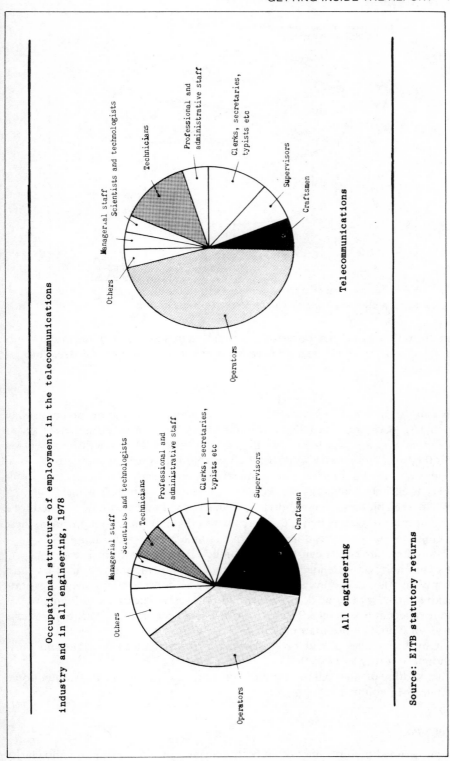

Figure 54 *Maximum number of segments suitable for a pie chart*

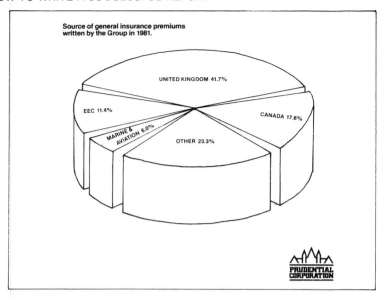

Figure 55 *Pie chart: insurance group's premiums*

even, birds flying out must be resisted. Certainly a pie chart is intended to show only generalisations but these ludicrous embellishments can only be a distraction.

Bar charts

The same urge to add an irrelevant third dimension is found in the preparation of bar charts. Again this is usually quite innocuous. The example at Figure 57[10] shows the British Vita assets as set out in their annual report. Here the third dimension takes the form of a letter V as in British Vita. No *y*-axis scale is shown and a third dimension to the bar precludes accurate reading, in any case. However, this simple display is entirely explicit as the columns are marked with their values.

Where the columns are not individually marked with their values, the *y*-axis of a bar chart must be clearly marked. Sometimes horizontal lines can supplement these markings and facilitate reading. Such an example is shown in Figure 58.[11]

Compound bar charts can be used to good effect as shown in Figure 59.[12]

As bar charts are intended to create immediate general impressions, they must not mislead the reader even momentarily. If the constraints of size necessitate breaking a bar, it must be done clearly and obviously. The break in Figure 60[13] is hard to detect at first glance. The US total defence expenditure (second bar from the top) is, of course, more than nine times that of the UK.

All broken scales should be broken as near the end as possible and in as pronounced a way as possible.

The widths of the pillars should not vary except to illustrate intentional differences in volume.

Pictograms

Straightforward pictures may often both enliven a turgid explanation and clarify

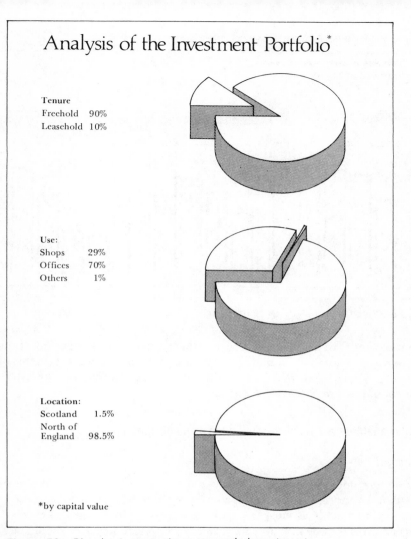

Analysis of the Investment Portfolio*

Tenure
Freehold   90%
Leasehold   10%

Use:
Shops   29%
Offices   70%
Others   1%

Location:
Scotland   1.5%
North of
England   98.5%

*by capital value

Figure 56   *Pie chart: property company's investments*

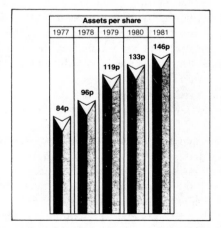

Assets per share				
1977	1978	1979	1980	1981
84p	96p	119p	133p	146p

Figure 57   *Three-dimensional bar chart successfully showing simple information*

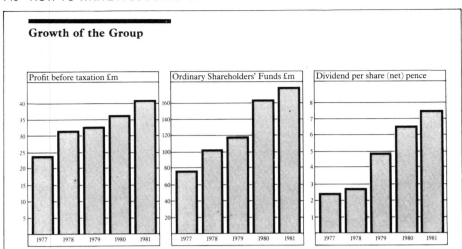

Figure 58 *Simple bar chart with clear y-axis marking and horizontal lines*

points. A very broad comparison such as that in Figure 61 can be demonstrated by a pictogram.[14] Figures are rounded and the simplistic presentation accounts only for quantity. There is no representation of quality or performance. Nevertheless the general impression survives effectively.

Tables enabling the reader to make his own calculations

Graphs

The most common of the type of illustration whereby the reader makes his own calculations and takes his own readings is a graph. Where more than one variable is represented the lines must be clearly distinguished by the way in which they are marked. This is done in Figure 62.[15] Ideally, however, the y-axis should be marked on both sides, particularly on highly informative and quite detailed graphs. It ensures that the reader's ruler is straight when he is taking readings from the graph. Sometimes this can be achieved by feint horizontal lines.

Where there is a clear break in the graph (see, for example, Figure 63[16]) between the first function (at the top) and the second (at the bottom), it is particularly important that the y-axis should include a clear, distinct break where the unit is the same throughout the comparison.

Sources must always be stated when presenting statistical information. If there is contradiction between two sources it may be appropriate to plot this discrepancy on a graph.

False zeros sometimes generate strangely emotive comments. There is no reason why the y-axis need start from 0, any more than the x-axis tracing monthly production need start at January. If most of the figures plotted are percentages or functions of an index of 100, they may well produce most of their readings between 80 and 120. In such a case, starting the y-axis at 0 would waste space, cramp the detail and generally be silly. The scale must not, however, distort the information in a way that is misleading.[17]

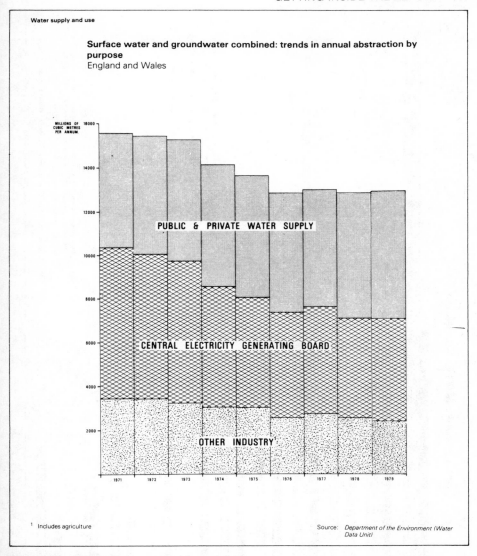

Water supply and use

Surface water and groundwater combined: trends in annual abstraction by purpose
England and Wales

¹ Includes agriculture

Source: *Department of the Environment (Water Data Unit)*

Figure 59 *Vertical compound bar chart*

The intervals on the axes must represent the accuracy of the sort of readings that the reader is likely to want to take. No other criterion is relevant.

Logarithmic scales cannot show 0 or minus quantities. They can be justified where it is necessary to show two widely removed variables on one graph, but they can be misleading and should only be used where essential.

Bar charts

While bar charts will normally be used for general impression, they may also show information of such detail that precise readings are more appropriate. Figure 64 shows such an example. It shows part (the Zinc and Lead columns) of a tabulation of heavy metals in mussels, expressed by sampling site.[18]

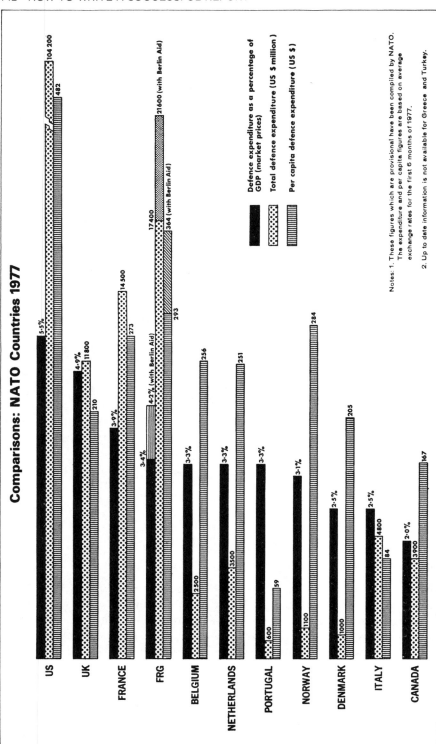

Figure 60   *Broken bar chart (see second line from top)*

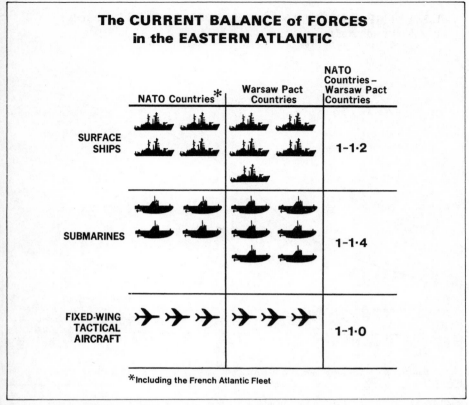

Figure 61   *Pictogram making very simple comparison*

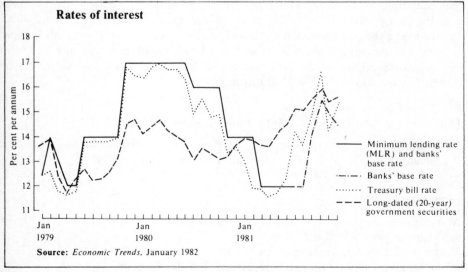

Figure 62   *Graph with four clearly distinguished variables*

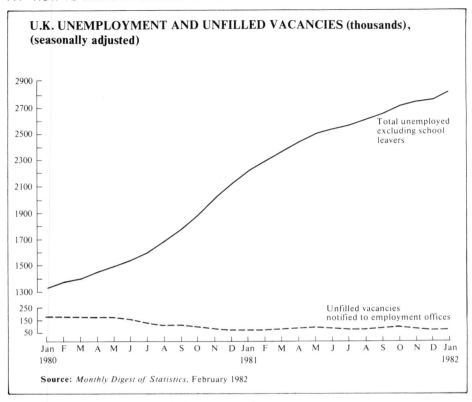

U.K. UNEMPLOYMENT AND UNFILLED VACANCIES (thousands),
(seasonally adjusted)

Total unemployed
excluding school
leavers

Unfilled vacancies
notified to employment offices

Jan F M A M J J A S O N D Jan F M A M J J A S O N D Jan
1980   1981   1982

Source: *Monthly Digest of Statistics*, February 1982

Figure 63   *Graph with clearly broken y-axis*

The following points are particularly noteworthy. The broken bar, in respect of the exceptionally high lead concentrations at Aberavon, is clearly shown and is equally clearly reflected in the scale. The sampling sites are listed in geographical order around the coast from Berwick-on-Tweed to Bowness. This is obviously more relevant and meaningful than alphabetical order or any other arrangements. (As in earlier shortcomings on the labelling of the *y*-axis, the *x*-axis should really be labelled at the top as well as the bottom.)

Diagrams representing the structure, working or mechanics of a system

The third type of diagram is that giving a picture of the functioning of any system, be it a machine, a sales area or just the organisation of a department.

Management structure

Management structures are traditionally shown in genealogical tables. The basic structure is often amplified by:
1   Lists of duties or areas of responsibilities.
2   A summary of the total staff represented in the diagram.
    Figure 65 shows detail of a management structure.[19] The summary at the foot

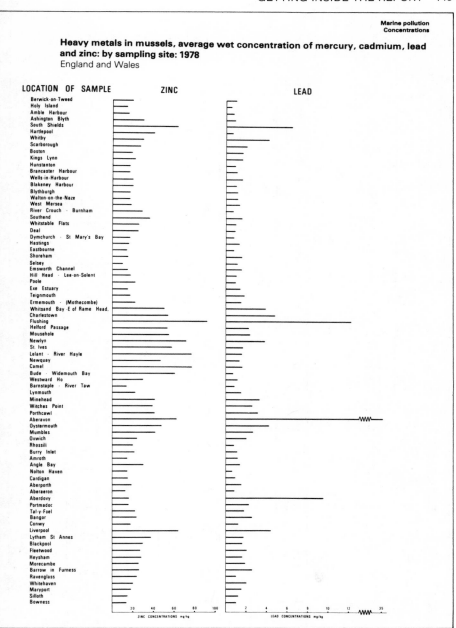

Figure 64   *Bar chart for detailed reading of information*

covers the whole table including many departments not included in the figure. The two trainees are properly divorced from the other particulars, as they are not part of any specific department. It is desirable for any such table to be dated and it is essential if individual names are included.

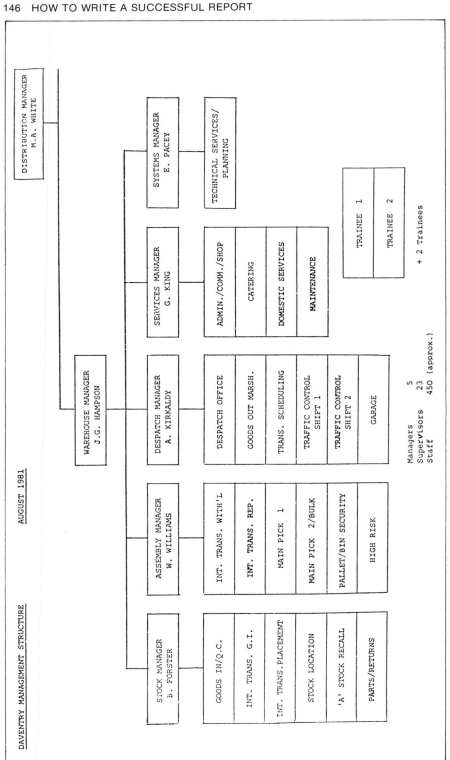

Figure 65 *Management structure diagram*

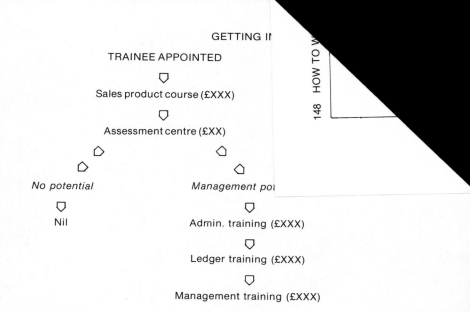

TRAINEE APPOINTED

Sales product course (£XXX)

Assessment centre (£XX)

No potential   Management pot

Nil   Admin. training (£XXX)

Ledger training (£XXX)

Management training (£XXX)

Figure 66   *Geneological tabulation (or tree) of accumulating costs*

Other uses of genealogical tables

Genealogical trees can, of course, be applied to very many other uses. For instance the simple tree in Figure 66 was used by Curry's Limited[20] to show the accumulation of cost involved in a scheme of management training. Algorithms and logical trees are, of course, a more complex extension of this principle.[21]

   Elaborate shareholdings may often be usefully set out in a similar way. Figure 67 is taken from a Monopolies Commission report on the proposed merger of a Canadian-based multinational distiller and The Highlands Distilleries Company Ltd.[22] This illustration appears to be extremely complicated at first glance. It is, however, no more than a reflection – and a clear picture – of a very complex structure. Shareholders who are not discussed in the accompanying paragraphs are, of course, omitted. There is no need to encumber the diagram with them.

Diagrams of machinery

Diagrams of machinery in cross-section are often appropriate to reports in the same way as they may be to technical manuals. Most systems must be simplified if the report is aimed at laymen. It must be labelled in simple terms. The schematic representation of a pressurised water reactor shown in Figure 68[23] is a very good example of such a picture.

Diagrams of systems

An even more symbolic approach is appropriate to the diagrams of systems of operation. Such a plan is the circuit diagram shown in Figure 69, describing the life of a returnable bottle sold over the counter in the off-licence trade.[24] It may appear rather elaborate, but it shows, by a consistent system of symbols, how the bottle enters or re-enters the circuit, is sold to the retailer, is sold by him and the various

Highland and R&B: group shareholding structure

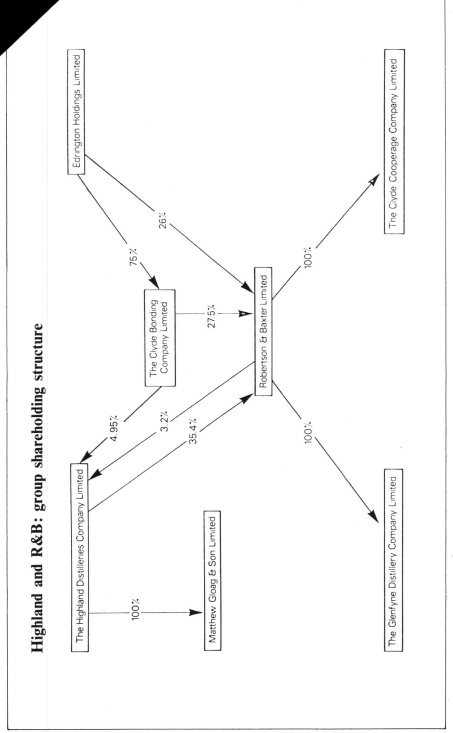

Figure 67 Explanation of complex shareholding structure

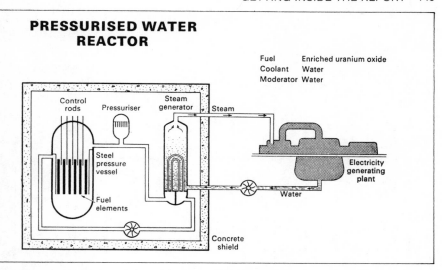

Figure 68 *Pressurised water reactor in simple diagram*

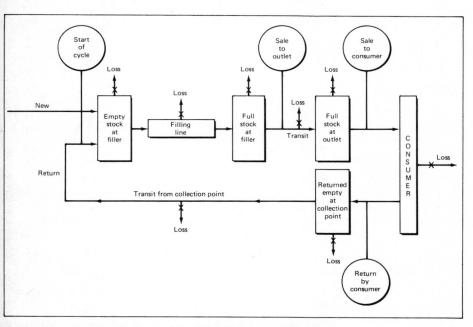

Figure 69 *Circuit diagram of the life of a returnable bottle*

points at which it may become lost. To explain the same procedures in words alone, even if it could be done in the same space, would certainly be less easy to follow.

Tables

The expression of numbers will be discussed in Chapter 11. Something must, however, be said here about the layout of tables. Tables with a $\sqrt{}$ or X configuration to show whether a particular quality is available or not are becoming increasingly

Plans for introducing further office technology

Case number	Description	Communicating WP	Stand alone WP	Combined WP and DP	Shared logic WP	OCR	Phototypesetting linked to WP	Computerized telex
1	Head office of oil company	√ now	√ now	√ now	√ probably	√ later in 1980	√ now	√ now
2	Finance organization	√ now						
3	University department		No - dispensing with present WP					
4	Organization sponsoring research		√ later in 1980					
5	Headquarters of chemical company	√ in 1-2 years	√ now	√ in 1-2 years		√ now		√ in 1-2 years
6	Division of chemical co.	√ in 5 years					Possibly in 1981	
7	Public administration departmental office	√ in 2-3 years	√ now	√ now	√ on order	√ next year	√ (probably)	
8	Research consultancy							
9	Public administration dept. office	√ in 5 years	√ progressively	Possibly in 1983	√ in 2-3 years			
	TOTAL	6	5	4	3	3	2	2

Figure 70 *Tabulation offering more complex information*

Table A2 Employees and trainees in the telecommunications industry analysed by sex and occupation, 1977/78 (percentages)

Occupation	Percentage of total (including trainees) by sex			Percentage of total under training October 1977		
	Male	Female	Total	Male	Female	Total
(1)	(2)	(3)	(4)	(5)	(6)	(7)
Managerial staff	6.2	0.1	4.0	2.9	0.0	2.0
Scientists and technologists	7.3	0.3	4.8	16.9	1.2	11.9
Technicians, including draughtsmen	22.0	0.9	14.4	41.5	1.0	28.5
Administrative and professional staff	7.9	2.1	5.8	7.8	2.8	6.2
Clerks, office machine operators, secretaries and typists	4.8	26.0	12.4	1.9	13.5	5.6
Supervisors, including foremen	9.2	2.6	6.8	1.9	1.0	1.6
Craftsmen	9.4	0.1	6.1	14.0	0.0	9.5
Operators	30.0	66.0	42.9	12.7	80.4	34.4
All other employees, excluding canteen staff and seafarers	3.2	2.1	2.8	0.4	0.1	0.3
Total	100.0	100.0	100.0	100.0	100.0	100.0

Source: EITB grant claim forms

Figure 71 *Well labelled tabulation*

popular. They do have merit, particularly in providing a simplified description for a committee of laymen, most of whom are unaware of the details and unlikely to be much interested in them.

Problems arise where more complicated options are represented in this way. Sometimes authors try to convey a fallacious accuracy in a rating scale of stars: ***, ** and * and so on. A simple descriptive phrase is likely to give a more precise indication. An example of this is shown in Figure 70[25] where the rather bland ticks are well supplemented by further explanation.

In tables made up solely of numbers, it is often a good idea to identify the columns by bracketed numbers as shown in Figure 71.[26] It is then easy to make reference to them, to circulate amendments or to make cross-reference to them. The practice can be taken a stage further by allotting numbers or letters to the lines. The columns and lines are well titled and, in the case of Colums 2 to 7, subtitled. It is always clear to what they refer. If the table were any more complex, horizontal and vertical lines might enhance it. This is very much a matter of opinion, however, as many people consider these distracting.

Maps and plans

Maps and plans require special attention. They must always have a scale and a

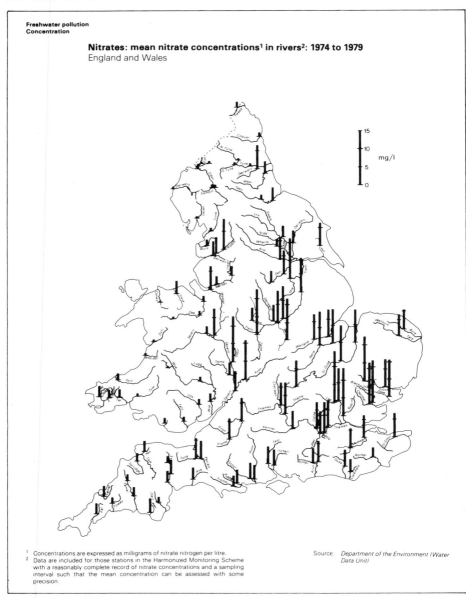

Freshwater pollution
Concentration

Nitrates: mean nitrate concentrations[1] in rivers[2]: 1974 to 1979
England and Wales

[1] Concentrations are expressed as milligrams of nitrate nitrogen per litre.
[2] Data are included for those stations in the Harmonized Monitoring Scheme with a reasonably complete record of nitrate concentrations and a sampling interval such that the mean concentration can be assessed with some precision.

Source: *Department of the Environment (Water Data Unit)*

Figure 72   *Imaginative map, but overcrowded in some parts*

north-point, even when these things seem obvious. Maps are sometimes too busy or overcrowded. The rather busy map in Figure 72 illustrates several points. This shows the mean nitrate concentrations in milligrams of nitrate nitrogen per litre of the rivers of England and Wales over a five-year period.[27] The idea is imaginative and general comparisons can be made, e.g. the notable increase in the Severn's content as it enters the West Midlands. The bars are essentially clarified by the horizontal notches at 5 and 10 mg intervals. However some parts of the map are extremely crowded and, therefore, not easy to follow, notably the Home Counties and southern part of East Anglia.

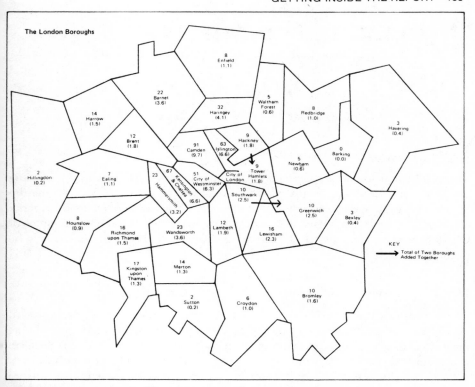

Figure 73 *Good use of impressionist map for simple return*

In many cases it will not be necessary for maps to follow literal geographical boundaries. An impressionist plan will do. The Arts Council layout of the London boroughs in Figure 73[28] suffices perfectly well for its purpose of indicating the number of respondents per 1,000 of population to their survey (and, in brackets, the number of theatrical respondents per 1,000). The arrow showing that the figures in the sections for Hackney and Tower Hamlets and for Southwark and Greenwich are totals are important.

Summary

Illustrations may clarify complicated issues or they may make quite simple information easier and quicker to assimilate. Nevertheless it is extremely important to avoid illustrations for their own sake.

No magic authority attaches to statics or to any graphic illustration. Sedgwick in C. P. Snow's *In Their Wisdom*[29] recalls 'some old mathematician saying that in an air raid he took refuge under the arch of probability'. This fatuous shelter was not enough for Sedgwick.

Before including an illustration of any kind, the report writer must ask himself:

1 Can this illustration stand on its own?
2 Is this the medium most suitable to the likely reader's needs? (Does the reader want a general impression, to take detailed readings, or to follow the mechanics of an equipment process of organisation?)
3 Is the display labelled and scaled so that it is quite clear what is being shown?
4 Does this display prove what is intended?

CHAPTER TEN

Organising the report

Outline of preparation

There are ten processes in the preparation of most reports (see Figure 74). In many cases these phases will be amalgamated. In some cases – such as where information comes from only one source – they will be over in the twinkling of an eye. In others – as when headings are not needed or where there is a standard framework – some of the steps will be non-existent. Nevertheless all steps of the framework should be borne in mind.

Identify the purpose of the report

The purpose of the report – expressed in the Introduction – must be expressed lucidly and unambiguously and should be kept before the writer at all times. Some people go to the lengths of pinning it up physically in front of them. Such an expedient is no good unless the writer keeps referring to it and relating his work to the object of the report. There is a danger that it will become part of the wallpaper (rather like the hearty quotations and glib maxims with which some offices are decorated).

The purpose (or aim or objective) may have:

1 Been given to the writer by a superior or another authority.
2 Be a traditional part of a routine; such as a monthly or weekly report or a visit report.
3 Been contrived by the writer himself on the basis of something which he has seen going wrong. It is no less important to stick to the objective just because the writer has drawn it up himself.

If the purpose is not kept in mind throughout the preparation and writing of the report, the writer will get distracted. Imbalances will occur. There will be temptations to ramble on about topics the writer happens to find interesting. He will be too detailed on aspects for which he chances to have a lot of information. Sloth will seduce him to avoid simplifying bits which he finds tricky. He will avoid issues that are embarrassing or controversial.

If the report is covering trials or experimental work, the objectives of the trials must be born in mind as well. These will very often be numerous, as in this case of Esso Petroleum trials on signature verification.[1] The following objectives were relevant:

1 To assess the performance of the system in terms of Type 1 (false reject rate) and Type 2 (false accept rate) errors.
2 To determine the security thresholds to set for different levels of access control.
3 To assess the degree of security afforded against the professional forger.
4 To assess the degree of variation in signature styles for different users.

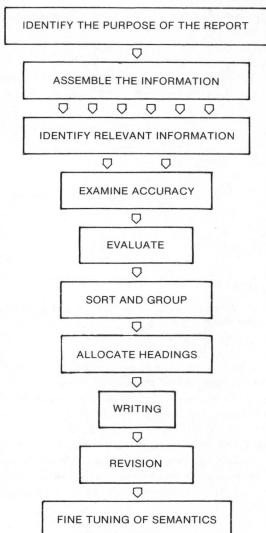

Figure 74   *Stages in preparation of a report*

5   To assess user opinion on both the technology and the implementation of the technology.
6   To assess the reliability of hardware/software.
7   To conduct the trials with an electromagnetic digitiser, so that it may be compared with the resistive type.
8   To assess the ergonomic design of the pen and terminal.

Assemble the information

Information and opinion (both the writer's and other people's) will emerge from many different sources for inclusion in the report. It will also come to light on unexpected occasions so a notebook and pencil should be kept in the writer's pocket or briefcase at all times during the preparation of a complex report of high cost of failure.

The net will – and must – be cast very wide at this stage. The detail will be thinned out later when the strictly relevant items are identified.

The list of possible sources is almost as limitless as the number of purposes for which reports are written. The following are among the most obvious:

Earlier reports
Correspondence
Minutes of meetings
Informal discussions
Technical trials
Fieldwork of every kind
Reference books
Questionnaires

Two examples will illustrate this.

Merchant banker's credit report

Compilation of credit report for a merchant bank will involve scrutiny and analysis of an astronomically wide diversity of published material: press comment, periodicals of every kind, industrial magazines, stock market reports and annual reports.

Annual reports will be examined not only for the overt claims of the chairman and directors and the bland figures of the audited accounts. Particular notice will be taken of the notes to the accounts which will give a more detailed idea as to the company's ambitions and problems. The published reports of other companies operating in the same trade will also deserve attention.

A substantial range of non-published information will also be tapped. The customer will be checked with other banks, possibly even indirectly with other customers. Earlier credit reports may be available. Most important there will be the need to analyse the voluminous details produced by the customer and elicited in discussion with him.

Area sales manager's report

An area sales manager will possibly examine his representatives' reports, reports of competitors' performance, retailers' stock turnover, local, and perhaps national, newspaper comment as well as the observations of such periodicals as *Marketfact* and *Which*. He will maintain a liaison with the customer relations and press departments so that feedback through complaints and other letters are reconciled with his performance results.

None of this information will come to light in the most convenient order or the most convenient form. It will probably not even be provided in uniform quantities. In certain circumstances the writer may be able to help himself by suggesting a format for certain types of return or submission. This must only be done if there is absolutely no danger of the form restricting the contributor in such a way that important information gets left out through lack of room.

Identify relevant information

A lot of information can be weeded out as being either irrelevant or too detailed in relation to other similar topics. While it is unwise to generalise on this very important process, two guidelines will be helpful:

(a) Relevance   The writer must apply all sorts of questions to the information he has assembled. For example:
1   Does this apply to this company?
2   Does this apply to these people?
3   Does this apply to these products?
4   Could this statute apply to this situation in the future?

(b) Balance   Once the relevance of the information has been established, it must be examined for balance. Aspects of equal standing should be discussed in equal detail. However, sometimes a particular bias to the report will be required. An exercise at UAC called for preparation of a general report describing UAC for a foreign reader with a particular interest in motor manufacture. The structure shown in Figure 75 was devised and was absolutely appropriate in the circumstances.

Where persuasive writing on a controversial subject is involved it is usually desirable to show both sides of the argument. This:
1   Shows that both sides of the question have been examined.
2   Should avoid the heavily distorted one-sided style, which is characteristic of extreme political journalism and lacks credibility.
3   Anticipates counter-arguments and thereby limits tedious extended correspondence.

For the report, *Industrial Democracy*,[2] to retain some validity despite the near-hysterical disagreements which were heard in the committee, Lord Bullock ensured that arguments both for and against were included.

It is at this stage that much of the information will be discarded, or at least set aside. This is indicated by the reduction of the number of arrows in Figure 74.

```
1.   UAC International

     (a) Location
     (b) Origin
     (c) Shareholding
     (d) Areas of business
     (e) Expansion
     (f) Other interests

2.   Divisions of UAC

     (Breweries, Foods, Medical, etc., described)

3.   UAC Motors

     (a) Origins
     (b) UK
     (c) Overseas
```

Figure 75   *Structure of general report for a foreign reader*

Examine accuracy

Most information can be taken at its face value but there will be some which must be validated. The following questions are typical of those which must be asked:

1   Have figures been irresponsibly and misleadingly rounded?
2   Are ratios meaningful?
3   Are percentages more expressive than bald numbers?
4   Is the fieldwork up to date?
5   (If names have been mentioned) Are staff-lists up to date? (Have this verified by telephone inquiry. Do not rely on rumour.)
6   Is the information sufficiently specific?
7   Does the information take into account recent legislation, safety instructions and working practices?
8   Does this apply to current equipment?
9   Are prices quoted up to date?
10 Are manuals to which reference is made the most recent editions?

Evaluate

Even when the technical accuracy of all the detail appears to be sound, there is still some evaluation to be done:

1   Information from different sources about the same kind of subject must be balanced and comparable.
2   Materials which have come from any biassed source must be trimmed back to realism. Such bias may be in the form of dishonest prejudice or it may just be the harmless gymnastics of advertising description.
3   Information must be as specific as possible. Generalisations which are the result of haste or of superficial investigation must be sharpened.

This phase is particularly important when preparing a comparison of claims by, say, manufacturers of office equipment, or some service such as office cleaning. The clichéd euphemisms of estate agents (*house of character, in need of some improvement*) have now passed into the lore of situation comedy. Yet the language of other trade is often no more helpful.

What are *hand-picked staff* in a security firm? Presumably they have been through a selection process like any other employee. To describe employees: 'All our drivers have been employed by the firm for a minimum of three years. No one is engaged who has not seen at least ten years' service, with good character, in the Police or Armed Services', is more specific and more helpful.

What is an *expert service*, or, more suspect, *professional staff*? Do they just mean that those providing the service have received some sort of training? Is professional just the opposite of amateur here? Some specified achievement or nominated referees who are in a position to give specific evaluation would be preferable and would enable a more accurate comparison to be made.

There is nothing morally wrong or commercially mischievous about these woolly descriptions. They are a healthy part of the exchanges of a competitive economy, they amuse the children and, frequently, help to sell a product or a service. However in preparing a balanced comparative report which is leading to a decision, they must be eliminated or replaced by more specific information.

Sort and group

This is probably the most important step of all. The items of information which have been identified must:

1 Be grouped into cohesive packages.
2 Be arranged into a sequence which helps the reader.

The order in which a report's sections are sequenced will depend, of course, on the reader's need and interest. It may be appropriate to start with the most interesting or the most important. The subject may be dealt with geographically or chronologically.

Recent Defence White Papers[3] have followed a train of thought from the general to the particular. They start with the global defence issues including the moral issue of arms control, then progress through nuclear defence policy and then conventional policy, particular small defence interests such as Hong Kong, community service, down to details of equipment, personnel handling and the details of how it is all funded.

The second report of the Department of the Environment's Working Group on Pop Festivals under Lady Stedman[4] demonstrates an extended chronological approach. First the law is discussed; in other words the framework within which the festivals must take place. Then the evidence submitted to the working group is summarised. The problems (of outdoor and indoor festivals, separately) are analysed. Possible approaches are discussed and then the report ends on the possibility of assistance from public funds; in other words the practicalities of sorting the problem out.

At this stage, definite headings are unlikely to have been allocated. A note as to the character of each group of information will have been made, but this is unlikely to be a sufficiently precise signpost to become the heading in the final report.

Allocate headings

The next stage, therefore, is to allocate headings. The headings must be:

1 Clear.
2 Unambiguous.
3 Different from each other. (If possible no heading should appear twice in the same report and certainly not in the same group of headings.)

Sometimes this function can be combined with the sorting and grouping procedure. They will take place simultaneously. Certainly in both processes the author will be guided by the objective of the report. The arrangement of the information and its description by title will depend on the angle from which the subject is tackled.

Because these two phases are so closely related, and sometimes simultaneous, one set of examples may be used to illustrate these two critical techniques. They are critical because if the information is not arranged in a logical sequence the reader will have difficulty in following it, the point and conclusion of the report will be obscured or lost altogether and the whole business will have been a waste of time. The second phase is critical because if the signposts are not lucid and precise the reader will not be able to pick out the bits that he wants.

On the Account Officers' Course at the European Training Centre of Citibank NA, a report writing module is included. A simple exercise in structuring and titling

(a)

```
OVERVIEW
ECONOMIC OVERVIEW
PUBLIC EXPENDITURE/BUDGET
BALANCE SHEET
```

(b)

```
COUNTRY OVERVIEW
ECONOMY
    Employment
    Energy
    Monetary
    International Trade
    Tourism
```

(c)

```
BALANCE OF PAYMENTS
EXTERNAL DEBT
INTERNAL ECONOMIC SITUATION
    Production and Consumption
    Budgetary and Monetary Policies
    Statistics
OUTLOOK
```

(d)

```
COUNTRY OVERVIEW (INFRASTRUCTURE
EMPLOYMENT
ENERGY
MONETARY
INTERNATIONAL TRADE
TOURISM
```

(e)

```
POPULATION
COMMUNICATION
EMPLOYMENT
GNP
ENERGY CONSUMPTION
INVESTMENTS
FISCAL POLICY
MONETARY POLICY
BALANCE OF PAYMENTS
    Goods
    Services
```

(f)

```
ENVIRONMENT
    General
    Economic Survey
GOVERNMENTAL POLICY
    (Local) Internal Situation
    International Relationship
INTERNATIONAL TRADE
    Oil
    Tourism
    Export/Import
```

Figure 76   *Six variations of grouping and titling of the same data* a report is set early in the course to demonstrate and practice the principles described here. The bank officers on the course are drawn from many nations and the authorship of the solutions discussed below is similarly diverse (British, German, Dutch, Spanish, Italian, Zimbabwean, South African and others), but the specifics are not important. They are issued with 30 disconnected points on a general economic issue. In this case it was the economic condition of Greece in a particular year. They work in pairs, to promote discussion, and are invited to sort these random details into clearly labelled groups for a report. No guidance is given on the purpose of the report, the number of headings or the desirability of sub-headings. They can devise any purpose for the report provided that the layout reflects it and is consistent in doing so. Six of the solutions are set out in Figure 76. It is perhaps surprising that only 30 pieces of data could simulate such diverse arrangements.

Figure 76(a) gives a very simple breakdown so that the sections will inevitably be long and the guidance given by the headlines slight. The headings are indeed very general. The first heading 'Overview' must be distinguished more precisely from the second 'Economic Overview'. What sort of overview does it give? The third and fourth suggest an accountancy approach to the problem. The national budget is compared with the way in which the economy has performed.

The approach in Figure 76(b) also demonstrates the need for an overview of some kind. Only one other heading of equal status is shown, 'Economy' which is, in fact, the subject of the whole report. The first section calls for no sub-division. On the other hand, the second section contains much diverse information; it is therefore properly and helpfully divided into what the author felt were the most important fields.

Figure 76(c) also demonstrates an approach based on an analysis of the Greek balance of payments. The external commitments are described first and then the internal difficulties. Care must be taken with a heading 'Statistics'. Is it really appropriate to segregate statistical information in this way? Is it being used as a repository for miscellany which will not fit under any other heading?

The approach in Figure 76(d) uses a straightforward division into six main headings; more first-rank headings than in any of the earlier examples. 'Employment', 'Energy', 'International Trade' and 'Tourism' are certainly important areas in the interpretation of these authors. 'Monetary', however, was an enormous heading in this answer and got out of hand as a receptacle for items which they could not place elsewhere.

If there is to be no extensive sub-division, then more first-rank headings are probably necessary, as in Figure 76(e). In this version each subject is treated discretely. The balance of payments was relegated to a less important placing than in some of the earlier examples, although it was a fairly long section and slightly divided.

Probably the most subtle of the suggested possibilities is in Figure 76(f). It has divided the material into three clear packages and has broken them down further in a helpful way. The sub-heading 'General' is of course totally uninformative in most circumstances, but is excusable as a sub-heading. The significance of the bracketed adjective '(Local)' is uncertain. It certainly adds nothing to the signpost.

Writing

Ideally at least one draft will be made before the final copy is produced. However, other pressures will sometimes (or frequently) make this impossible. In *I Like It Here* (Kingsley Amis), Garnet Bowen is seated in front of his typewriter 'his "rough draft" now unavailingly headed "First final draft"'. It had apparently 'got to page 19 again, the point where twice before he had ripped it up'.[5]

A celebrated historian emphasises that it is vital to get writing, to get something down on paper, however rambling and disjointed this may seem at the first attempt.[6] It can always be put right afterwards. The draft can be read aloud. The passage of time will magically suggest new and improved forms of words.

This is wonderful advice. If the report writer does not start writing as soon as he has assembled and sorted all his information, a mental constipation sets in. Indeed the longer the report is left, the more likely it is to assume bogyman dimensions. Quite minor report-writing tasks become a bugbear.

However it is vital to remember to do the revision.

Even a manuscript that is not going to get any typed drafting should be left overnight and re-examined in the morning. Erratic spellings, repetitious and *double entendres* which were not evident when first written will appear crystal clear the following day. If possible, the writer should read something completely different in the intervening period, in the train on the way home or at least in bed; a chapter or two of a well written novel or a reputable weekly. This will take his mind off the problem preoccupying him and he will look at it in a fresh light in the morning.

The mechanics of setting out the text of a report are explained in Chapter 11.

Revision

The report should be scrutinised in fine detail both in manuscript and in type/print. Type has the contradictory effects of:
1   Making a poor report (particularly a windy or vacuous one) appear better than it is.
2   Making spelling mistakes and word repetition appear more obvious.
In revising a report the following points must be borne in mind:
1   Balance between sections.
2   Avoidance of repetition.
3   Removal of contradiction.
4   Consistency of punctuation and accuracy of spelling.
5   Cross-referencing of paragraphs and figures.

Paul Johnson, criticising an article by Noam Chomsky, is astonished to find a very cumbersome sentence structure. Johnson goes on:

> Of course all of us may produce such horrors as we are setting our thoughts down. But we then cross them out, disentangle the syntax and start again. There is nothing to be ashamed of in getting a sentence wrong the first time. What shows contempt for the reader is the unwillingness to embark on even the most cursory revision.[7]

Just as an oral presentation will be rehearsed, it is highly desirable to try to report on a suitable reader. It is not always easy to get hold of someone with the time and patience. However the guinea-pig should:
1   Be as near the technical, intellectual and semantic level of the eventual reader-ship as possible.

2   Be prepared to offer constructive and detailed criticism.
3   Avoid nitpicking harmless points just to show that he has read it.

Fine tuning of semantics

Bowen in *I Like It Here*[8] on looking at a piece of obscure writing felt that he wanted to stand in front of whoever had written it with 'a peck, or better a bushel, of ripe tomatoes' and then he would throw one at the writer every time he was unable to justify a phrase 'on grounds of clarity, common sense, emotional decency and general morality'. The report writer must be just as severe with his own work, albeit less messy.

No doubt, in view of the strictures of earlier chapters, the writer will have taken great care to choose the most appropriate words available. There will still be scope for further checking before the report is finished. In particular:

1   Words which have been changed in the draft in order to provide variety must be checked to ensure that the sense of the passage has not been changed.
2   Where a word, clause or whole sentence has been inserted into a draft, the whole paragraph should be read (possibly aloud) to ensure grammatical consistency and to avoid repetition.
3   Use of words such as *recently*, *last year*, etc., which relate to a certain point in time should seldom be used unless supported by a specific date. These phrases become meaningless as time passes. However ephemeral the writer intends the report to be, the reader may keep it for much longer than he visualised.

Problems along the way

Editing contributions by several writers

The production of a report which is the compilation of the efforts of several writers gives rise to certain special problems. One member of the committee must be nominated editor, if one has not been appointed already. In particular the editor must watch for:

1   Uniformity of style.
2   Balance in contributors' treatment of similar aspects. Not only must he give them an indication of length, but also give guidelines as to whether prose, tabular or graphical treatment is suitable. If one sales area is described in four bar charts and a pie, it is unsatisfactory if the other area is described in the same document by 250 lines of prose.
3   Minutiae such as consistency in use of numbers, abbreviations, paragraph numbers and so on. The logic and importance of these tiny, and sometimes tiresome, details are described in Chapter 11. A whiteboard in the room which the committee is working in, or using as an office for periodic meetings, will be helpful. This can show such things as:
    a   Technical symbols used.
    b   Abbreviations and the point in the report at which they are introduced.
    c   Blocks of paragraph numbers allocated to individual contributors.
    d   List of appendices and the numbers allocated to them (so that other writers may make reference to them).
    e   Other documents to which cross-reference has been introduced.

The co-ordination of the contributions of a committee also produces wide problems of management. The members of the committee will be working at different paces on different parts of the work. Some will be on the draft of one part at a time when they are required to give their attention to the final proof of another. They will become isolated from one another and preoccupied with their own responsibilities for the time being. If different vested interests are represented or different attitudes of principle, disagreement is bound to arise and inevitably sometimes bitterness. After the 54 meetings of the committee of 22 which prepared *A Language for Life*, Lord Bullock always required them to lunch together. He placed great importance on these lunches and the harmony achieved and maintained by them.

Scissor-and-paste jobs

It will sometimes be expedient, or just unavoidable, to stick bits of earlier reports or other documents into a report. A first attempt may be cut up quite savagely, but certain paragraphs usefully salvaged. All the editorial problems described above apply here. In addition particular care must be taken with pronouns: *it*, *he*, *these* and so on. Do they refer to what is intended? Should the full noun be introduced?

Control of the manuscript

Great care must be taken to ensure that the manuscript and, later, the typescript is circulated safely during its preparation. It is unlikely that the whole document will get lost, although sillier things have happened. More realistic dangers to guard against include:

1   Pages becoming detached by accident. (Pages of a draft should therefore be numbered, contrary to the practice in many offices, and the total number of pages should be shown on the front of the draft; even if such a total number would not be appropriate on the end-product).
2   Specialists detaching their bits to play around with, while the rest of the report goes on its way. (This should never be allowed. It is almost impossible to keep track of a draft if it starts to be dismembered.)
3   Circulating several copies of a report in the mistaken view that it is likely to save time. (This should only be allowed if each recipient is to be responsible for amending a different section of the draft. If differing revisions are submitted independently without conference, the versions will be so diverse that they will be almost impossible to reconcile.)

For control of a draft, many organisations use a proforma. Figure 77 shows the job progress sheet employed by the National Nuclear Corporation. It is important that the progress table should have enough columns or boxes to allow for the maximum possible number of retypings. For several dates and signatures to be crammed into one slot is confusing and likely to defeat the object of the control which the form is intended to provide.

Time

The pressure of time is the factor about which the writer can do least. This was certainly a substantial problem with Lord Bullock's *Industrial Democracy*. To

```
                 ┌────────────────────────────────────────┐
                 │  JOB PROGRESS SHEET FOR GENERAL WORK     │
                 └────────────────────────────────────────┘

                                        JOB NO.................

                                        DATE RECEIVED.........

                                        INTERNAL/EXTERNAL ISSUE

  TITLE/NO ................................

  COST REF ...............................

  AUTHOR/DEPT ............................

  DATE REQUIRED ..........................


  SPECIFICATION

  PAPER (SIZE/WEIGHT)      A4/FOOLSCAP        70 g/85 g

  COVER...............................    BINDING............................

  NO OF COPIES ............................
```

PROGRESS	DATE
(1) TEXT	
EDITING	
TO TYPIST	
PROOFREADING	
TYPIST FOR CORRECTION	
FINAL PROOFREADING	
TO AUTHOR FOR APPROVAL	
RETURNED BY AUTHOR	
TYPIST FOR AMENDMENTS	
FINAL PROOFREADING	
TO OFFSET/XEROX	
COLLATING & BINDING	
COMPLETED AND PASSED TO AUTHOR	

```
  TOTAL NO OF PAGES.............        TOTAL NO OF FIGURES.............
```

Figure 77   *National Nuclear Corporation's job progress sheet for general work*

complete their task within a year they had to work long, arduous hours. Bullock himself signed the report in hospital, as a result of a mild coronary.

If a report writer has 24 hours to write a report, 24 hours he has. Apart from an initial pitiful complaint, there is generally nothing which he can do. However, there is one aspect of time that always remains within the scope of the writer and must remain within his control: that is planning.

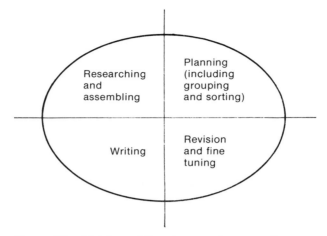

Figure 78 *Division of time in report preparation*

The allocation of time will depend on the complexity of the report and the amount of excavation necessary to winkle out the raw material. As a very general guideline, the division shown in Figure 78 will suffice. In most instances this represents an understatement of the time required for writing. However, as a simple cameo it gives a good indication of the general proportions in a well planned report.

Even in the best-made time-plans, there will always be unpredictable problems. A safety factor of 10 or 15 per cent should be built into all planning schedules, even if this means restricting the scope of the report or the number of drafts it will enjoy.

There will always be sickness, if not among the report writers, amongst typists, clerical staff, graphical artists and the many others in the chain. Photocopiers and other equipment will break down. The final draft will be drowned in coffee only a few hours before it has to be submitted. It is for these kinds of unwelcome eventuality that allowance must be made in every report plan.

Summary

Not in every report will the ten phases of report preparation be obvious or pronounced. Nevertheless on every occasion, each step should be considered before being discarded.

Particular care must be taken with the structure of the report in the sorting and grouping phase. If the information is poorly arranged, it will be difficult or impossible to follow. If the headings are carelessly chosen, information will be difficult to identify.

Even when small revisions are made to the script, the whole paragraph should be read to ensure that the change does not distort the sense of the whole.

The production of the report must be carefully planned. Sufficient time must be allowed, not just for writing, but for the equally important planning phases before and the revision stages afterwards.

CHAPTER ELEVEN

Typing or printing

Whether a report is submitted in manuscript, typescript or print will depend on its importance, circulation, length and expected life. The fine details of presentation are, however, not just a matter of administrative expediency.

Choice of script has been almost as important as the traumas of official language in recent history. Germany abandoned the Fraktur or Gothic script in 1941 because, despite its Teutonic appeal to Germans, it was unpalatable to the occupied nations of Europe.[1] Attaturk insisted on westernising Turkish official documents as part of his modernisation programme of the 1920s.[2]

Similarly the presentation of a report will affect its acceptability. This may be a question of style and courtesy such as the use of capital initials as discussed in Chapter 8. It may, however, affect the intelligibility of a report such as misuse of abbreviations, a carelessly insinuated diagram or poor spelling. It may just be a distraction such as inconsistent or illogical use of headings and print sizes.

All these are the product of the mechanics of typing or printing of the report. They are nonetheless ultimately the responsibility of the author who must make his intentions clear in his dictation or drafts.

Privacy markings

Privacy markings restrict the distribution and handling of the report. Some house styles list a sequence of privacy – or security – markings which all documents produced in the company must reflect. For example, in one professional firm:

CONFIDENTIAL might reflect the loosest level of marking which covers professionally sensitive material. This would be handled freely within the firm but not divulged outside except to the relevant client.

PRIVATE would be more sensitive.

PERSONAL would obviously be even more carefully treated and probably opened only by the addressee, not even by his secretary.

This produces a useful measure of control over the processing of sensitive material. However, such a scheme has important limitations of which users must be aware. The markings may not be understood outside the company. They will certainly not be accorded the same precise meaning. For example 'CONFIDENTIAL' as shown in the system above as the loosest form of restricted marking will be treated differently in a Government department: the same marking will attract lock and key and will be more limited in its circulation.

There is a danger of being over-cautious in classification so that privacy markings are used to excess. Worse, lack of confidence in the system will lead to a use of superlatives such as 'Strictly Confidential' to do duty as belt and braces. Like a word, a form of punctuation or any other feature of written communication, a privacy marking becomes devalued if overused. It becomes clichéd. Familiarity breeds contempt. This is just in the same way as excessive superlatives and over-lavish thanks or praise have a hollow ring about them.

Recipients will become blasé about privacy-marked material if it appears on their desks too frequently. Time will prevent them treating genuinely sensitive documents with the protection and security they deserve. In this way, the system either becomes slowed down and clogged by highly classified trivia or the plethora of markings are ignored. The latter difficulty is akin to the products of the cold canvass sales technique whereby unsolicited letters are marked 'Personal and Important'. This is now generally taken to indicate something that can be consigned to the waste-paper basket unopened.

Inclusion of appendices and tables

The content of tables has been discussed in Chapter 9. However some cosmetics are important. Tables should respect the same marginal disciplines as the rest of the text. If the table strays into the marginal space there is a likelihood that it may get chewed up by the binding – apart from appearing inelegant. If the temptation to include such an enormous table suggests itself, the writer must ask himself if it is not too elaborate, particularly for the main body of the report.

Coding of alternatives

Sometimes reports are concerned with comparing various products, properties or other alternatives. It is generally unhelpful to describe them as 'House A', 'House B' and so on. The reader will have to keep referring back to see which alternative is being discussed. On the other hand if the alternatives so described are complicated courses of action, e.g. 'To close the site at Reading, transfer the operation to Wolverhampton and to increase production at Manchester by 30%', these are laborious and complicated to repeat. Such a plan could indeed be more economically described as 'Option A'. Such a system was shown in Chapter 4 where a choice of plan for dealing with a problem of stock adjustment was effectively used by Warner-Lambert.

Abbreviations

Many generally accepted abbreviations are shown in dictionaries. Those shown in the *Concise Oxford Dictionary* are a good guide. Most of the major unions have been shown since the early 1970s. *SLADE* was added in the 1978 Addenda as was *ACAS*. That small set of Addenda[3] of 118 words also included *MLR*, *NEB* (as National Enterprise Board, the same abbreviation as *New English Bible* already being shown) and *PLO*.

In general the franchise of the dictionary will serve as an indication that an abbreviation may be used unexplained. Such inclusion suggests that British readers may reasonably be expected to be familiar with them. Exceptions to this rule are:

1   Abbreviations shown as particularly British or specialist usages which must be explained to American readers or to laymen, respectively.[4]
2   Abbreviations shown as colloquial, or slang such as *Trot* (Trotskyist).

If there is no indication of this sort that an abbreviation is generally understood, it is necessary to introduce it. This is usually done by showing it in brackets the first time it is mentioned as

```
Trade Union and Labour Relations Act (TULRA)
```

For example:

> We use the term 'word processing' (WP) technology to refer to all typewriters with sufficient electronic intelligence and storage to permit the modification and output of stored text. . . . For example, there is considerable variation in the claims made for productivity increases achieved through WP.[5]

A (draft) General Council for British Shipping report, *Tanker Safety and Pollution Prevention: Guidelines to Shipowners*, introduces Inter-Governmental Maritime Consultative Organisation (IMCO), Crude Oil Washing (COW) and Segregated ballast tank (SBT) which are not generally applicable, but are essential to the fluency of this particular report.

Some companies use inverted commas as well as brackets:

```
Enforcement Working Group ("EWG")
```

At first glance this may appear to be an unnecessary measure. However it is more than that. It is possible that the information which is to be abbreviated may already contain bracketed detail, as

```
W. H. Smith & Son (Holdings) Plc
```

It should be absolutely clear what is the abbreviation which the writer wishes to introduce into his report and what is part of the original information, thus:

```
W. H. Smith & Son (Holdings) Plc ("W. H. Smith")
```

or

```
W. H. Smith & Son (Holdings) Plc ("WHS")
```

Whatever form of introduction is used it must be done on the first occasion that the expression is mentioned in the report. Some writers choose to except a title: if introduced as part of a title, the abbreviation may pass unnoticed. Just as important, the abbreviation, once introduced, must be used again. Otherwise the reader, who has made a mental note of it on first encounter, reads to the end of the report, notices that there has been no recurrence of the abbreviation and reads the whole thing again.

Of course, some technical abbreviations can be accepted in a paper which is aimed at a strictly technical readership. Some companies take the sensible precaution of publishing a vocabulary in their reports. For instance, the National Nuclear Corporation's vocabulary for the letter C is as shown in Figure 79(a). They also produce a separate vocabulary of valve abbreviations, part of which is shown in Figure 79(b).

Very exceptionally the reader can be expected to know the meaning of an abbreviation, such as *P&L* (Profit & Loss) in an accountant's report, or *FX* (Foreign

(a)

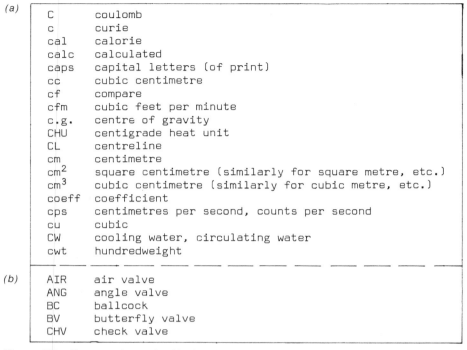

```
        C        coulomb
        c        curie
        cal      calorie
        calc     calculated
        caps     capital letters (of print)
        cc       cubic centimetre
        cf       compare
        cfm      cubic feet per minute
        c.g.     centre of gravity
        CHU      centigrade heat unit
        CL       centreline
        cm       centimetre
        cm²      square centimetre (similarly for square metre, etc.)
        cm³      cubic centimetre (similarly for cubic metre, etc.)
        coeff    coefficient
        cps      centimetres per second, counts per second
        cu       cubic
        CW       cooling water, circulating water
        cwt      hundredweight
```

(b)

```
        AIR      air valve
        ANG      angle valve
        BC       ballcock
        BV       butterfly valve
        CHV      check valve
```

Figure 79 *Extracts from the National Nuclear Corporation's vocabulary*

Exchange) and *TD* (Term Deposit) in a banker's report. To explain these would be patronising. However an assumption of this kind is exceptional. It should be restricted to internal reports addressed to internal readers whose understanding can be guaranteed.

Where the plural of an abbreviation is needed it is usual to add the *s* at the end of the whole abbreviation, regardless of logic; as in FOCs (and MOCs, come to that) although the plural relates to the Fathers (and Mothers) of the Chapel (one Chapel).[6]

Symbols

There is also a variety of symbols which have achieved general acceptability. In a financial report ( ) indicate deficit figures. For example:

1982	1983	1984
£'000	£'000	£'000
(14)	18	29

shows a deficit of £14,000 in 1982 and credit figures for the next two years. Of course, use of colours would clarify this further.

Square brackets [ ] indicate detail that has been inserted into a quotation to indicate a phrase popped in for clarity, e.g. to explain a pronoun

```
'He [the West Midlands Sales Manager] explained
that he had high hopes for the next 6 months.'
```

Other generally accepted symbols for technical work are to be found in *Hart's Rules for Compositors and Readers.*[7]

Quotation

The extravagant and slapdash use of inverted commas which has become fashion-able of late is discussed in Chapter 8, as they are really a function of style. However, some points on the physical reproduction of quotations may be helpful.

When to quote

Only quote directly as much as is necessary:
1   To show the original writer's precise intentions (as in terms of reference). The Scarman Report opens

> On 14 April 1981, . . . you appointed me to hold a local inquiry into certain matters connected with the policing of the Brixton area of South London. The terms of reference were:- 'to inquire urgently into the serious disorder in Brixton on 10–12 April 1981 and to report, with the power to make recommendations'.[8]

2   To show his precise wording. Later, the same report illustrated this also:

> This criticism of harassment was well summarised in the words of Mr Rene Webb, the Director of the Melting Pot Foundation . . . 'We do not object to what they do so much as to the way they do it'.[9]

What marks to use

There are two systems: double quotes " " as the primary (or outside) quotation marks and single quotes ' ' as the secondary (or internal) marks for quotes inside the original quotation and *vice-versa*, single quotes as primary and double quotes as secondary. In the USA double quotes are always the primary set. The same system is strongly advised for typewritten reports. Double quotes have only one job to do on a typewriter: the single quote also does duty as an apostrophe, exclamation mark and various other things. Printing practice in the United Kingdom is fairly evenly divided between the two practices.

Omission

If parts of a quotation are left out (as in the two Scarman quotations above), dots replace the omitted passage. Among various conventions is one where:
   . . .   3 dots represent less than a sentence,
   . . . . . .   6 dots represent a complete sentence or more.[10]

Questionable detail in the original

If a word in the quoted text is questionable, e.g. appears to be misspelt or to represent erratic mathematics, the Latin word *sic* (thus) should appear in brackets (and *italics* if available) immediately after the item questioned. There has been some overkill of this indicator in *Private Eye* but it can be used effectively to highlight suspect detail in this way.

Numbers

A uniform system for expression of numbers must be agreed for a report. This will often be laid down in a company typist's manual. In any case, the system must be uniform throughout the report. Three possible systems exist for cardinal numbers:

1 *Arabic numbers*   Arabic numbers (2, 3, 4, . . .) may be used throughout. The word *one* is usually used for 1 to avoid confusion with capital I. This system has the advantage of being economical on space. Some criticise it on grounds of inelegance.

2 *Words*   This is entirely satisfactory for small numbers, e.g. *six* and *sixteen*, but becomes absurd with such expressions as *nine-thousand eight-hundred and seventy-four*. There is a requirement to express numbers in this form in some legal documents, but its general application in report writing is very limited.

3 *Words up to ten*   A system which has a rather obscure and puzzling appeal is the use of words up to, say, ten and Arabic numbers thereafter. This weird compromise eases the conscience of those who for some reason are embarrassed by the naked digits for the lower figures without encumbering their reports with unwieldy expressions. However it produces uncomfortable contradictions such as 'It is hoped that between nine and 12 companies will be represented'.

In short, any of these systems will do and there seems little wrong – in most circumstances – with using Arabic numbers throughout.

If a number unavoidably occurs as the first word of a sentence, it is usual to write it as a word. This makes for more fluent reading and ensures that the number is not confused with, or mistaken for, a paragraph number.

Numbers over 1,000 must be punctuated by commas every three digits. If columnised a space at the relevant position will do. In prose commas are preferable (and essential if there is any danger of a number being split at the end of a line).

Emphasis

Words (as in the final paragraph of *In Place of Strife*):

> These are the major actions and policies which the Government proposes to strengthen and improve industrial relations in this country and which it will further discuss with the trade union movement and with managements. They are intended to retain the best aspects of our traditional system – its freedom, flexibility, tolerance and general sense of reasonable compromise, while at the same time enabling us to grapple with what is wrong. They are designed to build on the initiatives already being taken by management and unions and to reinforce, not weaken, their responsibility. They are an opportunity and a challenge. The Government proposes a joint effort with all those involved to remake and improve the relationships of people at work.[12]

or commas (as in the Sizewell B report):

> Satisfaction of these assessment levels should, in general, be sufficient for acceptability but, if reasonably practicable, it would be expected that suitable provisions be made to make the plant safer.[13]

are the most accurate form of emphasis. Exclamation marks, which have been discussed in Chapter 8, are a blunt form of emphasis covering the whole sentence in a thoroughly crude way. <u>Underlining</u>, BLOCK CAPITALS and **bold face** (the latter particularly popular with word-processor users) have the advantage of being specific to the word emphasised. However, they are over-emphatic and as a result may become confused with headings.

Courtesy

While precision and accuracy have quite properly been emphasised throughout these pages, it is important to remember the allied area of courtesy. The purpose of paying detailed attention to what may appear to be archaic styles of address and fine nickpicks of punctuation is to avoid giving offence. It is important that a well constructed, carefully drafted report should not be spoilt by a ha'porth of tar which is going to make the report less acceptable to the reader. Such slips occur in the following areas.

(a) Titles of organisations   The titles of organisations, companies, products and other proper nouns should be stated in the same form throughout. If Spicer & Pegler are so called at the beginning of the report, there must be no lapse into the more colloquial Spicers later in the report.

(b) Individual titles and descriptions   Such is the folly of human nature that inconsistency in forms of address or description can cause offence astonishingly easily. Examples include:
1   Use of Mr instead of Esq. if a report is addressed to someone by name (or, conversely, use of Esq. to an American unless he be a lawyer).
2   Omission of decorations in one case but not another.
3   Unconventional description of those with any kind of title or professional description.

Those seeking incontrovertible guidance in these quaint minutiae should refer to *Debrett's Correct Form*.[14] While much of it covers charming and, in some cases, possibly old-fashioned information on dinner-table seating and invitation-design, several parts[15] are highly pertinent to report writing. Furthermore its authority is undisputed, so that its pronouncements will prevent embarrassment in this strangely delicate area.

(c) Use of capital letters   In certain proper nouns the use of capital letters is undisputed. The names of countries and companies warrant them without question; as do months and days of the week, in all but a few Francophile (or perhaps francophile) firms.

The problem arises with such things as appointments. It can be argued that all appointment-titles should have capital initials; Managing Director, Sales Manager, Company Secretary and so on. In the 17th Century the problem would not have arisen as all nouns were allocated capital letters[16] (as they are to this day in German). Of late, however, a fashion has been advanced for showing appointments with lower case initials: chief executive, product manager. This unhelpful custom is of American origin and is unwelcome. It does not allow important detail – for such an appointment is – to be picked out at a glance.

Companies will often have their own style in this respect. Some (such as Ford

Motor Company) also extend their stipulations to the use of a Capital C for company when dealing with their own company. Those who are not blessed with such specific guidance or who intend to produce such a system are referred to in two books which provide general rulings in this area: *Hart's Rules for Compositors and Readers*[17] and *The Oxford Dictionary for Writers and Editors*.[18] Both are highly revered by lexicographers.

It must not be forgotten that in many particulars the use of capital initials will mean more than just fine distinctions of courtesy. The names of the political parties which are also common adjectives are good examples: a Conservative solution or a conservative solution, the history of Labour or the history of labour, a Liberal idea or a liberal idea.

Spelling

Unlike almost any other aspect of this subject, the rules of spelling are finite and, with very few exceptions,[19] not open to dispute. Lexicographers admit[20] that if usage insisted on a novel spelling they would record it. Patrick Hanks suggests that *overnite* may soon achieve this recognition.[21] For the time being, however, a particular spelling is certain. Changes are so infrequent that in this connection they may be ignored.

Unlike other unconventional aspects of report presentation, such as word use, punctuation or style, irregularities of spelling may therefore be described as wrong. Perhaps for this reason, many report writers deny any need for competence in this elementary field or are anxious to abdicate their responsibility and pass it on to the typist. The more common excuses include:

(a) 'I can always look it up in a dictionary.'   Indeed he may, but before he gets round to doing so, there has to be some doubt that the spelling is amiss.

(b) 'It's the typist's job.'   It is certainly the typist's job to query suspect spelling. However, the author's signature appears at the bottom of the report and it is his job to ensure that it is properly spelt. In this respect he must give particular attention to proper nouns and various homophones such as

accessary/accessory	forbear/forebear	sight/site
canvas/canvass	led/lead	stationary/stationery
complement/compliment	premises/premisses	storey/story
discreet/discrete	principal/principle	their/there

He must also check the similarities such as

allusion/illusion	later/latter	prescribed/proscribed

The last pair is particularly poignant as the two words mean the opposite of each other.

(c) 'Spelling does not matter.'   Whether the writer likes it or not, it does matter. Firstly, more and more homophones like those shown above emerge as the language expands. Frequently they have very important differences in meaning. Second, few things (not even erratic use of capital initials) irritate so much as misspellings. This type of ignorance, whether it threatens the clarity of the report or not, certainly makes the writer appear ludicrous.[22] Such mistakes destroy the credibility of the

report. Indeed because the edges are so well defined, spelling provides a sharp stick with which the critical or truculent may chastise the author.

There are certainly many anomalies in British spelling (fewer in American) for strange historical reasons[23] and freak mischances. Attempts have been made, notably by Bernard Shaw, to regularise it. He expressed his views in heavy correspondence in *The Times* for most of the first half of this century and supported it on many of his inimitable postcards to his friends.[24] Before Johnson's Dictionary, spelling was random and phonetic. Milton spelt *dumb* as *dumn*.[25] During the course of *Faerie Queene* Spenser spelt *hot* in six different ways.[26] However it must now be regarded as settled and, however bizarre, the conventions on which fortune has settled must be respected.

Forms of spelling calling for particular caution are the endings *-ize/-ise* and *-t/-ed*. The dictionaries offer both alternatives in many cases, but a report should be consistent. (It is worth remembering that all *-ise* words can be spelt with an 's' but not all can be spelt with a 'z'. Also watch out for the all too prevalent misspelling *analyze* that has arisen from a peculiar back-derivation from *-ize* words.)

There is an excellent little book published by Chambers entitled *Spell Well!* to help those who are seriously handicapped by their poor spelling. Oxford Dictionaries also offer *The Oxford Minidictionary* which achieves the same purpose. The minidictionary is a guide to meaning as well, and so also defines the words. Chambers does not, except to eliminate confusion.

Production of the typescript

Production of a typescript will be necessary whether the final copy is to be typewritten or set in type. The two most usual ways of passing the text of the report to the typist are, of course, a manuscript draft or dictation. The factors which will suggest the method are:
1 Importance of the report.
2 Familiarity with dictating procedures.
3 Speed of writing.
4 Time available.
For example this book was written in pencil manuscript, words and punctuation being changed by rubber. Its subject matter means that it must go under the semantic microscope. On the other hand, a factual report covering a series of routine site visits may be easier dictated.

It must be remembered that in judging paragraph and sentence length, five lines of most people's handwriting is the equivalent of only two lines of typescript. This is important for two reasons:
1 Sentences will look misleadingly cumbersome. (They should be read aloud to see if they are comprehensible.)
2 Paragraphs which may appear to be of reasonable length in manuscript may turn out brief and staccato.
Some notes on the two techniques follow.

Typing instructions

Typing instructions are an extremely personal matter. The only criterion by which they may be judged is that they require complete unequivocal comprehension by the typist. The major typing instructions should be attached on a sheet at the front, covering things as:

1   Number of copies.
2   Double or single spacing.
3   Type of paper.
4   Time and date for completion.

Detailed instructions should then be inserted in the margin of the text in a different implement to the main draft. These would include clarification of spellings, justification or sub-paragraphs, paragraph markings and indication of start of a new paragraph where this is not clear from line layout.

It is also a good idea to mark in a different colour any symbol or work which is to be verified before the draft is handed for typing:

```
The Sales Manager (East Anglia) Mr ✖    will be present.
```

The same applies to detailed cross-references within the report, as:

```
This point is amplified at Sub-paragraph  ✖   .
```

A marginal ✖ can augment this sort of reminder:

```
      It has now been agreed that the total
  ✖   sum available for this purpose is £✖.
  ✖   This will be available on ✖ July 1983.
  ✖   For further details see Appendix ✖ .
```

This will ensure that in the heat of the moment and the pressure which almost invariably characterises the closing hours of report preparation these details are discovered and included.

Dictation

The dictation of short reports has always been a time-saving expedient for those who are competent at dictation. (For those who are not good at it, it always has been and continues to be, time-wasting.) The dictation of longer reports, as a first draft, is becoming increasingly popular. This can be an excellent economy of time provided the draft is scrutinised sufficiently carefully. A typescript has a phoney respectability which is lacking in manuscript. So while some mistakes will become more evident, an even larger number are likely to be disguised by their appearance in typescript.

There are two common pitfalls in dictation, at opposite ends of the scale of preparation. They are:

1   Writing the whole report out in longhand and then reading it. Such a document could be typed by a copy-typist more cheaply.
2   Attempting to dictate without making any notes. This is unlikely to save time and will quite probably produce such a muddle that the whole procedure takes much longer.

The answer is a set of simple notes possibly set out on a standard form. Very simple notes are then inserted, giving a guide as to paragraph subjects (which may indeed become paragraph titles) in the left-hand column and the main points under each heading, in order, in the right. Cryptic notes are all that is required. The proforma should not be cluttered with complete sentences. A completed example is shown in Figure 80. In this way the writer has organised his ideas and prepared a set of notes to enable fluent dictation.

Ref.   GBS/123

TO: General Manager   Date: 1 May 1983
      cc Managing Director

1.   Intro
Gen. Man's memo 25 April
Discussed with SCL Ltd
Excluding Carlisle

2.   Item 1   Perimeter fencing
Renewal needed NW
Extension : lorry park
Cost of both £1,500

3.   Item 2   Security staff
Numbers from 8 to 10
Increase overtime 10%
Dogs: not required

4.   Item 3   Lighting
Perimeter lights OK
Are lights ordered?
Electricity bill up 15%

5.   Conclusion
All security satis.
Significant cost increase

6   Recommendations
Extend fence: lorry park
Increase budget for
security to cover overtime
and electricity

Figure 80 *Completed planning form for dictation*

In dictating, it is important to speak slowly and evenly, to speak into the microphone (or, if applicable, in the direction of the girl; rather than out of the window) and to avoid eating and drinking during dictation. These are basic suggestions, which may seem patronising. However it would not be necessary to make them if they were not regularly ignored.

As with all report writing, punctuation and spelling remain the writer's responsibility in a dictated report; not the typist's. This is particularly relevant with commas and capital initial letters. Commas can transform the meaning of a sentence. As for instance in the difference between defining relative clauses 'the product which we make at Birmingham' or descriptive 'the product, which we make at Birmingham'. The second is just giving a bit of extra information about the product. The first is identifying that it is the Birmingham (as opposed to the Leeds) product which is under discussion.[27]

The dictator must include the spelling of difficult words and of words with homophones. Proper names, unless specifically familiar to the typist, must always be dictated. Unless the typist knows the individual mentioned, she will not know whether *Alan* or *Allan*, *Brook* or *Brooke* (or *Broke*) is intended. To count on the most obvious spelling of a name being understood by the typist is subjective and hazardous.

It is civilised to greet the typist at the beginning of each report and to forecast how long the tape or dictation session will last. Thereafter it is important to make it clear every time a new document begins. Any remarkable points about the layout should be clarified at the beginning. For a long report an overview of its structure may be helpful. If the report is in draft, it must be declared whether double- or treble-spacing is required. Also at the beginning, the number of copies must be specified (with the distribution also being given at some stage).

At the close, it is important to remember to specify the signature block appropriate (if there are any alternatives). Appendices and enclosures must be listed.

Printed presentation

A display of common print types (type faces) is given in Appendix 1.

In choosing headings for printed reports, it is a good idea to choose type faces or styles as diverse as possible to emphasise the differences between the various levels of heading. Chapter or Section size should be as large (or bold) as possible. The lowest level of heading, however, must be clearly distinguishable from the run-of-the mill text. (As an example, the main subheads in the chapters of this book are set in text face bold, the sub-subheads in text face italic.)

The symbols used in proof correction are available in a large number of manuals.[28]

Translation

Where it is necessary to translate a report into another language, the translation must be checked by a native-speaker of the tongue in question. However good a British translator may be, there are bound to be some nuances, *double entendres* and colloquialisms which he misses. The problems of over-confidence in this respect were demonstrated during a visit to Poland by Jimmy Carter during his Presidency. In a speech in Polish he expressed his affection for the people of Poland by saying that he wished carnal knowledge of them. This was not the only gaffe perpetrated by inadequate translation on the tour.

Summary

The need for attention to detail in the typing or printing of a report cannot be over-stated. It covers consistency in the introduction and use of abbreviations. Symbols and numbers must also be used in a uniform and logical system. Quotations should be used only when it is appropriate to specify the precise form of words used.

This care must also be extended to explanation of the writer's intentions to the typist, be it in manuscript or in dictation. Of course, in many cases typists will be able to clarify questionable instructions or elements of the report. However, clear watertight instructions will always ensure that temporary staff can do the work. Otherwise ambiguities which may never occur to the writer may still suggest them-selves to the typist.

CHAPTER TWELVE

Binding and presentation

The manner in which the whole report is put together will depend on these factors:
1 The size of the document, both in paper size[1] and thickness.
2 To whom it is going, including to how many people.
3 Its cost of failure.
4 The number of times the reader is going to refer back to it, in other words the need for robustness.
5 Its expected life.

Binding for reports

The simplest form of binding is just a staple or pin at the top. However, there is then a progression through a number of various intermediary bindings right up to the kind suitable for a permanent printed document:

(a) Staples A paper-clip should never be used, however ephemeral the report and however imminent the need may be to dismember it for photocopying. Paper-clips get caught up with other papers and bits of the report get detached. Pins are an improvement but they can be hazardous and may shed blood on to the finished product. A staple has none of these disadvantages. The top left-hand corner is the most convenient place for easy reading. If need be, staple the report from the back and the front with longer reports. They can be placed down the left side for a more book-like appearance. If this is done, it is important that:
1 A big enough margin is left.
2 Enough staples are used including one each at the top and bottom. If this is not done the report will become dog-eared and scruffy.

(b) Treasury tags Notwithstanding the possibility of having staples in the report from both back and front, they will not manage to hold a report of more than about 25 pages. Even then, if the report is much handled it will be in danger of coming apart. A treasury tag through a hole will deal with up to about 100 sheets. (These approximations in sheet numbers obviously depend on paper thickness.) Care must be taken to ensure that the hole is an inch or so into the paper, to avoid the tag tearing loose.

(c) Slide binder A slide binder down the side of the report will not hold more than about 25 sheets and there is still a danger that some will drop out. A thin cover should be chosen unless there are very few sheets in the report. The report will not open flat but it gives a more elegant appearance than staples.

(d) Plastic comb This uses a machine to insert a comb into up to about 20 sheets. Various colours can be used to distinguish reports. The document will open flat and new sheets can be inserted or old ones removed.

(e) Velobind   This is a type of plastic-binding which can manage up to about 20 sheets, or, with a system of multiple punching, nearly one inch of paper. The report will not open flat. The equipment is about twice as expensive as that for conventional plastic comb binding.

(f) Wire binding   This is a similar process to plastic comb binding. Wire is used instead of plastic. About a dozen sheets may be bound and the report will open flat. However no new sheets can be inserted. The cost of the equipment is comparable to that of a plastic comb binder.

(g) Hot melt glueing   This is a much more sophisticated system than anything described up to now. Various systems for glueing the report exist. For example, one applies hot glue with a roller; another involves tape which is impregnated with glue. Cost ranges widely from less expensive to much more expensive than wire and plastic comb bindings.

(h) Perfect binding   In this process, the ends of the papers are frayed and glue is poured over the edge. It is ideal for a document such as a telephone directory. However it is only suitable for matte paper. It is not very robust and there is a danger that the glue will not have reached some of the pages.

It may be that for an internal report, a file cover, or transparent wallet will suffice. The principal stationers and manufacturers offer extensive ranges to cover the whole variety of price ranges and sizes. For example, that by Spicers[2] is particularly appetising. Nevertheless, even if a loose wallet is used, a staple should hold the report together inside.

Paper

The standard of paper used for a report is directly dictated by the amount of money which it is proposed to spend. It should be borne in mind when choosing paper that a complex report may well be enhanced by a choice of different coloured papers for each section. In particular:

1   Such distinctions by colour must be logical and rational. Random choice of papers will only confuse the reader who will seek a pattern where none may exist.
2   Easily distinguishable colours should be chosen.
3   On the other hand, very dark papers on which it is difficult to read print or typescript should be avoided.

If coloured papers are not justified, coloured partitions may be a cheaper expedient.

The leading paper manufacturers offer a wide range of papers at all prices and of all qualities. Of course price increases with more calendering, the process whereby paper is treated with clay. Not only is highly-calendered paper more aesthetically pleasing but it also reflects fingerprints. The more exciting colours also tend to be more expensive.

Papers of up to 100 grams per square metre (shown as g/m^2 or gsm) are only suitable for printing on one side. If two-sided work is attempted on the thinner papers, the text will show through, in the same irritating way as air-mail letters written in biro. On the other hand papers much over 70 gsm are not suitable for carbon work. The heavier papers are also more bulky.

Advice on paper choice will be forthcoming from any reputable distributor, e.g. Wiggins Teape.[3] Their Stratakolour (89 gsm and 176 gsm) range offers a good sequence of the paler colours. Their Keaycolour (120 gsm and 500 gsm) offers a particularly excellent range of 40 colours of heavier paper. The Kronor (120 gsm and 225 gsm) sits between the two in points of weight and colour range.

Covers

Many reports which are short and for internal circulation can make do with just a title underlined. Others such as the cover of an Esso report shown in Figure 81[4] will use a simple (in this case, very simple) cover sheet.

Some organisations will consistently use a more complex form of cover sheet, including perhaps a motif or logo and reference number. A good example of this more formal approach is shown in the National Nuclear Corporation Limited model cover in Figure 82.

In some companies, the fluency and security of report circulation is facilitated by a uniform outer cover regardless of the content of the report. Such a system is represented by the Trustee Savings Bank. The inner paper cover is arranged as shown in Figure 83,[5] including the initials of the author (KL) and the date. Then an outer board cover is superimposed, in TSB's case usually dark blue and plain, with a hole (shown by the dashed line in Figure 83) cut to show the title from the inner cover. Some companies have a motif or logo on the outer cover.

The range of boards available for this purpose is well illustrated by the products of G. F. Smith & Son,[6] one of the leading board manufacturers. Their ranges, Colorplan, Brilliant and Grandee, are the most comprehensive. Their complete range offers 98 colours and textures.

Many reports which have a public relations role, such as an annual report, will justify greater expenditure. Glossy covers with illustrations may be expected. The National Coal Board annual reports[7] are good examples of this more imaginative

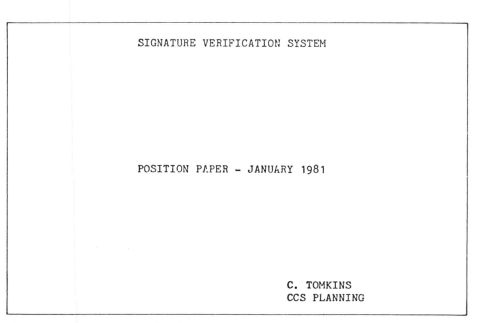

Figure 81 *Simple cover sheet*

REPORT NO.   NNC 1322
             Tech Memo P&S(R)1234

DATE   February 1982

DEPARTMENT   Technical

The assessment of the radiological hazards
at Hartlepool/Heysham I Power Stations
that could result from a dropped fuel stringer
accident during on-load refuelling

by

Mr J Ruskin and Dr T Carlyle

R167-NNC1322(1)

Figure 82 *Elaborate cover sheet with reference number*

TRUSTEE SAVINGS BANKS CENTRAL BOARD
Computer Division

UNIPAY   -   FUTURE DEVELOPMENTS

3160/12
KL

COMPUTER DIVISION
TSB Central Board
December 1980

Station House Stamford New Road Altrincham Cheshire WA14 1EP   Telephone 061-941 2458/9

Figure 83 *Inner cover sheet of TSB report. The material inside the dashed line indicates the hole on the outer cover*

approach. Their covers give a good insight into recent achievements and developments by the Board. They are relevant to the content of the report and are topical.
Both these aspects are important.

Distribution lists

Frequently a report cover will include the distribution list.

Standard distribution lists

Use of standard distribution lists may be helpful. For instance internal heads of
department could be List A, regional sales managers could be List B and so on.
However it is very important to ensure that unnecessary copies are not circulated in
this way. Everyone on each list should be given a serial number so that they can be
excepted like this:

```
Distribution:   List A (less 4)
                List B
                List C (6-10 only)
```

Blocking of distribution lists

If the distribution list is very long or the geographical distribution of the company
very wide, it may be a good idea to divide the list into such blocks as:

```
Internal
External: UK
External: USA
External: Continental Europe
```

Often information addressees can be blocked off in the same way.

Numbering of addressees

While it is slightly beyond the scope of report distribution and more part of general
office management, the system of referring to addressees by office number is worth
a mention. This system is rigorously enforced by the Ford Motor Company and is
very strongly encouraged by the company in their external correspondence.

In this way a distribution list in Ford will show a number against every name, as

```
J.Brown 1/155
```

The 1 indicates that the recipient is in their UK head office at Eagle Way,
Brentwood. The 155 shows the room number, on the first floor of that building.

Summary

The binding and presentation of a report is the last thing to be done to it. Yet it must
be given sufficient attention as it creates the first impression to the reader.

A cover will ensure the durability of the report. It may also improve its security.

Coloured papers or partitions may also ensure that a report is improved for reference.

The distribution list must be set out in a way that is at once simple and explicit. It must allow speed of handling by the mailing rooms but must never be so simplistic that it generates more copies of the document than the subject matter justifies.

PART THREE

REPORTS NEEDING SPECIAL CARE

CHAPTER THIRTEEN

Appraisal reports

In all reports, the writer carries a heavy burden in reducing events and opinion to the more concise form appropriate to his medium, without losing accuracy. Nowhere is this responsibility more acute than in the area of appraisal reports. Yet nowhere are the temptations to use evasive semantic euphemisms more in evidence.

In the space of perhaps a couple of A4 sheets, or whatever practicality allows, the reporter must account for an employee's complete performance in 365 days. Good days, bad days, hangover days, days of partial concentration, brilliant flashes of inspiration, hours of work beyond the call of duty must all be described in the space provided.

The language of an appraisal report

Words or numbers

A continuum of possibilities in presentation of this information runs from a prose essay to a matrix of boxes, which offer a range of points from 1 to 10. Personnel staff frequently favour the latter. It is clean, tidy and lends itself to definitive mathematical comparison. Those of a paternalist disposition favour the prose description. Probably for most cases the answer lies somewhere between the two.

The numerate system is too clinical. It gives a spurious accuracy to qualities that are incapable of precise measurement. The distinction between five points for, say, technical competence and four points is not as clean-cut and discrete as the distinction between those numbers suggests. The man who just gets five points will be as near the man who just misses the five grade as he will to the one who easily gets five.

It can be said that the all-prose version places too much dependence on the writer's skill with language. Perhaps this is so, but, without doubt, a more precise representation can be achieved with words than in the impersonal mystery of numbers.

Consider the difficulty of reducing these somewhat contradictory characteristics of a typing-pool supervisor to a simple numerate analysis. Imagine her to be 30 years old and called Emily:

1   She is an intelligent girl who has one 'A' level and is working for another by correspondence.
2   She supervises her pool of 10 girls very firmly. She is considerably more intelligent than any of them and feels that she could be doing a better job.
3   She is younger than two of the typists in the pool: two middle-aged women, who worked there before Emily came to the company. They resent her running the pool, but accept that she is more capable than they are. In general, she has maintained a reasonable working relationship with them.

4   Her sharp intellect enables her to impose very high standards of accuracy and neatness on the pool. However, she is often tactless in achieving these standards. On nine occasions the office manager has had girls in his office complaining of the harshness of Emily's criticisms.

5   She is of smart appearance and is always well dressed.

6   On five occasions during the year she was over an hour late. On one occasion she did not appear in the office until 12 o'clock. The typing pool ran unsupervised on a particularly busy morning. The result was chaos and the typing pool took several days to recover. She has long agitated for the pool to work on flexitime. However, the Board have turned this down twice and she is reluctant to take 'No' for an answer.

7   She participates regularly in the life of the Company Social Club. She has represented the company in badminton matches on several occasions.

8   She is always polite to her superiors and equals, although on one day last summer there was a certain amount of unpleasantness between her and the Personal Assistant to the Sales Manager.

9   In the absence of certain senior secretarial staff, she personally provides shorthand cover in emergency. She does this willingly and highly efficiently. Her shorthand at 120 words per minute is everything that it should be.

10 On her own initiative, she has re-drafted the company manual 'Instructions for Typists'. Her revised document of 40 pages has been adopted by all departments of the company.

A compromise between a numerical and a prose format may often be the answer.

Use of numerical ratings in an appraisal form

That part of the form which does consist of boxes and points must be imaginatively designed. It may be supported by a key – for the reporter's use – to guide him as to likely interpretations of the grades and thus ensure fairness and uniformity of marking.

The less important qualities must be restricted in the maximum points available. Consider the situation in Figure 84(a) which might be describing an interpreter's performance. It enables a very smart, inarticulate employee to score more highly than a very lucid interpreter who is less spectacular in appearance as in the lower part. This could be revised as in Figure 84(b) to reduce the maxima for the less relevant qualities.

The problems of designing a rating-scale are not to be underestimated. The Stewarts in the definitive study on this subject say that 'the design of rating scales is something that nobody ever gets completely right, because of conflicting demands and expectations'.[1]

Not only is the design of the forms tricky. The reporters have to guard against creep.[2] If the form offers five options, A to E, and the norm is C, lenient, feeble or wet reporters will tend towards B. B will then become the norm and the markings will be devalued. It is a similar form of devaluation to the devaluation of words described towards the end of Chapter 6.

However this can only provide background data and will indicate such things as a minimum standard of competence to be considered for promotion and so on. The onus for making the finer distinctions must rest on the flexibility of words.

(a)

	1	2	3	4	5	6	7	8	9	10
Smartness										✕
Lucidity			✕							

	1	2	3	4	5	6	7	8	9	10
Smartness		✕								
Lucidity										✕

(b)

	1	2	3	4	5	6	7	8	9	10
Smartness						////	////	////	////	////
Lucidity										

Figure 84   *Brief examples of* (a) *unmodified and* (b) *modified numerate rating systems*

Use of words in appraisal forms

The lapse into generalisation is almost inescapable in appraisal. However each one will lay the writer open to a request to substantiate the generalised comment. Such a request may come from above as in the case of the use of words such as *adequate* or *satisfactory*. It may come from the subject of the report as in unpunctual *on one or two occasions*. This immediately invites the inquiry from the appraised: 'What were the occasions?'

It must be possible to justify every word and every phrase. This, of course, is true of all reports, but of nothing is it more pertinent and more critical than the highly poignant phrasing of appraisal reports. To this end, a notebook of significant points about each employee may have to be kept. This will be entirely personal to the writer, but will ensure that he produces a balanced account of the whole period. Otherwise it is easy for events which happen to have taken place in the last three or four months to achieve a disproportionate significance.

This is not the sinister measure which it might appear. It is an efficient expedient to ensure fair, consistent and accurate appraisal. It is particularly the rather grey, nebulous man in the middle who will benefit from this type of record. The very good and the dreadful are easy. Their performances will be remembered in some detail for their excellence and their awfulness. It is with those whose achievements are routine and unmemorable that the writer will grasp at unfair generalisations if he has no such pocket record to assist his thinking.

Because of the shortage of space on a report, a specially direct style of writing is necessary. In particular:

1   Euphemism must be avoided. In military reports the expression 'a good mess member' was once fashionable to describe a species of avuncular time-serving senior non-commissioned officer who spent most of their time in the bar. This is evasive writing which relies on the reader interpreting the arcane code aright.
2   Litotes and understatement are generally unhelpful too. Terms such as 'not unindustrious' can cover the whole range from 'just avoids being bone idle' to the superlatives of hard work.

Attitudes to appraisal reports

The purpose of appraisal

There are three clear but interrelated purposes of appraisal:
1   To improve performance.
2   To highlight training needs.
3   To identify promotion potential.
The second and third will follow from the first. As with any other report, the design must reflect these objectives.

American management has for much of this century adopted a more structured approach to management appraisal than has been fashionable in Europe. British practice has followed American techniques rather slowly. The feeling that there is something slightly improper about analysing an employee's performance in anything except the most general platitudes has hindered developments in this field. However three phases can be detected. They represent refinements of the techniques which bring the design of reports nearer to the objectives which they set out to satisfy:
1   Personality reporting.
2   Performance criteria.
3   Job objectives.
Companies have introduced the stages at varying paces. Some may have good reason for a more cautious approach. Others, such as the Civil Service, have always been in the vanguard of progress. The dates indicated below are therefore only generalisations and there will be exceptions in both directions.

Personality reporting

Until the late 1960s and early 1970s such appraisal reporting as existed was restricted to broad-brush comments on the employee's personality. Tidyness, technical competence and like qualities were explained in the broadest language, with little regard to the particular requirements of his employment. In the main, this was done on unstructured forms with only occasional guidance as to the qualities to be discussed. Some use was made of numerate rating boxes.

The resulting reports relied heavily on the priorities of the reporting manager. Consistency was almost non-existent and interpretation of the description depended too much on the coincidence of the reporter and reader having the same values.

An example of such a design formerly used by Miles Laboratories Ltd is shown in Figure 85. Other Miles Laboratories forms will be used for comparison.

Performance criteria

The next development was the establishment of certain criteria against which he is judged. This became particularly popular around the mid-1970s.

The reporters are given particular criteria which they have to consider. Questions may be asked on the form: Is he accurate? Can he meet deadlines? It is important to recognise that not all criteria will apply in equal significance to all employees and to reflect these varying values in the completed report. A good example of this type of layout is the format with which Miles Laboratories replaced that in Figure 85. The significant pages of this are shown in Figure 86. The cover-sheet is a simple resumé of the appraised's date of birth, qualifications and employment but also including the important complementary boxes.

```
Actions for improvement
          By whom
          Implementation date
Training requirements
```

The same principles may be applied to courses assessing employees' suitability for promotion. The criteria shown in Figure 87 were laid down by a retail company on a course assessing potential branch managers. The report will then reflect these criteria, as shown in Figure 88. (The report does not discuss the criteria in the same order.) In such a case it will probably be desirable to supplement these criteria-related reports with a general summary of the candidate's performance and – where the standard achieved is as low as that – some remedial suggestions. Here, the comments shown in Figure 89 satisfied this requirement.

The criteria-based report might be further amplified by marks or accounts of the candidate's performance in any tests or exercises. In this supplementary capacity quite crude numerate pieces of data may still be helpful. In the case study under discussion exercise rating summaries such as that at Figure 90 were so attached. (The ratings shown are those of another candidate, as they are a better illustration than those of Mr XXX.) Here four exercises, of which one appears not to have been completed or, at least, not graded, are considered by criteria. The rating scale is from 0 to 5 with 5 being the best. It is important that these formats should provide a space for expansionary comments. In Figure 90 it has proved necessary to comment in such a column on this candidate's particularly good performance in one-to-one situations. (It would have been better to have spelt out the 'one-to-one' as '1-1' is confusing among the gradings.) It was also a good idea to make the important division, against Stress Tolerance, between his good performance one-to-one and his rather weaker showing in group-work and on paper.

Job objectives

The third stage in the chronological development of appraisal reporting ties the standards of performance directly to quantifiable achievements. An area sales manager might be expected to improve penetration of his area by 20 per cent. It can

PRIVATE AND
CONFIDENTIAL

STAFF APPRAISAL AND

DEVELOPMENT SCHEME

PERFORMANCE APPRAISAL FORM

Employee's Name and Initials	
Date of Birth Date Joined	Location/Department
Present Position	Date of last Appraisal Interview
Date of assuming present Position	Date of this Appraisal interview
Qualifications	

NOTES FOR GUIDANCE

1. Miles Laboratories Ltd. Staff Appraisal and Development Scheme is designed as a framework for individual development allied to the achievement of the company's objectives. For this purpose it is necessary to:

   (a) Clarify the individual's main duties and responsibilities
   (b) Set the objectives which he should aim to achieve
   (c) Assess his achievements against the objectives set
   (d) Establish his training and development needs

   The Scheme is also designed to assist in the planning of the individual's career and in furthering the Management Development plans of the company.

2. Before commencing any appraisal please study the Appraisal and Development Guide, and read through the form carefully.

3. Commence the appraisal by completing parts 1, 2 of the form.

4. You should remember to give your employee a copy of the Review Preparation Form, on which has been entered the time and date of his interview, at least a week before the interview is due.

5. This form should be formally completed after the interview and then forwarded under confidential cover to your manager, together with a copy of the job description on which the appraisal has been based.

Figure 85 *Personality report*

PART 1   PERFORMANCE REVIEW

Comment briefly on how completely and efficiently each of the Major Job Objectives has been attained. Wherever possible cite relevant figures or specific examples that support the evaluation. Comment on any circumstances unforeseen, or beyond the control of the Employee, that may have affected his performance.

Continued on pages 196-7

PART 2	EXPERIENCE AND TRAINING

Give details of experience gained, or training given, to the employee during review period to improve current job performance. Where formal training has been given, state course title, dates and organiser.

What additional experience and/or training do you propose to give the employee to improve his current job performance? Give details of proposed methods and suggested dates.

Figure 85 – continued

PART 3   MANAGERS SUMMARY OF OVERALL ASSESSMENT AND INTERVIEW

This section is completed by the Manager after the interview and should
contain an overall assessment of work performance and summarise the most
important aspects of the interview.

☐   Unsatisfactory

☐   Fair

☐   Competent

☐   Exceptional

☐   Outstanding

Areas for Improving Work Performance

Summary of Interview

APPROVALS AND COMMENTS

Assessment made by Employee's Manager

Date _____   Signature _____

                                       Appointment _____
                                                   (Employee's Manager)

Assessment Approved by Manager's Manager

Do you know this employee personally?   Yes/No

Do you agree with the assessment in   Yes/No
all respects?

Date _____   Signature _____

                                       Appointment _____
Additional Comments (if any)   (Manager's Manager)

**Private and
Confidential**

The object of this appraisal is to help improve a person's performance. on the front page of this form is an action sheet for the year. Please note any points on this sheet and give a copy to the appraisee, if they wish.

DETAILS OF PERFORMANCE

1.   KNOWLEDGE OF WORK
     Strengths   Improvements

2.   NEED FOR SUPERVISION (ALLOCATION OF PRIORITIES)

3.   DECISION MAKING AND PROBLEM SOLVING
     Strengths   Improvements

4.   RELATIONSHIPS (BOTH WITHIN THE COMPANY AND EXTERNAL)
     Strengths   Improvements

5.   ADAPTABILITY

6.   DIRECTION AND TRAINING OF SUBORDINATES
     Strengths   Improvements

Figure 86 *Criteria report (inside sheets)*

7.   SUMMARY OF RESULTS IN LAST PERIOD (ACHIEVEMENT OF ANY SET TARGETS)

8.   OVERALL ASSESSMENT OF ATTITUDE AND PERFORMANCE

COMMENTS

▷ Unsatisfactory
▷ Reasonably satisfactory
▷ Good
▷ Exceptionally Good
▷ Outstanding

Signature of Appraisor . . . .

Signature of Appraisee. . . . .

JOB SKILLS CRITERIA (not in order of priority)

1. Decisiveness
Readiness to make decisions, render judgements and take actions.

2. Stress or tolerance
Stability of performance under pressure and/or opposition. Ability to make controlled responses in stressful situations.

3. Planning and organisation
Ability to establish efficiently an appropriate course of action for self and/or others to accomplish a goal.

4. Delegation
Effective use of subordinates and other resources available. Knowledge of when, how and whom to delegate. Effective allocation of decision-making and other responsibilities.

5. Management control
Appreciation of need for controls and maintenance of control over processes, people and tasks and actions to ensure this.

6. Leadership
Ability to develop teamwork and maximise resources within a group to give most effective achievement of group objectives.

7. Problem analysis
Effectiveness in identifying problems, seeking pertinent data, recognising important information, and identifying possible causes of problems.

8. Judgement
Ability to evaluate data and courses of action to reach logical decisions. Unbiased, rational approach.

9. Initiative
Actively influencing events rather than passively accepting; sees opportunities and acts on them. Originates action.

10. Impact
Ability to create a good first impression on others and to maintain that impression.

11. Persuasiveness
The ability to convince others of courses of action and/or ideas.

Figure 87 *Example of job skills criteria*

```
Mr XXX - YYY BRANCH

The assessors rated Mr XXX just below the standard in all the
criteria under review.

Decisiveness: In two of the exercises he changed his original
        decision. He put off making important decisions.

Stress tolerance: Does not project himself in a stressful
        environment. There were long periods of silence in both
            the interview and the discussion.

Impact: Did not create a good impression on his colleagues or
        the assessors. Both District Managers described him as
        'untidy'.

Problem analysis: Showed some ability but never got to the root
        of the problem.

Judgement: The conclusions he arrived at were generally sound.

Persuasiveness: Powers of persuasion appear limited.

Delegation: Delegated on a number of occasions. Instructions
        need to be clearer, and report-back procedures instigated.

Leadership: Made little or no attempt to involve himself in a
        group discussion. He appeared unconcerned that the group
        would not achieve its objective. He spent most of his
        time with his head down and arms folded.

Initiative: Instigated some activities, but opportunities
        usually went begging.

Planning and organisation: Showed some ability to organise
        himself but not others
```

Figure 88 *Example of assessment report reflecting criteria*

be seen that this approach reflects very directly the philosophy of Management by Objectives.[3]

An example of this is a system used by another organisation in the distributive field. In the company each person has a Job Description including:
1   An Overall Objective (main role).
2   Main Objectives (key areas).
3   Standards of Performance (targets).
An illustration will be helpful to distinguish between the overall and main objectives. The example is that of the Secretary/PA to the company's General Manager and Administration Manager in their Northern Area – see Figure 91.

At least two weeks before the Performance Review, a Review Form such as that in Figure 92 is issued to the appraised. The example shown is for an Agency Manager (not the PA discussed in the job description above).

At this stage the Standards and the Performance Achieved would be completed. The objectives and their attainment would then form the basis of the Performance Review interview. During and after the interview the remaining boxes will be completed as a record of the discussion and a basis for future development.

Mr XXX has received formal training in many of the areas covered. His major problem appears to be lack of confidence. This prevents him from projecting himself and influencing events. The following suggestions may help him overcome these weaknesses:

1. Organising, preparing and presenting training sessions at branches other than his own.
2. Briefing meetings to branch staff.
3. Attendance of managers' meetings - make him contribute.
4. Relief management with set objectives.

Figure 89 *Example of general summary and remedial recommendations*

ASSESSMENT CENTRE

RATING SUMMARY

Name: Z Z Z

CRITERIA	EXERCISES					
	Business Consultant	Management Trainee	Customer Complaint	In Basket	Final Rating	Strength Average or Development Need
Decisiveness	2	5	/	2	2	
Stress Tolerance	3	5	/	1	3	1-1=4 GROUP + PAPER 2
Impact	1	3	/	1	2	
Problem Analysis	2	4	/	1	2	
Judgement	2	5	/	1	2	1-1 SITUATION GOOD
Persuasive	0	5	/	0	2	1-1 SITUATION GOOD
Delegation	0	0	/	2	2	
Leadership	2	0	/	2	2	
Initiative	1	5	/	1	1	1-1 SITUATION GOOD.
Plan and Organise	3	5	/	1	3.	
Management Control	2	0	/	2	2	

Figure 90 *Example of rating summary*

```
MAIN ROLE

To provide an efficient secretarial/personal assistant service
to the General Manager and the Administration Manager Northern
Office. Also secretarial service to the Management Information
Co-ordinator and Agency Services Manager.

To ensure the confidentiality of all information, files, etc.

To create a system of priorities to ensure that urgent matters
are handled immediately, but that other matters are processed
whenever possible within the day or to an agreed timetable.

KEY ACTIVITIES (Extracts)

1. Communications: Open all mail, including Directors', dis-
       tributing where necessary, and passing all relevant docu-
       ments to General Manager/Administration Manager....

2. Filing:....

3. Confidential files:....

4. Appointments/Diary: Book Conference Room as necessary for
       office meetings, managers' meetings, etc....
       Book hotels, lunches, dinners, etc., for visitors, con-
       ferences, etc., checking facilities to ensure adequate
       standards.
       Arrange travel and tickets as required.

5. Hospitality:....

6. General: Keep a record of car reports (mileage, etc.).
       Issuing of Free Issue authorisation forms.
       ....
```

Figure 91   *Example of job objectives*

The appraised's part in appraisal reporting

Mention of the performance review interview in the system described above raises the part played by the subject of the appraisal. It should go without saying that an interview must be held. Like all other forms of communication, the appraisal dialogue must be genuinely two-way to be effective. None of the three purposes of appraisal can be achieved if this is not so. IBM in the USA led the way in establishing a vogue for open reporting.[4]

Two questions arise:

1   Should the appraised see the report itself?
2   Is a scheme of self-appraisal useful?

Seen and unseen reports

The distributor's system just described provides not only for the report to be seen but for it to be passed to him at least two weeks before. This is admirable. In the heat of the moment, in what may – with the best will in the world – be a very tense interview, it is difficult to digest the full import of an appraisal form passed across the desk there and then.

PERFORMANCE REVIEW

(Agency Manager)

On ....(Name)

AREA OF REVIEW: Agent Service and Sales   Date:

STANDARDS   What performance standards were agreed at the start of the period?

PERFORMANCE ACHIEVED (ACTUAL)

1. Documentation   5.   Visits to Agents

2. Complaints   6.   Sales Activity

3. Work Monitor   7.   Commissions

4. Catalogues   8.   Staff Cover

SPECIAL FACTORS DISCUSSED DURING THE REVIEW

Figure 92 *Objectives-based performance review form*

JOINTLY AGREED ACTION FOR THE FUTURE

PEFORMANCE STANDARD CHANGES FOR THE NEXT PERIOD

It may, however, often be that in an open scheme, where the appraised sees the whole document, the report is less than frank. The reporter may leave dangerous nettles ungrasped. He may describe the subject's shortcomings in such mealy-mouthed, woolly terms that they are not sufficiently acutely pointed out.

There must be a system of safeguards to prevent anyone being too harshly over-reported or under-reported. The report must be endorsed by a grandfather (a manager at least one tier up from the reporter but who knows the appraised). Anyone who has received two very strong reports, in either direction, should have the third report written by someone else. A Management Development Committee, consisting of perhaps the personnel directors and two line directors, should review difficult or sensitive cases. This panel should then re-evaluate their decisions at annual intervals.

A useful possibility is an unseen report to supplement the open form. This must, of course, not contradict the spirit of the open form, but concentrates in its design on potential for promotion. Such a form, as designed and used by Miles Laboratories, is shown in Figure 93. The term Helicopter shown in Section 4 (Appraisal Category 6) describes the ability to see the whole breadth of a problem but then descend to hover close to one small part of it. Some cynics say that the analogy is of limited accuracy as in certain conditions a helicopter will throw up so much dust at low levels that the particulars are not easy to see.

Self-appraisal

Self-appraisal, if well carried out, can only improve the appraised's appreciation of his position. The Stewarts[5] speak particularly favourably of this type of increment to the dialogue. It may meet with some resistance from those of cautious or conservative attitudes. They will feel that they are in danger of exposing some of their own weaknesses which have gone unnoticed. They may also argue that it is the job of the manager, not the employee, to point out such shortcomings.

Plenty of time – probably 10 days, or at least 5 – must be allowed for completion of these forms. They should be supported by an *aide-memoire*. They must be closely related to the employee's job and, if possible, pre-determined objectives. The design of the form should provide some direct questions calling for straightforward answers. Again, Miles Laboratories have devised a first-class form of this kind. It is reproduced in Figure 94.

Summary

Appraisal reporting is inextricably involved with the whole treatment of appraisal. The purposes of the appraisal process, whether carried out by interview or in writing, must be to improve performance, to highlight training needs and to identify promotion potential.

It can have no other justification. Therefore the design of the form must reflect those needs and must be as closely related to predetermined objectives or targets as possible. If the documentation is designed in this way, words should give greater precision than numbers and rating scales.

Moreover, the form and the system which it supports, must be conducive to establishing a genuine rapport and two-way exchange between the reporter and the appraised.

Private and Confidential

ASSESSMENT

NAME OF EMPLOYEE'..

1. Has he/she reached limit of advancement?   If 'yes' state why.

2. Comment on his/her suitability for promotion, when and to what possible job?

3. How do you see this person's job changing in the next 12 months?

4. APPRAISAL CATEGORIES

No.	Category	Present Job Level Requirements		
		BELOW	MEETING	EXCEEDING
1.	Analysis			
2.	Imagination			
3.	Sense of Reality			
4.	Proactivity			
5.	Resilience			
6.	Helicopter			

7.	Leadership qualities

Excellent	Good	Satisfactory	Need developing

5. TRAINING/EXPERIENCE - What training or other experience is required in the next 12 months?
Please note these on front of form.

Signature of Reviewer......................................

Date..

COMMENTS OF SENIOR DIRECTOR/MANAGER

Signature..   Date.............................

Figure 93 *Unseen appraisal report*

MILES

STAFF APPRAISAL AND

DEVELOPMENT SCHEME

PRIVATE AND
CONFIDENTIAL

Employee's Name and Initials		Location/Department
Interview Date	Interview Time	Manager's Name

REVIEW PREPARATION FORM

It is the policy of Miles Laboratories Ltd. for each Manager and Supervisor to meet periodically with his (or her) own Manager in a formal Appraisal and Guidance Interview. Its purpose is to assist you to develop your particular talents and skills and increase your job satisfaction to the mutual benefit of yourself and the Company. By developing your abilities to the full your career potential will be developed at the same time.

An interview with your Manager has been arranged at the time and date shown above. As this interview should benefit both yourself and your Company, it is important that you prepare to derive maximum advantage from it. This form is simply a guide to help you prepare for a useful discussion during your interview. It is up to you how you use it; if you wish you may show it to your Manager or keep it for reference during the interview (although you need not adhere strictly to it). You should use the MBO worksheet to draft objectives, prior to the interview and this form should also subsequently be used to type up agreed objectives for signature.

The value of this interview to you will depend largely on what you yourself contribute to it. You may introduce for discussion any subject which, in your opinion are related to your satisfaction with your work, to your accomplishments and effectiveness in your current job, and any hopes you may have about your future career. Your Manager will be prepared to discuss your ideas about your job and your future and will try to comment on all of your ideas in as frank, practical and helpful manner as possible. He will also give you his own ideas on your work, which should be helpful to you.

Remember that the main subjects to be discussed are how to continue and improve your job performance and satisfaction, as well as your future in the Company. The results obtained from the interview depend on your active participation.

1. In your opinion, what are the most important duties of your present job? In other words, which parts of your job deserve to be given more care and attention than the rest?

2. Consider your performance in your present job: what have you done well in the last year and what not so well?

Figure 94 *Self-appraisal form*

3.   Were there any obstacles which hindered you in accomplishing what you wished?
     Are they likely to recur? If so, how could they be eliminated?

_____

_____

_____

4.   Is there any aspect of your job which you do not find satisfactory, or about which
     you would like more information? Do you have any suggestions about how to make your
     Company a more satisfactory place to work for yourself or for other employees?

_____

_____

_____

5.   What parts of your present job interest you most?

_____

_____

     What parts of your present job interest you least?

_____

_____

6.   Do you feel there are some areas of your job performance which could be improved,
     and, if so, what action do you think might be taken to achieve this by:-

     (a)   Yourself?   _____

     (b)   Your Manager?   _____

     (c)   Anyone else?   _____

_____

_____

7.   Looking ahead to the future, what kind of work would you like to be doing two to
     four years from now?

_____

_____

_____

8.   What do you think should be the major job objectives in your work for the next
     year, and how will you judge how well these have been met?

_____

_____

_____

_____

CHAPTER FOURTEEN

Accident reports

An accident (or incident) report is, by its nature, remedial. It must, of course describe the event for future reference. It must also apportion responsibility and above all, stop similar accidents occurring in the future.

Earlier chapters have given an indication of the excellence of Health and Safety Executive investigation reports. They have been used as models of lucid argument and simple clear layout. In most internal investigations it is not likely to be possible to produce such a polished document, nor will it be necessary. However the same virtues may be imitated where appropriate.

An internal report will probably be more centred around a sketch-map which will be supplemented by a number of statements. These will be taken from participants witnesses and experts (including technical inspectors).

Accident forms and diagrams

Two well designed accident proformae from Overseas Containers Limited (OCL) will illustrate the relevant points. Figure 95 shows a simple report form. The form is divided into five sections. The first two sub-sections describe the equipment and its driver. The item 'Haulier' (at Sub-section 1.2) is important in this case as OCL containers are hauled by prime-movers belonging to a variety of companies. The 'Description of Accident. . .' at Sub-section 1.3 will give only an outline description; something like:

> Trailer parked in authorised parking place. Steamroller ran into the back. Trailer sustained minor damage; no casualties.

Further details will be set out in a sketch-map and witnesses' statements.

The Inspection Report at Section 2 is generally self-explanatory. The date of inspection (Sub-section 2.2) is of particular significance in exceptionally humid or cold climates, where weather conditions may affect the damaged vehicle between the accident and the inspection. Methods of stow and restraint (Sub-section 2.4) are especially important to a container company. The former might be described as something like 'Pallets: one on top of another with boards every two'. The latter might be 'strapping (web)'. Nonetheless methods of stow and restraint have a relevance with even the most trivial loads involved in an accident, such as something carried in a wheelbarrow.

The sketch at Section 3, which is $2\frac{1}{2}$ inches tall in the original form, will only allow for the most rudimentary sketch. In many cases this will suffice. However in the majority of traffic accidents on public roads, for instance, this will have to be either replaced or supported by a separate sketch-map attached to the report form. Some notes on such sketch-maps follow later in the chapter: the great range of items which may be relevant for inclusion indicate how much room will be needed on occasions. The reporter's comments at Section 4 will include observations on delay in reporting the accident. Action taken (Section 5) can cover details of recovery.

DCL OVERSEAS CONTAINERS LIMITED
Beagle House, Braham Street, London E1 8EP

INCIDENT / ACCIDENT REPORT

REGION:-

DATE:-

PERSON REPORTING:-

POSITION:-

1.   **Details of Incident/Accident**

1.1   Equipment (Serial No's, Type, Etc):—

1.2   Haulier   Driver:-   Reg No:-

1.3   Description of Accident, Circumstances, Injury to Persons, Property, Etc:-

1.4   Witnesses:-

2.   **Inspection Report**

2.1   Condition of Equipment, M.O.T. Date, Tyre & Twist-Lock State, Structural Condition of Container, Etc.,

2.2   Date of Inspection:-   Location:-

      Persons present:-   :—

2.3   Cause (State Opinion and Reasoning):-

2.4   Cargo Details:-

      (a) Cargo:-

      (b) Weight:-

      (c) Type of Package:-

      (d) Method of Stow:-

      (e) Method of Restraint:-

3.   **Sketch of Incident : Accident:-**

      Time:—   Date:—   Direction of Travel:—
                                              Weather Conditions:—

4.   **Reporters Comments:—**

5.   **Action Taken (Quote EDR No's Etc.):—**

Figure 95   *OCL incident/accident report form*

The same company uses a triplicate form to describe damage to its trailers and containers. The form just discussed covers only the circumstances of the accident. The Equipment Damage Report is shown in Figure 96. The form, which is self-explanatory, provides seven diagrams which allow the inspector to show the precise damage to the trailer and container as seen from all possible angles.

The top form (white), which is shorter than the other two, ends below the reporter's signature. This is sent to the Insurance and Claims Department. The

OCL OVERSEAS CONTAINERS LIMITED
BEAGLE HOUSE, BRAHAM STREET, LONDON E1 8EP

Serial No. 312963

EQUIPMENT DAMAGE REPORT

REPAIR COMPANY COPY

Date of Damage	D	M	Y
Voyage No.			
E.I.R. No.			

Equipment Type	Size	Equipment Serial Number

MARK DAMAGE ON PLAN

FRONT REAR FRONT
LEFT SIDE RIGHT SIDE

FRONT REAR FRONT
ROOF UNDERSIDE

FRONT INTERNAL REAR

NOTE:
B-BROKEN M-MISSING D-DENT
H-HOLE R-RIVET OFF

CONTAINER LOADED/EMPTY

Damage to Contents

Signature of person reporting Date

Describe the extent of the damage or deficiency.

Describe how the damaged occurred (incl. vehicle reg. nos., drivers names, and damage to other property.

Damage first reported by:
Indicate where damage first noted.

Name & address of party in charge of equipment when damage occurred or first noted (Liable Party)

Estimated cost of repair	Estimate Ref. No.	State if no repair action taken.

Date letter of recourse sent to Liable Party
(attach copy to this form)

To:—
Please carry out the following repairs. Date D M Y

Repair order authorisation:

For OCL/OCL Agent

OM 017 (4/76)

Figure 96 *OCL equipment damage report*

second form (yellow) goes to OCL Head Office and the third (blue) goes to the repair company.

Two aspects are particularly noteworthy. Firstly the Insurance and Claims Department are spared irrelevant detail, by not receiving the repair instructions. As this extra detail is at the foot of the form all three can still be carboned together. Secondly, the three copies are in different colours; a commonplace precaution, but one that is overlooked too often in form-design.

Accident sketch-maps

All accident sketch-maps, whether part of a proforma or on a separate sheet, must be drawn at the scene of the event which they report. If circumstances, such as foul weather or the lack of suitable materials, prevent a reasonable copy being made, the fair copy must be produced as soon as possible afterwards. Rough notes lose their meaning and abbreviations that seemed clear at the time become undecipherable. They should be as near to scale as possible and a fine grid on the paper may help to achieve this.

The items listed below suggest some of the very wide range of things likely to be required in an accident report involving vehicles or equipment on a public highway. Of the routine reports considered here, that is likely to be the most complex. Other reports such as accidents to individuals caused by working parts of static machinery are simplifications of this.

The list represents a progression from the permanent (starting with the natural permanent then moving on to the man-made permanent) to the impermanent (first the natural impermanent such as the weather and then the artificial impermanent). This sort of progression may help to formulate an *aide-memoire* for anyone compiling such a report.

(a) Permanent natural features
Hills (which would impede visibility)
Hedges
Trees (including type, coniferous or deciduous; relevant in winter)
Ditches

(b) Permanent artificial features
Houses and other buildings (indicating approximate height)
Pavements
Walls, e.g. around gardens or school playing fields
Traffic lights
Road signs
Lane markings
Zebra crossings
Lamp-posts (including an indication as to whether the lights were on or off)
Double and single yellow lines

(c) Impermanent natural features
Sun direction at time of accident
Wind direction at time of accident
Wet stretches of road or floods

(d) Impermanent artificial features
Positions of parked vehicles
Positions of moving vehicles (before and after accident)
Skid-marks
Position of moving parts, e.g. on cement mixer in a traffic accident, but conveyor
    belts and other moving machinery in other accidents
Position of fallen or spilt loads
Oil patches (before and after accident)
Positions of people:
    those involved (including positions of bodies or injured thrown clear)
    witnesses
    present but not used as witnesses
    police

(e) Labellings   To this must be added:

North point

Actual measurement of the roads, etc. (a formal scale is either impossible or, at best, misleading in a sketch-map)

Name of streets

Names of towns as an indication of road direction, e.g. Newbury 15 miles

One-way systems

Formal accident maps

Scale maps will accompany the reports of printed investigation reports which result from formal inquiries. A detail of the map included in the Health and Safety Executive report on the Cardowan colliery accident[1] to indicate positions of injured men is shown in Figure 97 to illustrate some points of good practice. Note in particular the shading of the extent of the flame or hot gas. The length of pit involved made the diagram somewhat ungainly and thin. The critical section around the shearer has therefore quite properly been blown up, so that the positions of the individual men in that area can be shown accurately. The lines connecting the men's positions and names do not cross each other so that they are always easy to follow.

Statements

Statements, whether from witnesses or those involved, must be taken as quickly as possible after the incident. Whatever the type of report, the statements should be taken formally:

1   Surnames and initials should be used. The fashion in some companies to use Christian- or nick-names is not appropriate. Disciplinary or legal proceedings may follow compilation of the report.
2   Chatty colloquialisms should be eliminated.
3   Fact should be distinguished from opinion. If expert opinion is included, the expert's status and qualifications must be mentioned.
4   Hearsay must not be included.[2]

The statements must be prefaced by

a   The witness/participant's name.
b   Address.
c   Occupation.
d   Position in the company (if appropriate).

The statement should start with the witness' position at the time that the accident occurred. It is usually advisable to record this sort of evidence in chronological order giving some indication of the passage of time, where possible.

All statements must be typed. They should then be signed and dated (with the date of signature).

Summary

Whether an accident report is to be printed and generally circulated or only scrutinised in a department of a company, it will need as accurate illustrations as possible. This complements statements from those present and those involved.

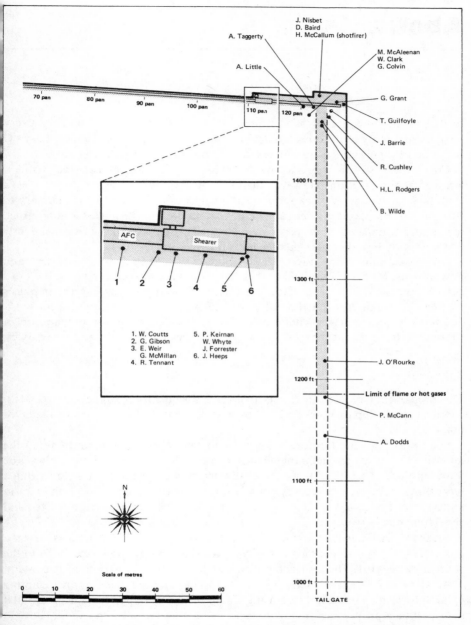

Figure 97 *Detail from the formal plan in the Cardowan Colliery accident report*

Compilation of such a report is a balance of speed, in the interests of getting detail down before people forget or circumstances change, and accuracy. This fine balance must be found. Only with an accurate report, with clear recommendations implemented by meticulous staff, can accidents be prevented from recurring.

CHAPTER FIFTEEN

Abstracts

In *Richard III*,[1] the murderers en route to do in Clarence give Brackenbury a very terse factual reply to his question. 'What, are you so brief?' asks Brackenbury. 'O Sir', one of them replies, 'it is better to be brief than tedious'.

Conciseness was described at the beginning as a fundamental characteristic of written communication. However there are degrees of conciseness. Sometimes a summary or abstract will be required. This may take the form of a summary to surmount a complex document as a guide to its content. Such a need was described in Chapter 5. It may take the form of an abstract to stand on its own independently of the report. In either case the general principles are the same.

One-page summaries are extensively used in commerce, industry and government. Much use is made of them for briefing senior executives in the Ford Motor Company, for instance. General George C. Marshall placed great emphasis on one-page summaries.[2] Churchill and Eisenhower were similarly disposed.

The principles described here also have an application in the preparation of summaries to appear at the front of many reports, as required by many house styles.

Approach

The preparation of such abstracts of longer documents is commonplace. Most people do it to prepare notes for their own use, even if they do not do it formally for other people.

It is most important before setting out on the task of sifting and editing the minutiae to identify the main theme or purpose of the original. This must always be borne in mind when producing the abstracted report, just as it must in writing a report from scratch. The message of a report is like the plot of a novel. In order to understand the story, it is important not to miss out the main twists and developments.

Jackson[3] has likened communication to driftwood in a river. Sometimes there is a great deal of it and sometimes virtually none. The analogy can be extended to the content of a report. The abstracter must watch out for these variations in content.

An abstract is essentially selective, but it must be balanced. It is easy and tempting to latch on to the unusual, the amusing and bizarre. This happens in the Press and it may well be a proper part of a newspaper's obligation to sell copy and its duty to entertain. However, this approach has no place in the preparation of abstracted reports. A cautionary tale will highlight the problem.

Sometimes, there are found crass oversimplifications which go beyond this task and stray into inaccuracy. Such was seen in the middle of the press silly-season in August 1982. A 500-word article by the Bishop of Winchester appeared in *The Times*[4] under the title 'Infidelity: not the worst sin'. The article was itself an edited version of a longer one destined for the following month's *Winchester Churchman*. The tenor of the bishop's argument was that the preservation of a marriage was more important and more appropriate to a Christian way of life than a great deal of acrimony and recrimination about infidelity. This is, at face value, a conventional enough interpretation of the Gospel. Given tabloid simplification of this concept, all Hell was let loose. The bishop was depicted blessing dirty weekends and all the rest of it.

Guidelines to preparation

Emphasis

The emphasis in an abstract is a balance – possibly even a compromise – between the original writer's aim and the abstract reader's interest and requirements. The abstracter must keep asking himself what parts will be particularly relevant to the reader. Some of this will be dictated by the reader's responsibilities or his scope of trade. For example:

1   If the company is a major multinational, a section of the original dealing with companies employing under 100 people will attract little or no coverage in the abstract and little or no coverage in the summary.
2   If the company brews lager and light ale, a section on stout is likely to merit little space.
3   If the company's sites are all in the Midlands, details of housing policies in North Yorkshire are unlikely to be of interest.

Key points

The principle of emphasis described above is the most important. It overrides all other considerations.

The abstracter must next look for key points in the original. This concept will be illustrated by reference to the Department of Transport/Home Office Green Paper on Road Traffic Law.[5] This was a provocative and far-reaching publication, on which many abstracts must have been made. In it the departments concerned proposed a simplification of road traffic law by the introduction of a points system.

1 Headings   The headings in the original paper indicate the way in which the writer has tackled the subject. The table of contents will give a good idea as to the sequence of headings and the balance of the paper. They do just that in the case study in question:

```
Fixed Penalty System - Improvements to
                       Present Machinery
Fixed Penalty System - Extension to Other
                       Traffic Offences
A Points System
Costs and Benefits
```

These explain the four divisions of the writer's treatment. In most abstracts all four parts will have to be represented. However the abstracter must take the process a stage further and look at individual headings and see what parts of these four chunks are relevant; for example, in the section on the Points System:

```
Classification of offences
Points values
Disqualification
Other penalties
Wiping the slate clean
Driving while disqualified
Vehicle defect and traffic sign offences
Fixed penalties vis-a-vis a points system
Legislation
```

Here some elimination may be possible. Most employers will not be interested in the paragraphs on 'driving while disqualified'. In most companies where a high standard of vehicle maintenance obtains, it will not be necessary to take up any – or not much – space in the abstract on 'vehicle defect and traffic sign offences'.

Annexes, of which there are 13 in this case, must be checked for relevance. However, their very nature means that they are unlikely to justify any inclusion in an abstract. There will be exceptions. A computer manufacturer, for instance, might be interested in Annex N: Capital and setting-up costs. This goes into the mechanics and equipment for introducing the new system.

2 Introduction As follows from the comments in Chapter 4, the introduction to the original is likely to be heavily weighted with important material. It is the same here. The background, purpose and method of working are set out in the five introductory paragraphs and will merit quite detailed explanation in the abstract. Some bits of the introduction can be ignored, for example:

a A paragraph describing the sequence of the report.
b Another explaining how the authors kept in touch with a comparable Scottish committee (unless, of course, the abstract is prepared for a reader in Scotland).

3 Important points Certain points are likely to be deserving of detailed scrutiny before the abstract-writer dispenses with them. That does not mean to say that they have all got to be packed in, but they must each be picked up and turned over before they are discarded:

a Listed matter, particularly if marked with bullet points. The authors of the Green Paper give six reasons why the anticipated behaviour of motorists can not be directly extrapolated from current reactions.[6]
b Anything that the original author has prefaced by numerical adverbs 'firstly', 'secondly', 'thirdly', etc. This indicates that these are separate aspects to the problem which the writer considers important.
c Proper nouns. In this case certain constabularies and certain government departments are named. Their particular experiences and comments should often be identifiable as to source.
d Acts of Parliament and regulations. These may have an important legal implication on the reader's business. It may be dangerous to avoid this. Sections and sub-sections are unlikely to be necessary.
e Numerate detail. For example 'Costs are based on the assumption that a new style minicomputer capable of handling 20,000 tickets a year will be required by each manually operated office.' In many abstracts that figure will give a helpful indication of the size of the problem.

f Comments on future developments. In most cases, the future is likely to be even more important than background.

Method

Mechanics

The following technique will usually ensure conciseness:
1 Read the original passage in its entirety to ensure an overview.
2 Strike out pieces which it is not relevant to abstract (as, for example the paragraph mentioned above on disqualified drivers).
3 Re-read the first paragraph. Then put aside (or close) the original and note any relevant points on a piece of rough paper.
4 If no points come to mind as being important, re-read to ensure that the paragraph is in fact, void.
5 Continue with subsequent paragraphs. (It is a good idea to note the paragraph or page numbers in the margin of the rough notes, to check detail subsequently.)
6 Write out the rough notes as a fair copy, without looking at the original.
7 Check the fair copy of the abstract against the original for accuracy of detail.

Direct copying

Direct copying of prose from the original is unlikely to be justified. However important two or three sentences may seem, they will almost certainly take up a disproportionate amount of room in the final abstract. What looks like an insignificant amount of material in a few lines of the original might take up nearly half of the one-page abstract if copied directly. Similarly it is unlikely that there will be room to reproduce tables. It may be possible to restate totals from the bottom of tables in the original.

Quotations

The dangers of copying, as a result of the importance of the original sentences or sloth of the abstracter, have been discussed. It should also be unnecessary to quote even lone phrases directly from the original. Exceptionally, they may constitute an important theme in the original and quotation would be justified.

For instance, in an abstract of the White Paper, *Industrial Democracy*,[7] which followed Bullock, the following would be a reasonable paragraph:

```
The authors see such a system as providing a framework for
satisfying the various parties' differing objectives, so
that conflict can be avoided. They use the expression
'partnership rather than defensive co-existence' to
illustrate their principle.
```

A quotation should never be included just because the writer cannot think of an alternative more concise form of expression.

Style

Long sentences are particularly dangerous in abstracts. On the other hand a telegraphic style without main verbs is likely to lead to ambiguity. Very short headings will sometimes help conciseness.

Comment

Imposition of the abstracter's own comment should be clearly identified in one of two ways:
1   By a change of style, possibly even introducing the first or second person ('I feel. . .' or 'You will note. . .').
2   A sub-heading *Comment* before the remark.

Attributability

As shown above, examples may often be identified by source. However, it is less likely that the abstracter will be able to afford the luxury of attributing observations to individual commentators in the original paper. Very exceptionally, the commentator's background may make it particularly important to name him. He may have experience of the trade, area or company concerned. This will be unusual.

Caveat

However good the abstract, something is bound to be lost if the original has been well written. Every word should have been put in the original for a purpose. When wording is removed and reduced, some fine shade of meaning or detail will go.

As Benny Green[8] said: 'If you are going to sum up Marcel Proust in four lines you are not going to get very profound'.

Summary

Some information can be struck out of the original as being irrelevant to the subject matter. The abstract should never be drafted straight from the original: a set of rough notes should be used as half-way stage.

Certain details such as itemised information, numbers and proper nouns are likely to be worth preserving in the abstract. Direct copying should never be undertaken, quotation very seldom.

Always bear in mind the purpose and theme of the original.

CHAPTER SIXTEEN

Telexed reports

Telex has two straightforward advantages over forms of reporting:
1 Speed – over a letter.
2 Permanence – over a telephone report.
On the other hand they are charged by the word and therefore length should be kept to the minimum commensurate with clarity.

Faults with telexed reports

The most common and most regretable faults with Telexed reports are those of length and of design or layout. They are largely complementary. A suitable design can save words.

Length

The length of a Telexed report is a balance. On the one hand there is the need to save money. On the other, there is the danger of economising to such an extent that further Telex traffic is generated to clarify the first report.

As with all reports the principle that every word means something slightly different and so every word must count for something is paramount. It has to be taken a stage further here and some rather more rigorous pruning has to be undertaken. A florid style, which may be appropriate and explicit in the more leisurely draft of a typescript report, has to be avoided. As a guide, the following principles may be borne in mind;
1 Eliminate personal salutations and signings-off: 'Kind Regards', 'Best Wishes'.
2 (As with all reports) Avoid padding words, as described in Chapter 6.
3 Remove prepositions, such as 'with', 'by' and 'from', provided that no ambiguity results.
4 Ensure that adverbs and adjectives add something to the Telex before they are used. If a Telex includes 'thoroughly', 'soon', 'recently' ask whether these convey a precise meaning or whether they are so much flannel which would be appropriate in conversation.
5 Expressions on the lines of 'as you know' and 'you will remember', which have a perfectly proper place in a prose report in the interests of tact, have none in a Telex. In the main, a Telex should have an antiseptic neutral tone. It is a functional way of passing facts and, sometimes, recommendations. Deference and courtesy are out of place.
6 Make maximum possible use of abbreviations.
7 Minimise use of punctuation.
8 Frequently the definite (*the*) and indefinite (*a, an*) article can be omitted.

The costs of sending Telexed reports are set out in the United Kingdom Telex Directory.[1] For centres up to 56 km apart the charge is 3p/min. Over that distance is

```
1.  XXXXXXXXX
2.  XXXXXXXXX
3.  XXXXXXXXX
WE PLAN TO INCLUDE THIS ESTIMATED CONTINGENT LIABILITY IN TOTAL
BRANCH REPRESENTATION LETTER. FOLLOWING ARE THE DETAILS OF THE
RELEVANT AMOUNTS:
                                    DOLLARS 1000
        EUROPE                          153
        AFRICA                          668
        MIDDLE EAST                     522
        SOUTH AMERICA                   420

                    TOTAL           1763
```

Figure 98 *Use of numbers and columns in Telexes*

it. 9p/min. To the Irish Republic it is 18p/min. Overseas charges are more substantial, e.g.

40p/min   Canada, Cayman Islands, USA
75p/min   Abu Dhabi, Dubai, Hong Kong, Singapore

Certain farther-flung countries, such as those of South America and certain parts of Africa, are subject to a minimum charge of £2.25.

Internal reports should be transmitted without delay. Internationally there may sometimes be some slight delay, usually of just a few minutes.

The rate of transmission is about 65 words/min (on an average of five letters per word).[2] It is relevant to consider this rate of transmission in connection with the charges shown above.

Design

This conciseness, achieving financial saving and speed of transmission, can often be achieved, without losing clarity, by a more structural approach. This is particularly important for Telexed reports which, by their nature, are rather more involved and complex than many Telexes. This can often be achieved by:

1 Numbering paragraphs.
2 Columnising sums of money and other numerate information.
3 Use of headings.

```
OUR TELEX REF. NO. 0373 OF 31.12.84 FORCED OUTAGE REPORT
CUSTOMER:  RURITANIA ELECTRICITY CORPORATION
LOCATION:  RUPERT POWER STATION, ZENDA, RURITANIA
TURBINE NUMBER 219999
                PRIME
                CUSTOMER UNIT NO. SEVEN
FIXED HRS/STARTS:  UNKNOWN NO RECORDS
FORCE OUT OF SERVICE DATE:  ESTIMATE DECEMBER 1985
CAUSE OF OUTAGE:  EXTREME OVERFIRING CONDITION
WORK REQUIRED:  COMPLETE REBUILD
```

Figure 99 *Headings in Telexed reports*

One major multinational, while not having a stereotyped layout, encourages the use of itemised points for the main argument with details indented, as shown in Figure 98.

Figure 99 shows how headings can be economical in the wording of reports, particularly those which follow a set of predictable form. Note how the reference to another Telex is made clearly and economically at the opening of the text.

Example

It will be profitable to look at these somewhat arid principles in relation to three Telexed reports. The European Vice-President of a multinational company has sent the following Telex to his heads of operations in three European countries, seeking precise, clearly defined information. The names of the countries have been changed to Transylvania, Atlanta and Ruritania. The product has also been translated to locomotives driven by solar-power. These are of various marks; Solar 22, Solar 550 and so on.

This is quite clear. The Vice-President seeks 3 definite bits of information:

1   1981 Sales Plan for Solar.
2   Proposed funding/manpower needs.
3   Major activities ancitipated.

The greeting 'Regards' is fairly fatuous but is part of the house style of the company concerned. (It will be noted that American spellings and idioms are used. This accords with the usual style of communication in that company.)

MARK TWAIN OF SAN FRANCISCO WILL VISIT ME OCTOBER 13 WEEK TO DISCUSS PROGRAMS AND FUNDING. PLEASE LET ME HAVE YOUR SALES PLAN FOR 1981 FOR SOLAR INCL. PROPOSED FUNDING/MANPOWER NEEDS BY INDIVIDUAL AS WELL AS MAJOR ACTIVITIES ANTICIPATED. PLEASE ARRANGE TO HAVE THIS ON MY DESK BY NO LATER THAN MONDAY OCTOBER 13TH.

REGARDS

W WORDSWORTH

First reply: Transylvania

This generally looks good. It is well spaced and easy to digest. It is surmounted by a clear heading. (The Re is superfluous, but clearly not a great extravagance.)
The Action Plan which is something which Wordsworth particularly wanted is easy to find and clearly itemised and numbered.

RE: TRANSYLVANIA - SOLAR SALES - 1981

ACTION PLAN

1. PUSH FOR GETTING SOLAR-22 DELIVERED. THIS IS MOST IMPORTANT FOR OUR IMAGE.

2. PREPARE FOR HIGH LEVEL VISIT TO TRANSYLVANIA EARLY IN THE YEAR, POSSIBLY FEBRUARY.
OBJECTIVE - RE-ESTABLISH FRIENDLY RELATIONS WITH ABS INCORPORATED IN SCHLOSS BERLICH-INGEN

   - MEET WITH DR FRANKENSTEIN, HEAD OF WUNDERSCHON GMBH TO PROMOTE FURTHER CLARIFICATION PROCESS
   - MEET WITH TOP MANAGEMENT OF TRANSYL-VANIAN RAILWAYS BOARD TO REVIEW THEIR PLANS FOR THE IMPENDING IMPLEMENTATION OF THE SOLAR PROGRAMS

- MEET WITH DIRECTOR OF MINES AND OTHER
GOVERNMENTAL OFFICERS CONCERNED IN
SOLAR LOCOMOTION
- MEET WITH MINISTER OF ENERGY WHO HAS
EXPRESSED INTERESTS IN SOLAR POWER.

3. FORMALLY INVITE DR C DRACULA, CHAIRMAN
OF TRANSYLVANIAN RAILWAYS BOARD TO VISIT
THIS COMPANY AT THE HIGHEST LEVEL.

4. PREPARE FOR RENEWED APPROACHES ON JOINT
VENTURES WITH ABC FOR THE ALPINE LINE.
THIS TIME RATHER THAN FOR COMPLETE NETWORK

5. CAPITALISING ON HARVEY DESIGN AND CON-
STRUCTION WORK DEVELOP DEFINITE RESEARCH
PROGRAM WITH ENERGY DEPARTMENT AND ABC INC
TO ENHANCE CONTRIBUTION OF SOLAR TECH-
NOLOGY TO TRANSYLVANIAN POWER GENERATION
INDUSTRY.

SUPPORTING INFORMATION

EXISTING SITUATION

Here different marks of equipment are described. It is questionable whether the original inquiry calls for so much detail. However, by putting the names of the equipments first, the author has given a good lead-in to each paragraph and it is easy to follow.
'We trust no new surprises will pop up' is probably superfluous.

SOLAR-60 OUT OF SERVICE BECAUSE Z200
PLATES ARE CRACKED AND MUST BE REPAIRED.
JOINT VENTURE FORMED WITH ABC INC BUT
PROGRESS VERY VERY SLOW. THIS FACE-
LIFTING PREREQUISITE MUST RECEIVE MANAGE
MENT SUPPORT.

SOLAR-900 LOCOMOTIVES STILL NEED TO
UNDERGO FINAL TEST AND WILL PROBABLY BE
DELIVERED TO TRANSYLVANIAN RAILWAYS BOAR
AROUND THE END OF THE YEAR: WE TRUST NO
NEW SURPRISES POP UP.

SOLAR-550 FINAL GO AHEAD SIGNAL EXPECTED
BEFORE THE END OF THIS YEAR. JOINT VEN-
TURE WITH ABC INC PROCEEDING WITH ENGIN-
EERING AND PRELIMINARY ORDERING OF
MATERIALS.

SOLAR-590 STILL OUT OF SERVICE TO ALLOW
FOR IMPLEMENTATION OF NEW SAFETY
MEASURES.

GENERAL COMMENTS

SPECIAL COMMISSION ON EXTENSION OF LAKE-
SIDE LINE JUST SUBMITTED REPORT WHICH
DEFINITELY FAVORABLE. FINAL GO AHEAD
SIGNAL EXPECTED FROM MINISTRY OF TRANSPORT
SOON. THIS MAKES SOLAR LOCOMOTION A
REALITY IN THE LAKESIDE AREA.

PROF U VALKYRIE CHAIRMAN OF TRANSYLVANIAN
PUBLIC TRANSPORT COMMITTEE VISITING US
NEXT WEEK. WE EXPECT HE WILL BE POSITIVELY
IMPRESSED AND AFTER HIS RETURN WILL FAVOR-

The paragraphs on the visits of **Valkyrie** and **Goshawk** could probably be more economically expressed with a lead-in sentence on the general subject of visits and then two sub-paragraphs on the two visitors.

ABLY REPORT TO MINISTRY OF TRANSPORT AND TO CHAIRMAN TRANSYLVANIAN RAILWAYS BOARD WHO HAS NOT YET VISITED US.

MR F GOSHAWK HEAD OF SOLAR DEVELOPMENT AT TRANSYLVANIAN RAILWAYS BOARD WILL BE VISITING US LATE NEXT MONTH. WE EXPECT ALSO THIS WILL BE PREPARATORY FOR THE VISIT OF THE CHAIRMAN.

COMPETITION

ADLER IS MAKING STRONG CLAIMS ABOUT HUGE CURRENT SOLAR LOCOMOTIVE ACTIVITIES BASED PRIMARILY ON RURITANIAN PROGRAMS. THEY ALSO STILL BRAG ABOUT THEIR TOTAL DEDI-CATION TO SOLAR LOCOMOTED TRANSPORT.

FUEL

MNO COMPANY INC HAS RECENTLY STARTED GET-TING INTO COAL TRANSPORT JUST LIKE SO MANY LARGE TANKER COMPANIES. THIS IS ALSO INTENDED TO SUPPORT DIVERSIFICATION PRO-GRAMS OF TRANSYLVANIAN GOVERNMENT WHICH CALL FOR SEVERAL NEW LARGE COAL BURNING PLANTS.

COMMENTS

There was a heading 'General Comments' earlier. It is therefore confusing to find another 'Comments'. It is highly questionable whether the subject-matter of this paragraph can be so described in any case.
He still has not given his manpower needs, one of three items requested.

YESTERDAY WE HAD A VISIT HERE BY STEPHEN CRANE WHO INDICATED THAT THERE ARE NOW HOPES FOR THE NEXT NOVEMBER ELECTIONS TO TURN IN FAVOR OF SOLAR LOCOMOTION AND THINGS MAY CHANGE. WE ARE GLAD THAT THROUGHOUT THIS HIATUS WE HAVE BEEN ABLE TO PRESERVE OUR FUNDAMENTAL BUSINESS RELATIONS WITH THE KEY PEOPLE IN THE INTERESTED ORGANIZATION NOTWITHSTANDING ALL CHANGES OCCURRED MEANTIME, JUST LIKE IN OTHER INDUSTRIES WHERE WE DO EXPORT BUSINESS HERE.

REGARDS

H W LONGFELLOW

Second reply: Atlanta

The heading is clear. Thereafter it is not easy to follow.
The text would be greatly enhanced by some sort of division and structure.

REF: ATLANTA SOLAR LOCOMOTION PROGRAM

LAST OCTOBER 6, L DA VINCI AND MYSELF MET IN ATLANTIC CITY JULES VERNE, GEN MANAGER OF JONAH ON POSSIBILITIES IN ATLANTA NUCLEAR PROGRAM.

OUR COUNTRY HAS PREPARED A PLAN FOR 300-400 MILES OF TRACK FOR SOLAR-POWERED LOCO-MOTIVES TO BE IN OPERATION DURING LAST DECADE OF THE CENTURY. THIS PROGRAM WAS TO HAVE BEEN COMPLETED FEW YRS AGO, BUT

DUE TO LOCAL INSTABILITY IT HAS BEEN POST
PONED FEW TIMES. NOW AS FROM LAST ELECTIC
CAME OUT A 4 YR GOVNT., WE HAVE INDICATIC
THAT THE PROGRAM WILL GO AHEAD IN NEAR
FUTURE.

The Telex has sometimes taken
the need for economy of
punctuation to absurd lengths.

The sentence: 'To revitalize our
. . . industry and government' is
a bit long and cumbersome for a
Telex.

TO REVITALISE OUR COMPANY'S IMAGE ON SOLA
LOCOMOTIVE INDUSTRY IN OUR MARKET WE THIN
THAT YOU SHOULD ENDEAVOR YOUR EFFORT TO P
TO HAVE HELD IN NEXT MONTH A SEMINAR ON
SOLAR-550, DEDICATED TO LOCAL UTILITY
INDUSTRY AND GOVERNMENT. THIS SEMINAR WOL
BE COMPLETED BY APPROPRIATE CONTRACTS WIT
PEOPLE OF ABOVE ENTITIES. MEANWHILE TO
OBTAIN INFO ON POSSIBLE FUTURE COOPERATIC
FOR LOCAL PROGRAM WE MET WITH JONAH.

The two paragraphs on Jonah,
which are somewhat peripheral
to the general information, could
have been rolled into one.

JONAH - A PRIVATE OWNED COMPANY ATLANTARA
HAS ABOUT 20 PCT SHARE - MANUFACTURES
INDUSTRIAL EQUIPMENT, OVERHEAD CRANES,
POWER PLANT BOILERS, RAILWAY ROLLING STOC
AND STEAM TURBO GENERATORS.

JONAH - IS FREE UP TO NOV TO COOPERATE WI
US ON A LOCAL PARTICIPATION PROGRAM FOR
SOLAR POWERED LOCOMOTIVES AND ANCILLARY
VEHICLES BUT JONAH HAS BEEN APPROACHED BY
OTHER SUPPLIERS AND THIS MEANS WE HAVE TC
MOVE FAST AND MEAN IT, VERY FAST. BY OTHE
SIDE STRONGHYLE HAD CONTACTS WITH SANTORI
THE OTHER LOCAL COMPANY SIMILAR TO JONAH
AND PARTIALLY OWNED NEPTUNE.

The paragraph 'We think it's
time . . .' suggests scope for
strong pruning. For example,
'We think it's', 'above
mentioned', 'up to now'.

WE THINK IT'S TIME TO OFFICIALLY APPROACH
OUR COUNTRY ON THE SOLAR LOCOMOTIVE PROGR
AND THIS MUST BEGIN WITH THE ABOVE MENTIC
SEMINAR. THIS FACT WAS ALREADY TRANSMITTE
TO SAN FRANCISCO BY SOLON'S LETTER OF AUG
21 BUT UP TO NOW NO REACTION HAS BEEN
RECEIVED.

Here he starts to get dreadfully
chatty. This conversational style
is too long-winded.

ALSO I HAVE TALKED WITH TIMAEUS AND A
POSSIBLE SUPPORT WHEN MATTER STARTS TO
DEVELOP CAN COME FROM OUR RURITANIAN CAPA
BILITIES. ALSO IT APPEARS BECAUSE OF SOLA
PROJECTS NOW STARTING AND ALREADY COMMITT
FOR THE NEAR FUTURE, THE AVAILABILITY OF
THE LOCAL INDUSTRY, ALTHOUGH ESSENTIAL
BECAUSE OF THE NATURE OF THE SOLAR LOCO-
MOTION PROJECT, MAY HAVE TO BE COMPLEMENT
FROM OUTSIDE. WITH A CORRECT APPROACH FRC
US MAYBE OUR RURITANIAN OPERATION CAN
BECOME A POSSIBLE PARTNER TO COMPLEMENT
THE LOCAL INDUSTRY.

HOWEVER WE MUST STRESS THAT ANY DECISION
ON SOLAR LOCOMOTION IN ATLANTA WILL BE
LINKED TO ATTRACTIVE FINANCIAL PACKAGE
EITHER BY COOPERATIONS OR BY OTHER COUNTF
IES SUPPORT. IT MAY BE POSSIBLE ALSO THAT

A POLITICAL DECISION WOULD BE COMPLETELY
SEPARATED FROM THE FINANCIAL ASPECTS.

AS YOU KNOW CRITIAS FOR THE LAST COUPLE OF
MONTHS HAS BEEN PART OF DICUSSIONS WITH
LOCAL MANUFACTURERS. YOU MAY ALSO GATHER
HIS OPINION ON THE SUBJECT.

Once again, his report does not
include the critical manpower
needs.

PLEASE ACKNOWLEDGE.

BEST REGARDS

H G WELLS

Third reply: Ruritania

There is no heading here, but if
there was a reference to the Telex
which it is answering, all would
be well.

This is the first report to include
the manpower needs. It must be
presumed that the reader would
recognise these rather bland
figures as such.

These short paragraphs provide a
direct statement of what the
intentions and objectives are.

Although this paragraph is long,
its content appears to be
extremely pertinent to the subject
matter. The short direct
statements are easy to follow.

A good economical style is being
used here.

ANTHONY HAWKINS VIST YOU TO DISCUSS 1981
CONCERNING SOLAR LOCOMOTIVE ACTIVITIES:

RISCHENHEIM	18 PCT
TARLENHEIM	27 PCT
RASSENDYL	22 PCT
TOTAL	67 PCT

THE ABOVE PERCENTAGE WAS SUBMITTED WITH OUR
PRELIMINARY BUDGET FOR 1981 TO M MITCHELL
WITH COPY TO B FRANKLIN. I AM DESCRIBING
BELOW MAJOR ACTIVITIES IN WHICH WE WILL BE
INVOLVED DURING 1981:

CONTINUE NEGOTIATIONS CONCERNING FINAL-
IZATION OF PENDING MATTERS IN RELATION TO
TARLENHEIM LINE SOLAR TRAIN CONTRACT.

FINALIZATION OF MANUFACTURING ASSOCIATION
AGREEMENT WITH RUPERT PLATES INC.

FOLLOW UP WITH RUPERT PLATES MODIFICATION
OF PLATES FROM SOLAR-222 FOR SOLAR-550?

SOLAR-900 LICENCES. CONTRACTS WITH MINISTRY
OF TRANSPORT AND COMMITTEE FORMED TO CARRY
OUT VIABILITY STUDY TO INTRODUCE SOLAR-900
LOCOMOTIVES IN RURITANIA. REPORT TO BE
READY SOMETIME BY MID-1981 RECOMMENDING
ADOPTION OF ONE OR TWO TECHNOLOGIES NAMELY
SOLAR-900 OR SOLAR-901. THIS IS EXTREMELY
IMPORTANT FOR FUTURE OF SOLAR LOCOMOTION
IN RURITANIA. VICE-PRESIDENT M MITCHELL AS
WELL AS B FRANKLIN HAVE ALREADY BEEN TWICE
IN RURITANIA DURING LAST FEW MONTHS AND
MET KEY PEOPLE WITH GOVERNMENT, RURITANIAN
RAILWAYS, UTILITIES, ETC.

ACTIVITIES IN CONNECTION WITH RURITANIAN
PUBLIC TRANSPORT FORUM. I AM A MEMBER OF
THE MANAGEMENT COMMITTEE OF THE SAID
ORGANIZATION REPRESENTING OUR NATIONAL
EXECUTIVE. ALSO PARTICIPATE IN PERIODIC
MEETINGS OF RURITANIAN RAILWAY AND TRAM
SOCIETY OF WHICH WE ARE ALSO MEMBERS.

PROVIDE COMMERCIAL SUPPORT AND GUIDANCE

WHEN SO REQUESTED BY REGIONAL RAILWAY
MANAGERS FOR EASTERN LINE CURRENTLY CON-
VERTING TO SOLAR. IF REQUIRED PROVIDE DIRE
ACCESS TO TOP MANAGEMENT OF EASTERN LINE.

PROVIDE GUIDANCE TO RURITANIAN RAILWAY
EXECUTIVE WITH REGARD TO PUBLICITY CAMPAI(
WHICH THEY PERIODICALLY RUN IN RURITANIA
IN LOCAL NEWSPAPERS AND MAGAZINES IN
CONNECTION WITH USE OF SOLAR POWER. EVENTL
ALLY PREPARE, IF REQUIRED, NEW PRESENTATI(
PARTICULARLY CONCERNING SOLAR-900 AND SOL/
901 SYSTEMS TENTATIVELY SOMETIME IN 1981.

PREPARE STRATEGY FOR NEW GENERATION OF SOL
LOCOMOTIVE TO BE OFFERED IN RURITANIA IN
1982/3.

The last paragraph seems a bit of
waffle. This is a pity as it
detracts from a lucid and punchy
report.

THERE WILL BE MANY OTHER DAY-TO-DAY ACTIV-
ITIES THAT WE WILL CARRY OUT IN CONNECTIO(
WITH RURITANIAN RAILWAYS WHICH WOULD BE T(
LONG TO LIST IN THIS TELEX. SHOULD YOU NEE
ANY FURTHER INFORMATION PLEASE LET ME KNO(

BEST REGARDS

A HOPE

Summary

A Telex is a highly functional way of making a report. Embellishment and ornament
are not appropriate.

Particular care must be taken to ensure conciseness and clarity of design and
layout of the text. Certainly a numbered, columnised and well headed layout will
often produce both conciseness and clarity.

CHAPTER SEVENTEEN

Reports of the future

Every generation believes that it is at a watershed of history. The events of the moment always loom larger than those of the past or obscure and imprecise prophesies of the distant future. The decisions, upsets and problems of today effect everyone's lives tomorrow and in the immediate future. Therefore they seem more important and more melodramatic than they will appear with the perspective of hindsight.

It is the same with new equipments and new technological developments. Their novelty gives them the element of surprise. Their supporting publicity gives them what is sometimes a disproportionate importance and urgency.

There are now a number of new innovations in instructional technology. In both variety and capability, they are substantial. That epithet will do, however. Anything stronger would be overstated and silly; for the time being. Nevertheless it would be churlish and irresponsible not to examine these developments seriously and as thoroughly as space allows. They have undoubtedly had an effect on report preparation and will continue to do so.

Resistance to change

There have been many Luddite reactions to new office technology. Some have been inspired by anxiety and some by misunderstanding and lack of knowledge. A few are the product of varying degrees of bloody-mindedness. There is much natural conservatism about everyone where their jobs and conditions of work are concerned. Unions and progressive philosophies notwithstanding, the *status quo* is known and safe. The almost universally high unemployment has exacerbated fears of any new labour-saving equipments. A report[1] published in 1980 declared that 21,000 jobs had by that time already been lost through word processing and that 170,000 would have been lost by 1990. (The figures do not take into account new jobs created in other trades by the related technology. This is not in any case relevant to people's entirely genuine fears about their own jobs.) It is not only fear of losing jobs that creates this alarm, but anxiety about restructuring of staff.

Some people feel that new techniques are in some way undignified. McCabe and Popham[2] see this as a logical extension of the feeling, prevalent well within the working life of people still on the job, that a typewritten letter was offhand. Certainly the attitude of many managers to typing on a word processor is of that school.[3]

The insecurity of new techniques of data storage generates quite a lot of alarm.[4] This is again an expression of disquiet at the unknown and is part of a general swing towards free information.[5] However the insecurity of paper-based records should never be underestimated.[6]

A lot of people are put off new equipments by the desperately complex documentation that supports the packages. There are widespread claims of easily comprehensible documentation, but too often these claims are unfounded.

More specific anxieties have related to possible damage to the eyes from the Visual Display Units (VDUs), which are an integral part of many new equipments. These fears have been shown to be quite without foundation. VDU-use does not damage the eyes and does not aggravate defects. On the other hand it is quite likely to make users more aware of the deficiencies in their eyes. In this way, older users whose eyesight is getting worse will believe, erroneously, that the VDU, rather than advancing age, is causing the damage.[7] They may certainly be prone to tiredness, soreness of the eyes and screwing up of the eyes because of the visually exacting nature of their work. Damage will not result though, and variation in colour of VDU print or brightness can usually alleviate these difficulties.

Equipments and their use

Word processors

These valuable machines, which have already become commonplace, offer the following advantages in the preparation of reports:
1   Justification of type at both ends of the line.
2   Important flexibility in the adaptation of standard reports to suit individual situations.
3   Ease of correction.
4   Ability to rearrange the sequence of sentences and paragraphs.
5   As an extension of point (4), the possibility of inserting completely new detail into the report.[8]
6   Availability to all staff, because of the high standard of the finished copy regardless of mistakes.[9]
7   Ability to perform simple calculations.
8   Avoidance of widow-lines (sitting on their own) and other cosmetic improvements.
9   Speed, particularly with reduction of proof-reading time.[10]
10   Aids to hyphenation.
11   Centring of report title pages, quotations and other indented material.
12   Ability to retain vocabularies, for example of abbreviations.
13   Ability to process lists, for instance of addresses.[11]
These are, of course massive generalisations. Every individual manufacturer will emphasise different advantages and the performance will vary accordingly.

The term *word processing*, which originated in about 1966, is perhaps misleading. It has been properly criticised.[12] There are some serious dangers in the equipment. If managers preparing reports are mindful of them, there will be no problem.

(a)   The machine is only as good as its user. When word processors were introduced into a large number of firms in the mid-1970s, staff were frequently of the opinion that the machines would somehow write the reports themselves. Opinion is now generally better educated. However, some managers still delegate responsibility for compiling word-processed reports to too low a level.

(b)   Standard formats and standard paragraphs must be updated regularly. They should be scrutinised about every six months both to ensure that:
1   The statutes, regulations, prices and names are up to date.
2   The forms of words used are still vigorous and meaningful.

(c) Ideally, nobody should ever use a standard paragraph or standard report format unless they know who last revised it and when they did so. To this end standard passages and layout should be annotated on the master-copy with these pieces of information.

(d) Nobody must use a standard passage unless they agree with every single word of it. The greatest advantage of a word processor is its ability to select and edit. If standard passages are regurgitated without thought in a report, not only is precision lost but the report might as well be performed on a cheaper, more conventional machine.

(e) Changes in print faces must never be used where emphasis would be more accurately achieved by punctuation or word choice.

The Equal Opportunities Commission[13] have been quite rightly critical of the lack of training given – or more accurately, taken up – on word processors. Manufacturers provide training on a variety of scales, sometimes for all users and sometimes for a cadre of staff who can train the company's employees.

The reluctance to take up the training is more evident among managers who accord a low priority to this type of learning. Certainly training must be supportive of other functions: it can never be justified as an end in itself. Furthermore, as finances become more and more straitened, training is an obvious area for particularly stringent cuts. However, when users (including managers) are not completely trained in the capability of word processors, the equipment is not used to its full capacity in preparation of reports and the economy is a false one.

Prolific governmental advice on making the most of new developments has been available, both before and after the 1979 General Election.[14] It can be obtained particularly from the Department of Industry Technology Point, Station Square House, Saint Mary Cray, Orpington, Kent BR5 3RF.

The ease of producing (or creating, as the vogue-word has it) a lot of documents by word processing is helpful. Work of a standard and routine kind can be done while the operator is out to lunch or engaged on other tasks. The corollary to this is that a great deal of junk mail will be produced.[15] Important reports may get swamped by spurious and unnecessary papers. Particular control of the generation of unnecessary paperwork must be exercised.

It is important in allocating work to word processors to bear in mind that between 75 and 80 per cent[16] of the work which they do is similar to that done on a conventional typewriter. Most of all, in drafting a report for reproduction by a word processor, it must be remembered that it has no mind of its own. A quotation from Anne Clark well summarises its limitations: '... although the word processor can do many complex operations, it cannot think, speak (yet!), take dictation, file incoming mail, and has no initiative. It is only an obedient clever slave.'[17]

Prestel and similar information systems

While word processors make it easier to reproduce reports, systems such as Prestel present information that can be updated in minute accuracy. Prestel and other data sources are therefore both a source of information and a form of report itself. For example, motor manufacturers make use of a data presentation system to link dealers direct to the manufacturer's central database which furnishes details of stock location and market information. Airlines use them for aircraft cargo and passenger states. Other possible applications include details of injuries sustained, financial information, rates of exchange, hospital bed states, vehicle pool and man-power availability.

It should be made clear that Prestel is the registered trademark of British Telecom. Many other data systems exist. The best known publicly available systems are Ceefax (BBC) and Oracle (ITV). Among the better known and most widely available systems is IBM Viewdata Service,[18] which is compatible with Prestel.

Data systems may be divided into two kinds:

1 *Videotext* This is the generic term for TV-based systems. These may be received on a modified TV set and consist of a number of pages of information. Ceefax and Oracle are forms of Videotext.
2 *Viewdata* Viewdata links the telephone to the screen. It can usually put more words on the screen than Videotext. Prestel is such a system.

The main advantages of using data systems either as a source of information for reports or as a report form itself are:

a Instant information can be transmitted over many thousands of miles.
b Information can easily be updated as stocks change, vehicles break down and so on. The information can therefore be presented to the reader without generating additional paper as changes occur.
c Information can be passed to work-stations in places other than offices.

On the other hand there are several significant limitations:

1 It cannot be read at places other than suitably equipped and bulky work-stations; for instance, not on a train. (Portable viewdata systems are being developed[19] and will fit in a briefcase. It remains to be seen how easy they will be to handle or read. They will be compatible with Prestel or private data systems.)
2 Without two screens it is difficult to compare two sources of data. This is a particular disadvantage in compiling a report when many information sources will often need to be spread in front of the writer.
3 A report on a VDU is less personal than one on paper where greater variations in presentation are possible.

While not strictly a disadvantage, the size of a VDU screen limits the number of words that can be seen at once. (For example, IBM Viewdata Service will show 24 lines of 40 characters each.) Although this ensures concise writing and places a great emphasis on word choice, it may lead to ambiguity. It is certainly productive of a very factual impersonal style.

During the Falklands War a very effective scheme of videotext reporting was used in the Whitehall Press Centre. Background information reports, frequently updated, appeared on a GEC 4000 (GEC Viewdata System) for the information of correspondents. To initiate the system of reporting, 1,200 frames were fed into the system and indexed over a Bank Holiday weekend.[20] This form of report was complemented by Ministry of Defence oral press statements.

Possible developments from this type of reporting are that less reliance will be placed on paper-reporting for routine updating of returns. This will save a lot of time-consuming paper-reporting. However it would be unfortunate if it developed into a reluctance to commit anything to paper. There is also a danger that the emphasis on the work-stations in which the VDUs are housed will make managers less flexible.

Microwriters

A less spectacular development, but one that will improve flexibility, is the introduction of the Microwriter.[21] This small,[22] hand-held device enables a manager to record information as he moves about his site without the encumbrance of pencil and paper. The advantages of this will be particularly apparent to those who work out of doors and in foul weather. Indeed, for all managers who have to write at speed and write up their notes some time later, the Microwriter will avoid problems of illegibility and, thus, inaccuracy.

The device has six controls and letters are recorded by depression of various combinations. As an analogy only, it could be said that the system was something on the lines of morse. The technique can be understood within an hour and mastered within a couple of days, achieving about 150 per cent of handwriting speed.

The portable recorder will plug into an automatic printer, a TV monitor or a cassette for storage. It can also save dictation time as it is compatible with many word-processing systems. Its memory runs to 8,000 characters, about 1,500 words.

A good example of highly successful trialling is by a Vice-President of Commonwealth Inns (a franchise of the Holiday Inns Group). The Microwriter has been a great boon to the Group Executive Housekeeping and their Bristol-based area manager. Both travel extensively and have to write up the reports of their findings in detail on return.[23]

One commentator[24] describes it as 'the biggest thing since man discovered the pencil'. It is certainly a splendid means of recording details for a report; particularly in uncomfortable circumstances. It may also provide a very adequate first draft. However, it is essential that the copy produced by a Microwriter is regarded, at best, as a draft or a source of data. The manufacturers state: 'Most professional people are involved in detailed drafting of letters, documents or reports requiring meticulous accuracy in the choice of words'. This will undoubtedly need sharpening when the microwriter copy has been got back to the office.

Facsimile

Transmission of complicated diagrams, proposals and plans accurately at great speed over great distances has been vastly improved by facsimile.[25] It saves time, compared with the post, and achieves 100 per cent accuracy, which can never be attained by Telex. Facsimile is extensively used by police forces and has many business applications. It can transmit anywhere in the world within about 40 sec. Fine definition of detail can be conveyed in up to 16 shades of grey. This produces a high standard of accuracy in photographs and half-tones. It is, however, not cheap and will for the foreseeable future probably remain only a supplementary form of report. It will be used for reports calling for immediate transmission of complicated detail in diagrammatic form. It can also be used for passing drafts requiring immediate and urgent comment.

Script editors

Allusion has been made in these paragraphs to the particular need for scrutiny and editing of draft reports produced by mechanical means. Not surprisingly, the market place is now offering mechanical means of editing. There are two main types of editorial assistance on offer.

(a) Simplification aids Particularly in the USA, thought has been given to machines which will prune and edit reports of over-lavish forms of expression. This may seem laudable, leading as it should to concise writing and elimination of padding words. It is not as simple as that.

The principal protagonists of this type of device are Bell Laboratories of New Jersey.[26] Their Writers' Workbench mechanism was described by Adrian Berry in *The Daily Telegraph.*[27] He cites two particularly revealing examples of the system's limitations. The opening of Dickens *Tale of Two Cities*, 'It was the best of times, it was the worst of times, it was the age of wisdom, it was the age of foolishness', is reduced to 'The times were the best and worst, wise and foolish'. Lincoln's Gettysburg address is similarly emasculated. After the obvious shortening of 'Fourscore and seven years ago', it continues with 'our grandfathers created a free nation here. They based it on the idea that everybody is created equal'. (This replaces '. . . our fathers brought forth on this continent a new nation conceived in liberty and dedicated to the proposition that all men are created equal'.) The inaccuracy and shift in meaning in the simplification speaks for itself. For example, the word *based* can in no way convey the meaning of Lincoln's *dedicated*. The imprecision of *here* is equally inept.

Four months later Berry returned to the phenomenon. In a rather longer article he described a Yale University programme which sought to enliven prose by packing it with lively and provocative words such as *murder threat* and *bomb-plot*. The same programme suggested that the word *nationalised* was a reasonable replacement for 'seized financial and operational control' regardless of the slightly different emphases conveyed by each of the words in that expression.

(b) Spelling error detectors Various word-processing equipments[28] provide systems for checking and correcting spellings. These are able to compare spellings in the report against vocabularies of probably about 20,000 words held in the word processor.[29] The facility is certainly valuable in the case of proper nouns, such as the names of foreign suppliers who are frequently mentioned in the reports. The machine is however quite unable to identify whether the correct word of a pair of the easily confused homophones described in Chapter 11 is being used (*complement/compliment, prescribed/proscribed* and so on.)

The main disadvantages then, of these editorial aids are that:
1 They tend to be over-simplistic. It seems that it will never be possible for any mechanism to make the fine distinctions and subtle judgements on which the precision of a report in English rests. These are essentially individual human choices to convey human ideas and opinions.
2 Even if these types of equipment, such as a spelling checker, are used as rudimentary supportive types of assistance, there is a danger that too much reliance will be placed on them. Drafting will therefore become slapdash and inaccurate.

Mechanical translation

A field of peripheral mechanical assistance, but one important to those dealing with foreign clients and customers, is that of mechanical translation. A long way back, in 1962, Boorstin[30] wrote of a Mark II machine that could translate Russian into 'rough but meaningful English'. The idea goes back as far as 1949[31] and although there have been advances since then, the subtleties of idiom cannot be translated. *Out of sight, out of mind* continues to be translated as *invisible idiot*.

Electronic mailing

Speed and the very reasonable pricing of electronic mail make this form of report despatch more and more appealing. Fedida and Malik[32] estimate the cost of transmitting one A4 page electronically as 4p, as opposed to their estimate of a first-class letter handling at 20p. (The latter seems a bit conservative.)

One of the leading systems is Comet Electronic Mail, originally produced by CCA of Cambridge, USA and now by BL Systems Ltd of Redditch. It provides a useful system for making quick written reports when the recipients are difficult to locate by telephone. The reports can be left until the addressee rings into his office when the system presents him first with the titles of all reports awaiting his attention and then with the text of those he chooses to read.

The system offers the following advantages:

1   It is time-saving from the originator's point of view. He does not have to spend hours trying to contact an elusive addressee by telephone.[33]
2   It avoids postal delays.
3   It is time-saving from the receiver's point of view. It is easy to hold the reports until he has time to read them.

Electronic mailing will become increasingly useful for reports from remote sites to their controlling offices and for the self-employed or those with very small, or no, secretarial staffs. Contrary to the general trend described in these pages, electronic mailing produces more permanent records. Its replacement of telephone reports by a more permanent record runs counter to the current fashion for temporary displays.

Conferencing systems

Teleconferencing obviates the need for a great deal of travel. It may also reduce the number of paper reports. However there must be proper concise records kept of all such exchanges. If a report of the discussion was appropriate in the days before teleconferencing was available, then it is no less necessary now.

Sociological trends

The cautious attitudes towards many new forms of report writing have been discussed. In parallel with these sorts of attitudes must be considered wide sociological changes which bear on the language and the way in which it is used in reports.

Results of television

It is appropriate to start with an equipment and its influence. Television was not discussed in the last section as it is not purely an office equipment. The influence of broadcasting on people's attitudes generally has been evident since Hitler's use of wireless. The influence of television on remoter regions of the UK has been particularly important in the last two decades.[34] The broadcasting hours have increased steadily and the coming of breakfast television and cable television will make them increase dramatically.

The effects of this exposure on the style of managerial communications are these:

(a)   TV news coverage is becoming so extensive that the role of newspapers is becoming to pass comment on facts already well known to the reader. This produces a style that is emotive and sometimes facetious. This will rub off on readers and will make its way into managerial reports; just as other styles were described as rubbing off in Chapter 8.

(b)   The pressure of journalistic techniques on public figures reduces their replies to a clichéd and empty style of reply. Those, such as cabinet ministers, general secretaries of trade unions, chairmen of nationalised industries, who are subjected to excessive exposure in this way develop a patter of vacuous phrases. *At this moment in time*, *having regard to all the circumstances* are of this genre. They are extremely infectious and pad our reports with nonsense.

(c)   Advertising evolves a style of language which devalues superlatives. This is not restricted to television, but it is more pronounced and more evident. It has a spiral effect and adjectives and adverbs become less precise.

Attitudes on the role of the BBC in preserving certain standards and values in English use have been widely discussed. Dr Robert Burchfield has said: 'I believe that the BBC does have a kind of custodian role. . . . It should not be in the forefront of recognising and giving ready acceptance to new fashions and trendy usage.'[35] Although he was writing about pronunciation, his comments may hold good for word use as well. Peter Elliot writing in *The Guardian*[36] quoted an earlier BBC style book. 'It is not for the BBC to set trends. Our role must be to follow not to pioneer.' In 1919 Robert Bridges[37] said that he believed that the introduction of broadcasting (and telephones) called for particular vigilance in the use of language.

Whatever is said, one thing is certain. The use of language in all the media will be followed. It will be followed in management reports, too. It is not necessarily the language of the BBC style book that will be followed. It is the wording of the advertisement, the interview under pressure and the impromptu press statement that will be subconsciously imitated.

Linguistic trends

Some trends have already become well established in the use of British English since 1945:

(a)   Literacy and semantic awareness have improved. There is no doubt that this may, in part, result from the dominant presence of broadcasting of both types. It is also related to the increase in the number of periodicals available. Hoggart shows an increase from 1,000 to 5,000 in the period 1857–1957.[38]

(b)   As a result of these developments, regional forms of spoken English and idiom have become more widely acceptable.[39] This has made itself felt in the tone and style of commercial writing. Some authorities[40] – and some who are less than authorities – will comment adversely on this type of swing. It cannot be denied, though, that

elimination of linguistic distinctions based purely on regional or social categories, can only enhance written and spoken communication.

(c) To complement these, everyone's educational expectations have increased.[41] These aspirations were given official encouragement by the 1944 Education Act. Whether they have been satisfied by the services offered by local education authorities is a matter for subjective comment well beyond the scope of this book.

(d) American office and other technology brings more American English into the workplace. This calls for diligence, where British and American phrases have similar meanings, and a need for consistency in preparing reports. The influence of American (and more recently Australian) English through films is not seriously diminished whatever temporary swings of fortune may affect that industry.

(e) Variation in print size and more imaginative designs in advertising tend towards a great emphasis on presentation at the expense of words. This trend was forecast and described by Marshall McLuhan in the 1960s.[42] It is unwelcome, denigrating the precision of word choice.

(f) Mention has been made of the increasing vogue for accountability. The examples given have been in appraisal reporting in Chapter 13 and in local government information in this chapter. This may produce a danger of rather cautious and, therefore, inaccurate wording of reports. This must not be permitted.

Changes in values

The British sociological climate since the Second World War, since Beveridge and more especially since the return of the Wilson Government in 1964, have been characterised by two emphases. Sometimes these have bordered on obsessions.

There is an awareness of the needs of those who are handicapped in various ways. These handicaps, which are veiled in a fine range of euphemism, are taken to cover not just physical misfortunes but also alleged handicap of being female, of being a mother and so on. The effect has been that more importance is being given to people being able to work hours which suit them and, if possible, at home. Flexitime, which was first introduced into West Germany's highly work-conscious society around 1967,[43] is now a well established part of British office practice. Many of the information-retrieval systems available will enable more people – married women with children and others – to work at home.

The second priority which has been emphasised is a need for more leisure. This is given a great boost by the publicity material for many word processors. Coupled with increased unemployment, which no government is going to be able to reduce to any significant extent, this is likely to lead to increased work-sharing.

Both these trends will lead to the need for increased control over the preparation of reports. Reports being produced by a variety of (sometimes part-time) staff in a variety of places, working variable hours, may necessitate issue of model reports and definitive statements of company standards. In no way must this be allowed to impinge on the precision, accuracy and variety of content.

What is needed

A flood of well marketed and intriguing devices is now available to change the way in which reports are written. Reports are prepared by a wide range of writers on a wider range of subjects using more words than ever before.

Various criteria must be applied to the equipments to judge whether they fulfil a useful function or are well packaged gimmicks.

1   They should improve the accuracy of the report.
2   They should improve the speed at which it is produced.
3   They should improve the efficiency of the staff; including providing a means for relieving staff of repetitive time-consuming duties.
4   They should improve the clarity and precision of the report.
5   They should be ergonomically convenient.

However, in no report can the human contribution be eliminated entirely. If this is so, the report is not worth submitting. More important, it must not appear that the human hand is absent. Ian McIntyre has written[44] pithily of a comparison of the current *BBC Year Book*: 'Today such publications give an impression of having been run off on a word processor, untouched by human brain'.

It will follow, of course, that there is bound to be human error. However elaborate the mechanisms for reducing errors in repetitive work, human error is also bound to feature in the programs, operator performance and original data.[45] Future developments must strive to make the equipments as foolproof as possible and easily accessible and comprehensible.

Summary

Technological developments have introduced two contrary but important developments into report preparation. Ephemeral reports calling for regular updating are presented in a less permanent form. On the other hand, many useful devices such as the Microwriter exist for giving new accuracy and permanence to reports from the field which hitherto have been submitted by telephone with all the attendant frustrations and inaccuracy.

Sociological trends have caused a shift away from somewhat elitist styles of English. These have been accompanied by rather more emotive tones borrowed from advertising journalism. Whether they are welcome or not, they are here and represent the way in which (younger) managers are inclined to communicate.

There is no doubt that paper reports will continue to play a major role in managerial communication. There will be occasions when VDU-linked systems are not available, when confidentiality calls for greater privacy or above all, as Teague says, when it is a good idea to be personal:

> Above all, the printed word will remain, for there is no reason why we should ever cease to benefit by use of a major faculty that is so pleasantly personal to each reader and yet so generally available to mankind at large.[46]

*   *   *

So this book has come full circle. It started by suggesting that communication was a subject of infinite extent. These pages have given important guidelines in report compilation. They are however just valid for a particular time.

Technology and language are changing every moment. The historian Pieter Geyl[47] has described history as 'an argument without end'. Likewise the preparation of reports must keep pace with new developments in equipment and expression.

A report must be up-to-date without being trendy. It must be acceptable to the most conservative without being archaic. In this dilemma lies the problem, but also the subject's fascination.

PART FOUR

APPENDICES

Type faces

If the report is to be typeset and printed rather than reproduced directly from a typewritten master you then enter the world of typography. What typeface should the report be set in? This problem should be discussed with the typesetter. However the following points should be borne in mind.

1   Most typesetting nowadays is done photographically (on a photosetter) rather than by casting metal type. This gives more scope for different typefaces and different sizes to be used. Typesizes are measured in *points* (1 point = 1/72 inch).

2   Most typefaces are either *serif* or *sans-serif* – with or without the crossline flushing the stroke of a letter. Examples of commonly used serif faces are Times, Century, Plantin and Baskerville; of sans-serif faces, Univers, Helvetica and Transport. Some typefaces, such as Optima, are neither fish nor fowl in being not quite sans-serif.

3   When specifying a typeface, remember that some typefaces are known by different names depending on the particular make of photosetter used. Thus Helvetica, Megaron on the VIP photosetter and Helios on the Compugraphic photosetter are all the same face.

4   The final appearance of the report will depend not only on the typeface and size used, but also on the amount of white space (known as leading or feed) left between lines. This calls for expert advice.

This book has been photoset in 10 point Times (with 2 points feed) with the Appendices set in 9 point Times, again with 2 points feed. The Chapter titles and running heads have been set in Megaron.

A piece of text set in various typefaces is reproduced overleaf for comparison. Each is set in 9 point with 2 points feed.

TIMES   There was a disappointing start to the year mainly due to bad weather and a drop in the number of visitors; the situation improved in July and August and a good Christmas trading period enabled the Trust to finish ahead of 1980 in terms of the volume of sales. The increasing cost of running shops and restaurants is a matter of concern to all retail traders but efforts are constantly being made to reduce them.

PLANTIN   There was a disappointing start to the year mainly due to bad weather and a drop in the number of visitors; the situation improved in July and August and a good Christmas trading period enabled the Trust to finish ahead of 1980 in terms of the volume of sales. The increasing cost of running shops and restaurants is a matter of concern to all retail traders but efforts are constantly being made to reduce them.

BASKERVILLE   There was a disappointing start to the year mainly due to bad weather and a drop in the number of visitors; the situation improved in July and August and a good Christmas trading period enabled the Trust to finish ahead of 1980 in terms of the volume of sales. The increasing cost of running shops and restaurants is a matter of concern to all retail traders but efforts are constantly being made to reduce them.

OPTIMA   There was a disappointing start to the year mainly due to bad weather and a drop in the number of visitors; the situation improved in July and August and a good Christmas trading period enabled the Trust to finish ahead of 1980 in terms of the volume of sales. The increasing cost of running shops and restaurants is a matter of concern to all retail traders but efforts are constantly being made to reduce them.

UNIVERS   There was a disappointing start to the year mainly due to bad weather and a drop in the number of visitors; the situation improved in July and August and a good Christmas trading period enabled the Trust to finish ahead of 1980 in terms of the volume of sales. The increasing cost of running shops and restaurants is a matter of concern to all retail traders but efforts are constantly being made to reduce them.

MEGARON   There was a disappointing start to the year mainly due to bad weather and a drop in the number of visitors; the situation improved in July and August and a good Christmas trading period enabled the Trust to finish ahead of 1980 in terms of the volume of sales. The increasing cost of running shops and restaurants is a matter of concern to all retail traders but efforts are constantly being made to reduce them.

Numbering systems

Combination of Roman and Arabic numbers

This is popular in Europe and is demonstrated by the layout of the Organisation for Economic Co-operation and Development Road Research report, *Traffic Control in Saturated Conditions*.[1] The first part of the table of contents is shown below to demonstrate the Continental preference for using Roman numerals for chapters or sections and then devolving to Arabic.

The breakdown is extended by decimals if required. For instance Sub-section III.3 is developed:

    III.3
        III.3.1
        III.3.2
        III.3.3
        III.3.4
        III.3.5
        III.3.6

Use of letters and small Roman numbers

Many house-styles use strictly prescribed sequences of letters and, in the lower levels of subordinate paragraph, small Roman numbers. Price Waterhouse use

1.
  (1)
  (2)
  (3)
    a.
    b.
    c.
      (a)
      (b)
      (c)
        i
        ii

Decimal numbers for the main divisions

Shannon Free Airport Development Company use similar combinations, but require decimal numbers for the first sub-division. They direct most specifically as follows:

1. *SECTION HEADINGS*
  1.1 *Sub-Section*
    (a) Paragraph
    (b) Second paragraph
  1.2 *Second Sub-Section*
2. *SECOND SECTION HEADING*

Their instructions then direct small Roman numbers in brackets for further sub-divisions, followed by unidentified dashes for subsequent divisions

    (b) Second paragraph
      (i) Sub-paragraph
        – Sub-sub-paragraph
        – Second sub-sub-paragraph
      (ii) Second sub-paragraph

However their instructions preface these latter divisions with the caveat that they should be used only 'if it is absolutely necessary'.

The Trustee Savings Banks Central Board system takes the decimal markings a stage further:

3.1
  3.1.1
  3.1.2
  3.1.3
  3.1.4
    (a)
    (b)
  3.1.5
    (a)
    (b)
3.2

The National Nuclear Corporation, which produces long and complex – sometimes massive – reports, extends such a system yet further:

section	1
sub-section	1.1
clause	1.1.1
paragraph	1.1.1 (a)
item	1.1.1 (a) (i)
	1.1.1 (a) (i) 1

All-decimal system

In a shift of fashion since the late 1960s, the most popular scheme of numbering is the all-decimal system. Such arrangements in their pure form make no provision for any symbols other than the decimal combinations. They are thus absolutely clear, but sometimes a bit cumbersome. They have, therefore, the clarity and precision of a Dewey library cataloguing system.[2]

The *Manual for Civil Service Typists*[3] now provides for use of a decimal system.

Selected suggestions for further reading

Here is a highly selective list of books suitable for reading by everyone to whom the content of this book has proved to be of interest – unless the notes indicate that the book in question deals with some specialism. The titles of works dealing with the more esoteric aspects are to be found in the detailed references in Appendix 4.

The notes describing the books explained in detail below contain many superlatives. This is deliberate. The books shown here are recommended, with very few qualifications.

FOR READING (AS OPPOSED TO REFERENCE)

English language

Fowler's Modern English Usage (revised by Sir Ernest Gowers; OUP)
This is, of course, legendary and a work of great scholarship. It was first published in 1926 and appear under the name H. W. Fowler, his brother having died some nine years earlier. It was revised by Sir Ernest Gowers (*q.v.* below) in 1965. It is a mine of fascinating information, grammatical, semantic and etymological.

It is arranged as a reference book in alphabetical order. The articles are couched in fluent prose and may be read straight through if desired. The entries include individual words with comments on their use, as well as phenomena such as *archaism, Briticism, pronouns* and *unattached participles.*

It may be argued that despite its revision it has not really kept pace with the times. Indeed nearly 20 years have passed since the revision. It is highly prescriptive by modern standards and the business report writer may find that it gets too bogged down in Classical allusion. However it is bliss to the authoritarian and will provide hours of entertainment and distraction to anyone interested in the language.

The King's English (H. W. and F. G. Fowler; OUP)
First published in 1906, it was the work of both H. W. and F. G. Fowler. It enjoyed a second edition in 1907 and a third in 1931. It describes style and custom rather more than giving a clinical glossary of individual words and syntactical functions. It is not arranged like a dictionary but in a series of chapters; Vocabulary, Syntax, Airs and Graces (which includes humour, metaphor and other embellishments), Punctuation and so on. Every chapter is beautifully simple to read and copiously illustrated by examples, albeit, of course, from pre-1931 publications.

Nevertheless, although the Fowler brothers illustrate and describe, *The King's English* is still strongly prescriptive. It is responsible, for instance, for such dogmas as 'Prefer the Saxon word to the Romance' quoted earlier in these pages.

The Complete Plain Words (Sir Ernest Gowers; Pelican paperback, HMSO hardback)
Gowers will make easier reading for many people than the Fowlers' books. It was first produced as *Plain Words* in 1948 at the request of the Treasury. In 1954 *The Complete Plain Words* appeared, incorporating *The ABC of Plain Words* which Gowers had produced three years before.

Sir Ernest Gowers was an experienced civil servant who was tasked with the improvement of Civil Service English. The book was aimed at civil servants who had been guilty for several decades of writing in the style of an even earlier era. In other words they were writing in Victorian English at the beginning of the second half of the 20th Century. So perhaps the malaises which Gowers sought to rectify no longer apply.

However, the book reads like a novel. It is full of examples, many of which are hilarious and a few of which defy credibility. All aspects of English usage are covered but there are five (out of 14) helpful chapters on word choice.

Good English, Better English and *The Best English* (G. H. Vallins; Andre Deutsch and, if you are lucky, Pan)

G. H. Vallins died in 1956, ten years before Sir Ernest Gowers (*q.v.* above). However, in a funny way these three books have aged better than *Complete Plain Words*. There are probably two reasons for this. He is slightly less prescriptive and the target at which he aimed the books were perpetrating more up-to-date evils than the antiquarian scribes whom Gowers was hammering.

The progression through the three books is simple. *Good English* deals with the basics. (In a review quotation from *The Sunday Times* on the front of the Pan Edition, it is described as 'the best book on the subject':) *Better English* advances to idiom, metaphor and similar subtleties. *The Best English* puts the principles into the context of great English literature.

It is desirable that the practical report writer should work through them in order and stop when he thinks it is getting a bit academic.

Usage and Abusage (Eric Partridge; Penguin)

This celebrated and much published work is laid out on very much the same lines as Fowler's *Modern English Usage*. The articles are shorter and generally less bound up with obscure academic allusions. It was first published in Britain in 1947 (20 years after Fowler). For these reasons, it is more readable to most people.

For all its brevity it still contains a wealth of relevant detail as to etymology, quotation and precedent.

Eric Partridge died in 1979, aged 85, after a lifetime dedicated to the language. Most of the last 35 years of his life was spent in the British Museum library pursuing this great affection. His output was prodigious. About 80 works are attributable to him. Only two can be shown in this appendix. Anyone wishing to sample a wide range of this great man's work should cast their eyes over the tribute anthology *Eric Partridge in His Own Words* (edited by David Crystal, published by Andre Deutsch).

Strangely this magnificent contributor to the understanding of English was never decorated.

The Facts of English (R. Ridout and C. Witting; Pan)

Here is a paperback in the same general direction as Partridge's *Usage and Abusage* but it is very much simpler. It will be particularly helpful to clerical staff, typists and those more at home with numbers than words. This is not intended as a patronising comment. The book gives good practical explanations of points that the occasional or inexperienced report writer might confuse: use of apostrophes, *affect/effect*, commonly used Latin phrases (such as *ad hoc, per annum, prima facie*).

The authors are a text-book writer and a journalist. They give suitably direct and uncomplicated advice.

The Use of English (R. Quirk; Longman)

This is a particularly readable account of the main issues in English language development. Professor Quirk is the Quain Professor of English Language and Literature at the University of London and is widely regarded as the guru of all aspects of practical English use. The book uses literary rather than commercial examples and is, quite properly, historical in its treatment. However its relevance to report writing is obvious as soon as a few pages have been read.

The Plight of English (B. Cottle; Arlington House)
Basil Cottle of the Department of English at Bristol University has produced this brisk and, at times, fierce treatment of some solecisms in English use. The authoritarian style may be too strong for some readers.

The author does not compromise his views, as is indicated by the strident sub-title 'Ambiguities, Cacophonies and Other Violations of Our Language'. However it is a good harbour for the report writer who is all at sea with his use of grammar and needs the security of a peaceful haven.

New Words for Old, *Weasel Words* and *Words Fail Me* (P. Howard; Hamish Hamilton)
These are fascinating and highly readable short essays on individual semantic usages. Each one discusses a particular cliché, vogue-word or extended expression. Many of the articles appeared in the author's occasional column in *The Times*, of which he is Literary Editor. Others were written specially for these books.

The three books first appeared in 1977, 1978 and 1980, respectively. There is no doubt that the tone of his comments is, in the main, less prescriptive in the later articles.

As to why his views are less authoritarian, Philip Howard suggests a variety of reasons, while stressing that such a complex matter does not permit a quick or simple explanation:

> You could say that I have developed a more realistic and sensible view of the way the language works. You could say that I have been influenced by my friends in the field like Randolph Quirk and Bob Burchfield. You could say that I have become embarrassed by the shrill tone of voice in the earlier pieces. You could say that I am growing middle-aged and I dare say there would be an element of truth in all the explanations.[1]

His items on word use continue to appear in *The Times* but his next book will be an examination of whether English is dying and what is happening to it.

Language Change: Progress or Decay? (J. Aitchison; Fontana)
Jean Aitchison of the London School of Economics has written a delightful book in this Fontana Original. It is aimed at linguistic reactionaries and conservatives who wish to imprison language in a straitjacket. Her dedication 'To those of my friends, and particularly Tony, who think that language change should be stopped' indicates the aim of her crusade. Her highly entertaining text is laced with quotations from widely diverse sources. Linguists, novelists, playwrights and others daily involved in the use of language are used as witnesses and demonstraters for her analysis of the general direction in which language, and English in particular, is travelling.

Punctuation

You Have a Point There (Eric Partridge; Routledge and Kegan Paul)
This is an unsurpassed guide to punctuation by the author of *Usage and Abusage* (*q.v.* above). Every punctuation mark (including such things as italics) is picked up, turned over and examined in fine detail. Examples are shown and trends described.

The book summarises the various uses with a chapter on Orchestration of the marks. This metaphor demonstrates admirably how the various marks must be drawn together to complement each other. Finally there is a chapter by John W. Clark of the University of Minnesota on practices in the United States.

Mind the Stop (G. V. Carey; Penguin)
Carey's book is much simpler and shorter than Partridge (*q.v.* above) (124 pages, as opposed

to 226). It is therefore less profusely illustrated. Many find that its advice is more direct and it is therefore easier to consult for quick guidance.

Carey first produced the book in 1939. A revision was published in 1958. The revision shows most commendable sensitivity to even the smallest changes in custom that have occurred since the first version. There is a useful little chapter on proof correction.

G. H. Vallins, author of *Good English*, etc. (*q.v.* above) says in another book[2] that he covers punctuation only loosely as it has been dealt with once and for all by Carey and Partridge.

American English

British and American English (P. Strevens; Cassell)
Strevens' little book is probably the best simple guide to American English for those who need to write occasional reports for American readerships. Seven easy chapters include an explanation of the reasons for the divergence of the two versions and some plain direct guidance on grammatical habits in the two countries. The book ends with a very short pair (American–British and British–American) of 'Contrasting Word-lists' (approximately 200 words each).

What's the Difference?: An American–British/British–American Dictionary (N. Moss; Arrow)
Moss provides much more comprehensive vocabularies (in both directions) than Strevens (*q.v.* above). The author was born in Britain but was educated largely in the United States.

It is a light-hearted paperback which can be read for entertainment as well as used for reference. It is probably more suitable for interpreting American writing than as a guide to word-choice. It contains many colloquialisms. It was first published in 1973 and revised in 1978. Quite a lot of the American terms shown have now achieved general acceptance in Britain.

Dictionary of American Slang (edited by H. Wentworth and S. B. Flexner; Second supplemented edition, Crowell)
This book only just gets into the list. Much of it is provocative. Some of it is obscene. Many of the terms included appear to be one-off nonce words of individual writers. There are 22,000 definitions, mostly supported by quotations. These are drawn from a very wide range of sources.

It just squeezes into the list as American reports sometimes contain words hovering about on the edge of received language. It is also fascinating in the breadth of its source material. Unless the user is strong-willed or has plenty of time he should be wary of opening it. (Hence its placement under 'Reading' rather than 'Reference'.) This original was produced in 1960. The Supplement contains items added in 1967 and 1975.

History of English language

A History of the English Language (A. C. Baugh and T. Cable; Routledge and Kegan Paul)
This book traces the history of the language from the earliest indications of the Indo-European family to the *New English Dictionary*. The chapters are arranged chronologically and end with a long chapter on 'The English Language in America'. The second of two appendices shows, by passages from different eras quoted in quick succession, how spelling has changed. It is very readable and a detailed table of contents enables the reader, if he wishes, to be selective.

A History of English (B. M. H. Strang; Methuen)
This is another history of the language which is very agreeable to read. Professor Barbara Strang describes it in her Preface as 'a book for beginners in linguistic history'. She sets out to dispel 'the fairy-tale – not to say nightmare – quality' of the subject. She succeeds in doing this

brilliantly. To add to the relevance, she starts with recent changes and works her way back to the period before AD 370.

The English Language (Volume 1): Essays by English and American Men of Letters 1490–1839 (edited by W. F. Bolton) and *The English Language (Volume 2): Essays by Linguists and Men of Letters 1858–1964* (edited by W. F. Bolton and C. D. Crystal) (Cambridge University Press) These two volumes are ideal source-books for anyone who wishes to follow the development of the language in original material. They show important and relevant passages from the period of Caxton and the demise of Middle English through the critical phase of Defoe, Addison, Swift, Johnson and the threat of the English Academy, via Webster to George Orwell and Anthony Burgess. There are reasonable, but not overwhelming, notes and every entry has a helpful paragraph of half-a-dozen lines as an introduction.

Textbooks

Writing Technical Reports (B. M. Cooper; Penguin)
This is a Pelican original which is deservedly popular and widely used. It was first published in 1964 and has been reprinted many times. Of the seven chapters, the content of the first six could generally be applied to most non-technical reports. The seventh deals with illustrations. There is an appendix on various sources of information which may be useful in compilation.

Except for some of the simplistic comments on word use, the book avoids the temptation of many handbooks on written communication to produce many authoritarian generalisations which do not fit every situation.

Communication in Business (P. Little; Third edition, Longman)
Of all the general guidebooks on business communication, this is probably the best. It is most comprehensive, covering oral communication, meetings, essays, notices and non-verbal communication. Three chapters on wording, one on summaries and one on reports are particularly relevant to the subject area in question here. Although the book is so wide-ranging it contains much important specific information. There is, for instance, an appendix on the use of postcodes which is astonishingly interesting for such a prosaic subject.

Business Communication (R. T. Chappel and W. C. Read; Fourth edition, Macdonald and Evans)
This comprehensive book also covers all aspects of communication. One chapter covers reports, but others touch on closely related areas. Two other chapters on the reporting responsibilities of committees are useful. It is a little unimaginative in its comments on style and word use. However it provides some first-class guidance for the authors of simple informal communications.

Effective Business Communications (H. A. Murphy and C. E. Pack; McGraw-Hill)
This is not useful as a guide to British business report writing. However, it is helpful to those who deal with American report writers or who have to write reports for American readers, as an insight to the way in which the American managerial mind works.

It is not lissome; over 700 large pages. Part 4 (three chapters) covers reports and contains many examples.

However, the reader must be warned that the authoritative and rather glib style describing some of the comparisons may be misleading. Not only is this a bit high-handed but the lessons drawn from the examples essentially represent American practice and contradict what would be acceptable in Britain.

The Successful Consultant's Guide to Writing Proposals and Reports (H. Bermont; Bermont Books)
This one is a highly specialised book of 55 (unnumbered) pages. It is not cheap. However it gives direct practical guidance on the drafting of consultant's proposals and reports. A good and a bad example are discussed.

The author starts his Introduction: 'There are books on how to write a proposal, and there are books on how to write a report. But for the consultant, these books as separate entities are meaningless. In our profession, the proposal and the report are linked in so many ways that they virtually become one process.' He then develops his guidelines to satisfy that need.

Employee Reports (A. Hilton; Woodhead-Faulkner)
Here is a very highly illustrated book which helps in the design of reports aimed at employees. The author, who is editor of *Accountancy Age*, stresses that he does not suggest formulae or models but wishes to stimulate managers into thinking more seriously about employee communication.

His 60 figures run through all the obvious types of illustrating: pie charts, graphs, etc. He also shows cartoons and other less conventional forms of display.

Practical Performance Appraisal (V. and A. Stewart; Gower Press)
This contains ten chapters on the benefits and mechanics of installing, monitoring and generally using an appraisal system. It is generally regarded as the definitive study of its subject. Its content therefore has an inextricable bearing on appraisal reporting.

Statistics and tabulations

(These books are listed in increasing order of simplicity.)

Statistics for Management (J. Ashford; Institute of Personnel Management)
This is a 400-page tome on the technicalities of statistical method. The book is derived from a self-instruction course in statistics which the author prepared for the National and Local Government Officers Association. It is an invaluable reference book for anyone dealing in detail with tabulations, numerate displays and illustrations. Some parts (such as the explanations of probability and estimation) are not suitable for the faint-hearted layman. Nor are they intended for him.

Wheldon's Business Statistics (G. L. Thirkettle; Ninth edition, Macdonald and Evans)
This is a much revised and frequently reprinted authority on statistical method and presentation. It is highly respected. There are detailed explanations and examples of all the principal forms of visual display. The chapters on Sampling and Surveys are particularly lucid and useful. A detailed system of headings makes the book particularly easy for reference.

Statistics in Action (P. Sprent; Penguin)
This book gives a useful insight into statistical method. It concentrates on statisticians' interpretation of data and does not cover display. It is particularly strong on probability and stochastic processes.

Use and Abuse of Statistics (W. R. Reichmann; Penguin)
This is an excellent, plain guide to all aspects of statistical handling and display. The diagrams are simple and it is suitable to be read through from beginning to end. Various complicated processes are relegated to appendices. An agreeable, chatty style and plenty of analogies make this book very easy to read.

How to Lie with Statistics (D. Huff; Penguin)
This short book is an entertaining explanation of the principal ways in which statistics and statistical presentations can mislead. It has a wide-ranging (for a 125-page book) selection of simple illustrations and many amusing but relevant cartoons by Mel Calman.

Word processing and technology

Word Processing: A Systems Approach to the Office (H. M. McCabe and E. L. Popham; Harcourt Brace Jovanovich)
Two American academics have produced a paperback commentary on the advantages of word processing and some of the difficulties in reconciling traditional Luddite attitudes with the new equipment.
   They take pains to explain the fundamental changes of approach and organisation necessary to accommodate word-processing systems and use them to their fullest advantage. The book is lavishly illustrated with diagrams, photographs and 11 case studies from a good spread of (American) commerce and industry; and a nine-page glossary is a model of simplicity and explicitness. It is well worth any difficulty which may be encountered in getting hold of an American publication.

Introducing the Electronic Office (S. G. Price; National Computing Centre)
This short (160-page) paperback is a glorified glossary which those new to office technology will find extremely useful. This description as a glossary is not intended in any way disparagingly. The book defines terms and describes equipment in valuable detail, explaining their performance and limitations.

The Impact of Microprocessors on British Business (S. G. Price; Francis)
This is a more philosophical treatise on the implications of office technology. It has 20 three- or four-page chapters on aspects such as 'Education and Training', 'Job Satisfaction', 'Management Capability and Role'.

The Future of the Printed Word (Edited by P. Hills; Frances Pinter)
Philip Hills, Director of the Primary Communications Research Centre, Leicester University, edited this collection of 13 essays which discuss the effect of technological change on written communication. He has contributed one himself on 'The place of the printed word in teaching and learning'. His article and those by Patricia Wright (MRC Applied Psychology Unit, Cambridge) on official information, Linda Reynolds (Graphic Information Research Unit, Royal College of Art) on design and the new technology, Yuri Gates (PIRA) on present and future printing techniques and Professor A. J. Meadows (Department of Astronomy and History of Science, Leicester University) on economic and social factors will hold particular interest for report writers.

Viewdata Revolution (S. Fedida and R. Malik; Associated Business Press)
Here is a clear explanation of the technology and implications of viewdata communications, in language entirely comprehensible to the layman. Information retrieval, electronic mail, the electronic diary and other topics are discussed.

The Fringe

The State of the Language (Edited by L. Michaels and C. Ricks; University of California Press)
Here is a selection of essays, published in January 1980, of varying appeal and varying relevance to report writers. The editors are Professor of English at the University of California, Berkeley, and Professor of English Literature at Christ's College, Cambridge.

They compiled the work of 63 contributors from both sides of the Atlantic. The British ones include Randolph Quirk, Robert Burchfield, Kingsley Amis, D. J. Enright, Anthony Burgess and David Lodge. All aspects of language-use are covered including feminist parlance (Angela Carter) and the argot of homosexuality (Edward White) as well as the use of language in politics (Enoch Powell) and broadcasting (Denis Donoghue). Many of the essays are subjective to the point of bigotry. Most of them are instructive and nearly all are entertaining.

The Story of Language (M. Pei; George Allen & Unwin)
This is a fascinating and wide-ranging book on the broader aspects of words and language. Without getting bogged down in the technology of sociolinguistics, it compares all the major languages of the world in a highly readable way.

The 48 chapters are discrete and diverse ('Dialects', 'The Saga of Place Names', 'The History of Writing', 'Slang and Vulgarisms', 'Language and Economic Relations', 'The Far Eastern Tongues', 'The Translation Problem') so that it is easy to dip into the book. Many individual words are discussed, as is shown by the word-list at the back totalling about 7,000 items.

FOR REFERENCE

Reference books described in detail in this book

The Concise Oxford Dictionary of Current English (OUP).
Chambers Twentieth Century Dictionary (Chambers).
Collins English Dictionary (Collins).
Webster's New Collegiate Dictionary (Merriam-Webster).
Roget's Thesaurus (Longman and Penguin).
Debrett's Correct Form (Futura).
The Oxford Dictionary for Writers and Editors (OUP).
Rules for Compositors and Readers at the University Press, Oxford (OUP).
Spell Well! (Chambers).
The Oxford Minidictionary (Oxford).

Reference books not described in this book, but of obvious content

Longman's Dictionary of Business English, (J. H. Adam; Longman).
Dictionary of Management (D. French and H. Saward; Pan).
A Dictionary of Economics and Commerce (Edited by S. E. Steigler and G. Thomas; Pan).
A Handbook of Management (Edited by T. Kempner; Penguin).
A Dictionary of Foreign Words and Phrases in Current English (A. J. Bliss; Routledge and Kegan Paul).
The Complete Desk Book (S. Feldman; Hamlyn).
Room's Dictionary of Confusibles (A. Room; Routledge and Kegan Paul).
The Word Processing Handbook (Drake International; Informative Publications International).

Works on wider aspects of managerial communications with indirect bearing on reports

Communication in Organizations (E. M. Rogers and R. Agarwala-Rogers; Collier Macmillan).
Communicate (C. Northcote Parkinson and N. Rowe; Pan).
Communication in Organizations (Edited by L. W. Porter and K. H. Roberts; Penguin).
Communications (R. Williams; Penguin).

Industrial Administration and Management (J. Batty; Macdonald and Evans).
The Effective Executive (P. F. Drucker; Pan).
The Reality of Management (R. Stewart; Pan).

Books that will be helpful to those who do not have English as their first language

Oxford Advanced Learners' Dictionary of Current English (OUP). (Generally regarded as the leading dictionary for those learning English as a foreign language.)
Chambers Universal Learners' Dictionary (Chambers). (Rather cruelly lambasted by Auberon Waugh[3] when it came out for the unhelpful banality of its example uses. However, many foreign people have found this paperback extremely useful.)
Practical English Usage (M. Swan; OUP). (Guidelines on grammatical use.)
Current English Usage (F. T. Wood, revised by R. H. and L. M. Flavell; Macmillan). (Good guide to word use and idiom.)

Notes and references

To avoid unnecessary repetition, the following reports, etc., have been cited in the references under an abbreviated title. The complete references are as follows:

Bentley Colliery Report Health and Safety Executive, *The Accident at Bentley Colliery, South Yorkshire, 21 November 1978*, HMSO (1979).

Cardowan Colliery Report Health and Safety Executive, *The Explosion at Cardowan Colliery, Stepps, Strathclyde Region, 27 January 1982*, HMSO (1982).

Lyric Theatres Report Arts Council of Great Britain, *Report to the Arts Council of Great Britain and the Greater London Council on Lyric Theatres in London* (1975).

Bullock, A Language for Life Department of Education and Science, *Report of the Committee of Inquiry appointed by The Secretary of State for Education and Science under the Chairmanship of Sir Allan Bullock FBA*, HMSO (1975).

Bullock, Industrial Democracy Department of Trade, *Report of the Committee of Inquiry on Industrial Democracy*, Cmnd 6706, HMSO (1977).

Scarman Report Home Office, *The Brixton Disorders 10–12 April 1981: Report of an Inquiry by the Rt Hon. the Lord Scarman OBE*, HMSO (1982).

Information Technology and Women's Jobs Communication Studies Planning Ltd/Equal Opportunities Commission, *Information Technology in the Office: the Impact on Women's Jobs* (September 1980).

Chapter 1 Introduction: meeting the reader's requirements

1 Liv Ullmann, BBC2 TV (3 October 1979).
2 Bullock, *A Language for Life*.
3 *The Teaching of English in England* (The Newbolt Report), HMSO (1921); see also J. Aitchison, *Language Change: Progress or Decay?*, p20, Fontana, Douglas (1981): 'Every generation inevitably believes that the clothes, manners and speech of the following one have deteriorated'.
   Allanbrooke in Arthur Bryant's *The Turn of the Tide*, Collins (1957), speaks disparagingly of the standard of British youth circa 1940, the same youth who are now the disparaging older generation.
4 L. Pearsall Smith, 'Needed words', in W. F. Bolton and D. Crystal (Editors), *The English Language, Volume 2, 1858–1964*, p114, CUP (1969).
5 S. J. Baker, *The Australian Language*, p12, Currawong Press (1978).
6 J. R. Hulbert, *Dictionaries, British and American*, p16, Andre Deutsch (1968).
7 P. Howard, *New Words for Old*, p xiii Hamish Hamilton (1977).

8   D. Jackson, *Times Educational Supplement* (30 December 1977).

9   A. J. Ayer, *Language, Truth and Logic*, Penguin (1971).

10 D. Henshaw, *The Listener* (24 September 1981).

11 For Johnson's attitude, see E. L. McAdam and G. Milne, *Johnson's Dictionary: A Modern Selection*, Macmillan (1963), Papermac (1980). See the Preface to the Dictionary p3 *ff*.

12 J. Rae, *The Observer* (7 February 1982): 'Grammar was a predictable victim of the self-indulgent Sixties. It was associated with authority, tradition and elitism. Grammatical rules, like so many other rules at the time were regarded as an intolerable infringement of personal freedom.'

13 J. Rae, *op. cit.*

14 It is quite clear that a rule which is not an observable rule has no place in report writing or any other communication.

15 W. Safire, *New York Times* regularly and, among others, *International Herald Tribune*, 'Weasel words to the wise' (20 November 1978). J. Aitchison, *op. cit.*, p223, makes a relevant comment.

16 *The Times* (26 August 1982).

17 J. Simon, *Paradigms Lost*, Chatto & Windus (1981).

18 R. Graves and A. Hodge, *The Reader Over Your Shoulder*, Jonathan Cape (1944). Percentage guides as to the frequency of words in different senses may have a use. There their use ends however.

19 E. M. Rogers and R. Argawala–Rogers, *Communication in Organization*, p12, The Free Press, Collier Macmillan (1976); see also G. Poulet in R. Mackesey and E. Donatio (Editors), *The Structuralist Controversy*, p56, John Hopkins University Press (1972). He saw books as objects, like animals in cages, waiting for a buyer. Their fate and the treatment depends on the purchaser.

Chapter 2   The purpose of reports

1   M. A. Lourie and N. F. Conklin (Editors), *A Pluralistic Nation* Newbury House, Rowley, Mass. (1978); J. L. Dillard, *Black English*, Vintage Books, Random House New York (1973).

2   R. West, *The Spectator* (29 August 1981).

3   General Secretary TUC (1960–69).

4   K. Hawkins, *The Management of Industrial Relations*, p175, Penguin (1978).

5   *Cf.* (and be warned of) a specialist sense, as well: 'to do with verbs' as used by Lockhart, *Languages of the British Isles Past and Present*, 'The verbal system is of almost incredible complexity', Andre Deutsch (1975).

6   G. Wagner, *On the Wisdom of Words*, George Allen & Unwin (1968).

7   N. M. Henley, in M. A. Lourie and N. F. Conklin, *op. cit.*

8   F. Rossi-Landi in R. Williams (Editor), *Contact*, Thames & Hudson (1981).

9   Although, see Chapter 7 for discussion of the important phenomenon of Diglossia.

10 *The Committee to Review the Functioning of Financial Institutions*, p16, HMSO (28 February 1978).

11 *New Statesman* (3 October 1980).

12 D. J. Allerton, *Essentials of Grammatical Theory*, p21, Routledge & Kegan Paul (1979).

13 H. Street, *The Law of Torts*, p288 Butterworths (Third edition, 1963).

14 H. Street, *op. cit.*, p289.

15 A. Huxley, *Point Counter Point*, Penguin (1957).

16 See also D. Crystal and D. Davy, *Investigating English Style*, Longman (1979).

17 *Bentley Colliery Report*.

18 *Cardowan Colliery Report*.

19 Health and Safety Executive, *PWR*, HMSO (1979; reissued 1982).

20 Health and Safety Executive, *Sizewell B*, HMSO (1982).

21   Department of the Environment/National Water Council, *Copper in Potable Waters by Atomic Absorption Spectrophotometry*, HMSO (1980).
22   Chemical and Allied Products Industry Training Board, *Working at the Future: Strategy for 1977/82* (September 1976 unpublished).
23   This is reproduced in full in Chapter 5.
24   *Ibid*, p9.
25   Price Waterhouse, *Notes on Written Communication* (compiled by Simon Mort), (unpublished).
26   *Companies Acts 1948, 1967, 1976, 1980 and 1981.*
27   *Guide to the Requirements of the Companies Acts*, published for the Institute of Chartered Accountants by Gee & Co. (Eighth edition, November 1981). It is important to refer to the most recent edition: sometimes more than one edition is produced a year.
28   A. Likierman, *The Reports and Accounts of Nationalised Industries*, Civil Service College Handbook 20, HMSO (1979).
29   English Tourist Board, *Annual Report for the Year Ended 31 March 1982.*
30   Cement-Roadstone, *Annual Report 1981.*
31   Guest Keen and Nettlefolds, *Report and Accounts 1981.*
32   Westland Aircraft Ltd, *Annual Report and Accounts for the Year Ended 30 September 1981.*
33   John Menzies, *Annual Report 1982.*
34   Johnstone's Paints, *Report and Accounts 1981.*
35   Midland Bank Plc, *Annual Report 1981.*
36   Cadbury Schweppes Ltd, *Annual Report and Accounts 1976*; Cadbury Schweppes Plc, *Annual Report and Accounts 1981.*
37   *The European Monetary System*, para. 46, p12, Cmnd 7405, HMSO (November 1978).
38   *Report of the Inter-Departmental Working Party on Road Traffic Law*, HMSO.
39   *Ibid*, p iv.
40   The 1982 paper was an exception. It was delayed until after the Falklands operation and then presented in its original form.
41   *The United Kingdom Defence Programme: The Way Forward*, Cmnd 8288, HMSO. A short 47-paragraph statement of general priorities was issued in June 1981 a few months after a reshuffle of Defence Ministers.
42   Ministry of Defence, *Statement on the Defence Estimates* (1982).
43   *Putting Asunder: A Divorce Law for Contemporary Society*, SPCK (1966).
44   *Ibid.*, para 6, p3.
45   *Ibid.*, para 9, p6.
46   *Ibid.*, para 29, p21.
47   *Ibid.*, para 38, p27.
48   Quite a lot of the objections had been raised during The Royal Commission on Marriage and Divorce 1951–55 (The Morton Commission) (Cmnd 9678) which illustrates that the moral issues confronting such an investigation are almost timeless, being less bound by political change and commercial necessity than are other affairs.
49   Bullock, *A Language for Life.*
50   Bullock, *Industrial Democracy.*
51   Conversation with the author (6 August 1982).
52   This arrangement is exemplified and discussed in Chapter 5.
53   The Prime Minister, *et. al.*, *Industrial Democracy*, White Paper, (Cmnd 7231), HMSO (May 1978).

Chapter 3   Making information more digestible

1   Colt Car Company report (May 1982; unpublished).
2   *Vandalism*, a note by Central Policy Review Staff, HMSO (1978).
3   See Civil Defence Department, *Manual for Civil Service Typists*, HMSO (Third edition, 1974). See especially examples at Appendices II and III, pp 33–34.

4   Cabinet Office, Advisory Council for Applied Research and Development, *Industrial Innovation*, HMSO (1978).
5   Cabinet Office, Advisory Council for Applied Research and Development, *Information Technology*, HMSO (1980).
6   Centre for British Teachers Ltd, *Malaysian Monthly Report for January 1981* (unpublished).
7   *Bentley Colliery Report*.
8   *Lyric Theatres Report*.
9   The National Trust, *Annual Report 1981*.
10 Central Policy Review Staff, *Services for Young Children with Working Mothers*, HMSO (1978).
11 Organisation for Economic Co-operation and Development, *Traffic Control in Saturated Conditions*, Paris (1981).
12 *Information Technology and Women's Jobs*.
13 National Coal Board, *Report and Accounts 1981/82 March 29 1981–March 27 1982*, pp 1 and 102.
14 *Manual for Civil Service Typists*, p13, HMSO (Third edition, 1974).
15 *QANTAS report from Airport Manager London to Manager UK and Ireland* (14 May 1979; unpublished).

Chapter 4   How to lay out a report

1   M. Bradbury, *The History Man*, Arrow Books (1977).
2   Centre for British Teachers Ltd (unpublished).
3   Esso Petroleum Company Ltd (January 1981; unpublished).
4   Engineering ITB RP/1/80, *Employment and Training in the Telecommunications Equipment Manufacturing Industry* (1980, unpublished).
5   *Putting Asunder*, SPCK (1966).
6   Home Office, *Alcoholism and Social Policy*, Research Study No. 65, HMSO (1980).
7   The *Concise Oxford Dictionary of Current English*, p860, OUP (Seventh edition, 1982); E. Partridge, *Usage and Abusage*, p260, Penguin (1973).
8   Home Office, *op. cit.*, p1.
9   QANTAS report on ticket offices (unpublished).
10 Manpower Services Commission, *Open Tech Task Group Report* (June 1982).
11 Engineering ITB, *op. cit.*
12 Cabinet Office, Advisory Council for Applied Research and Development, *Industrial Innovation*, para 1.4, p12, HMSO (1978).
13 *Cardowan Colliery Report*, p v.
14 *Information Technology and Women's Jobs*, para 1.4.1, p4.
15 Trustee Savings Bank's *Economic Trends No 4* (unpublished).
16 *Information Technology and Women's Jobs*, para 1.4, p2.
17 Manpower Services Commission, *op. cit.*, para 6, p6.
18 Manpower Services Commission, *op. cit.*, para 5, p6.
19 Health and Safety Executive, *PWR*, p82, HMSO (1979).
20 Argos Project 1 (Ref SC 77), *A Two Terminal Office Within the Random Storage Area*, Daventry Greenshield Management (unpublished).
21 *Ibid.*
22 Warner-Lambert (Eastleigh), *Efferdent System (Stock adjustment) Report* (unpublished).
23 Bullock, *Industrial Democracy*.
24 Building Research Establishment (A. A. Ogilvy), *Bracknell and Its Migrants: Twenty-one Years of New Town Growth*, HMSO (1975).
25 This is the Director who compiles the report to the Centre in London discussed in Chapter 3.

26 *Bentley Colliery Report.*
27 Price Commission, *Whitbred and Company Ltd – Wholesale Prices and Prices in Managed Houses of Beer, Wines, Spirits, Soft Drinks and Ciders*, HMSO (1979).
28 *Ibid.*
29 Some points on the content of this report are contained in Chapter 13.
30 A. Gibson, *Spectator* (19 May 1980).
31 *Bentley Colliery Report.*
32 *Ibid.*
33 Price Commission, *op. cit.*
34 Price Commission, *op. cit.*
35 V. Bogdanor, *Standards in Schools*, National Council for Educational Standards (1979).
36 Bullock, *A Language for Life.*
37 *Ibid.*, para 208, p288.
38 *Ibid.*, p543.
39 *Ibid.*, p513.
40 *Scarman Report.*
41 *Ibid.*, para 5.69, p96.
42 *Ibid.*, Part VIII, p125.
43 *Cardowan Colliery Report.*
44 Manpower Services Commission, *Training for Trainers: First Report of the Training for Trainers Committee*, HMSO (1978) and *Direct Trainers: Second Report of the Training of Trainers Committee*, HMSO (1980).
45 Trustee Savings Bank Central Board Computer Division, *Unipay – Future Developments 3160/12 dated December 1980* (unpublished).
46 *Ibid.*
47 Manpower Services Commission, *op. cit.*, p4; Bullock, *Industrial Democracy*, p v.
48 This is a series of papers published by HMSO for the Civil Service Department. They relate to teaching at the Civil Service College and their aim is to promote modern theories of management and administration in the Service.
49 *Lyric Theatres Report*, p3. In this case it did appear on its own under the slightly misleading heading: 'Introduction'.
50 *Flixborough Report*, p232.

Chapter 5 Forewords, summaries, appendices and other attachments

1   Bullock, *A Language for Life*, p iii.
2   Chemical & Allied Products Industry Training Board, *Working at the Future: Strategy for 1977/82*, p1 (September 1976).
3   Bullock, *Industrial Democracy.*
4   *Ibid.*, p169.
5   *Ibid.*, p169.
6   British Vita Plc, *Annual Report* (1981).
7   National Coal Board, *Report and Accounts 1981/82*, p2.
8   Shannon Free Airport Development Company, *Guidelines on the Format of Written Reports: an Aid for Staff Who Prepare Reports for the Management Committees of the Company* (prepared by F. Beech 1981), (unpublished).
9   *Information Technology and Women's Jobs.*
10 *Ibid.*
11 *Ibid.*
12 *Flixborough Report*, para 213, p35.
13 Organisation for Economic Co-operation and Development, *Road Research: Traffic Control in Saturated Conditions*, p6, Paris (1981).
14 *Flixborough Report*, p vi.

15 Economic and Social Committee of the European Communities, *Annual Report 1980*, p3, Luxembourg (1981).
16 *Information Technology and Women's Jobs.*
17 *Scarman Report.*
18 See, for example, Department of the Environment/National Water Council, *Copper in Potable Waters by Atomic Absorption Spectrophotometry*, HMSO (1980).
19 Building Research Establishment (A. A. Ogilvy), *Bracknell and Its Migrants: Twenty-one Years of New Town Growth*, HMSO (1975).
20 Department of the Environment: *Central Unit on Environmental Pollution Paper No. 9*, HMSO (1976). In this case the International Standard Book Number is also given.
21 Department of the Environment/National Water Council, *op. cit.*
22 *Scarman Report*, p164.
23 *Information Technology and Women's Jobs*, p89.
24 Council for Science and Society, *Childbirth Today* (1980).
25 Public Health Laboratory Service, *Laboratory Diagnosis of Venereal Disease*, p25, HMSO (1972).
26 *Ibid.*, p34.
27 *Scarman Report*, p95.
28 *Ibid.*, p95.
29 The Royal Society, *General Notes on the Preparation of Scientific Papers*, p10 (Third edition, 1974).
30 Organisation for Economic Co-operation and Development Surveys, Paris, 1982 and other years.

Chapter 6   Choosing words

1 A. Wesker, *Words as Definition of Experience*, Writers and Readers Publishing Co-operative, London (1976).
2 Note in (particularly) Switzerland, Belgium, Yugoslavia and Canada: E. Haughan *in* J. B. Pride and J. Holmes (Editors), *Sociolinguistics*, p104, Penguin (1972); M. Pei, *The Story of Language*, pp262 and 273, George Allen & Unwin (Second edition, 1966).
3 R. E. Nicholson, *A Literary History of the Arabs*, p159, CUP (1956).
4 T. M. Lindsay, *A History of the Reformation*, Volume 1, pp149*ff*, T. & T. Clark Edinburgh (1933).
5 C. A. Ferguson *in* P. P. Giglioli (Editor), *Language and Social Context*, p239, Penguin (1972).
6 R. Harris, *The Language Makers*, pp171 and 179, Duckworth (1980).
7 P. Howard, *Words Fail Me*, Hamish Hamilton (1980).
8 See also F. Rossi-Landi *in* R. Williams (Editor), *Contact*, p28, Thames & Hudson (1981).
9 E. Sapir *in* D. G. Mandelbaum (Editor), *Culture, Language and Personality*, p1, University of California Press (1949).
10 All the works of Simeon Potter are worth exploring for this kind of detail.
11 J. Goody and I. Watt *in* P. P. Giglioli, *op. cit.*
12 P. Hanks reviewing J. Branford's *A Dictionary of South African English* (Oxford University Press, Cape Town, 1980) in *English in Africa*, Vol. 8(1), (March 1981).
13 I. Jack, *Spectator* (10 April 1982) mentions *che* = friend, mate whence *che-coat* = anorak; the *Camp* = the open spaces of the Falklands countryside (from *campo* = country).
14 J. A. Sheard, *The Words We Use*, p15, Andre Deutsch (1970).
15 B. M. H. Strang, *A History of English*, Methuen (1974).
16 Cardinal Newman, *Loss and Gain: The Story of a Convert*, Burns & Oats (1962).
17 H. W. Fowler and F. G. Fowler, *The King's English*, p11, OUP (1973); *cf* the more

balanced criticism of this line of thinking by G. H. Vallins, *Better English*, p811, Pan (1953).

18 See also G. H. Vallins, *The Best English*, pp31*ff*, Pan (1963).

19 F. W. Westaway, *The Writing of Clear English*, pp64–5, Blackie (1926): 'prefer a word of English (*sic*) origin to a word of classical origin'.
C. R. Cecil, *The Business Letter Writer*, p26, Foulsham (1980).
R. Gunning, *The Technique of Clear Writing*, p38, McGraw-Hill (Revised edition, 1968).
W. Strunk and E. B. White, *The Elements of Style*, Macmillan (Third edition, 1979) does it in a fairly constructive way; even B. M. Cooper, *Writing Technical Reports*, Penguin, which is so admirable in other ways, does so on its p114.

20 C. R. Cecil, *op. cit.*, pp26–7.

21 A. C. Baugh and T. Cable, *A History of the English Language*, pp188*ff*, Routledge and Kegan Paul (Third edition, 1978).

22 *Ibid.*, pp167*ff*.

23 N. Rogers, *Wessex Dialect*, p2, Moonraker Press, Bradford-on-Avon (1979).

24 W. N. Francis, *The English Language*, pp101*ff*, Hodder & Stoughton (1975).

25 A. C. Baugh and T. Cable, *op. cit.*, p179.

26 Readers wanting further guidance on these kinds of problems are referred to A. Room, *Dictionary of Confusibles*, Routledge and Kegan Paul (1979), or for a very conservative and rather severe treatment of malapropisms, see Kingsley Amis, *Getting it Wrong*, in L. Michaels and C. Ricks (Editors), *The State of the Language*, p24, University of California Press (1980).

27 A. Room, *op. cit.*, p40, extends the area of confusion to *constantly*.

28 *The Oxford English Dictionary*, Volume V (Letter I), p43, OUP (1933).

29 D. Wright, 'The basic dilemma of management training', *Industrial and Commercial Training* (February 1981).

30 W. H. Mittins, *et. al.*, *Attitudes to English Usage*, OUP (1970): (a study by the University of Newcastle among 457 educated users of the language) at p14 showed 37% allowing *inferred* when strictly it should have been *implied*, but only 12% allowing *implied* where it should have been *inferred*.
J. Simon, *Paradigms Lost*, p xv, Chatto & Windus (1981), goes so far as to say that to accept *imply* for *infer* is 'also a form of prescriptiveness and dogmatism', stemming 'from some sort of populism, Marxism, bad social conscience, demagoguery, inverted snobbery or even moral cowardice'.

31 See also Chapter 11's coverage of spellings.

32 C. Connolly, *Enemies of Promise*, p22, Penguin (1961).

33 *The Times* (21 October 1981).

34 Bank of America Senior Auditor's report (unpublished).

35 Colt Car Company report on vehicles of various manufacturers 1982 (unpublished).

36 A. Hills, *The Guardian* (18 August 1980).

37 C. Reid, *The Listener* (29 October 1981) reviewing BBC Radio 4's 'Suez'.

38 S. Potter, *Changing English*, p42, Andre Deutsch (1975).

39 B. Foster, *The Changing English Language*, p198, Penguin (1976).

40 S. Potter, *Our Language*, p87, Penguin, (1982).

41 Described by P. Howard, *The Times* (3 January 1980).

42 *The Daily Telegraph* (17 April 1979).

43 *Spectator* (12 May 1979).

44 *The Guardian* (2 August 1979).

45 C. L. Beeching, *A Dictionary of Eponyms*, Clive Bingley, London (1979).

46 Bernard Levin, *The Times* (22 November 1978).

47 G. L. Brook draws attention to Shakespeare's *Hamlet* where it has an entirely neutral sense (*Hamlet*, Act I, Scene iii).

48 See extensive use about the activities of J. Lansman in Benn/Healey confrontation of September 1981. See also use in connection with South African Springboks, BBC Radio 4 News (20 September 1981).

49 P. Jenkins, *The Guardian* (9 July 1980).

50 K. Hudson, *The Language of Modern Politics*, p57, Macmillan (1978) on Mr Justice McKinnon's 'wogs, niggers and coons' judgement.
J. Branford, *A Dictionary of South African English*, p125, OUP (1980) has 'Kaffir . . . now a punishable offence in some parts of Southern Africa'.

51 *cf* The charming, if archaic formal business termination in Indian business writing: 'Assuring you we will do the needful' (informant of 1980).

52 For example, see H. M. Townley and R. D. Gee, *Thesaurus Making*, p175, Andre Deutsch (1980). A list of recent archaisms: *aliens, blitz, charabanc, Great War, Hackney Cabs, motor cars, spivs, wireless sets.*
See also J. Simon, *Paradigms Lost*, p64, Chatto & Windus (1981) where *cuckolding* is described as an archaism. The 'more serious' word *adultery* is considered appropriate.

53 J. Swift, *A Proposal*, in W. F. Bolton (Editor), *The English Language: Essays by English and American Men of Letters 1490–1839*, p117, CUP (1966).

54 *Ibid.*, p117.

55 For representation of this attitude see T. Baistow *The Guardian* (13 August 1979); I. Robinson, *The Survival of English*, pp99*ff*, CUP (1975); J. Simon, *op. cit.*; E. Newman in various manifestations including Cally Curtis films and various publications such as *A Civil Tongue* and *Strictly Speaking*.

56 L. Pearsall Smith, *Needed Words*, in W. F. Bolton and D. Crystal (Editors), *The English Language: Volume 2: Essays by Linguists and Men of Letters 1858–1964*, p114, CUP. He writes of 'purists who seem insensitive to the genius of the language'.
G. H. Vallins, *The Best English*, p13, Pan (1960).

57 See also A. Wesker in *Words as Definitions of Experience*, Writers and Readers Publishing Co-operative, London (1976) who asks what happened to German in the 1930s to allow itself to be used in that way. In the same slim volume R. Appignanesi in an Afterword deprecates the comfortable use of military terminology and, especially, acronyms in Vietnam.
Chief Supt Plowman spoke of *low-profile* and *saturation*. Scarman has said of *low profile* that is was 'a modern jargon phrase which we all use, but it doesn't really help'.

58 G. Orwell, *Politics and the English Language* in W. F. Bolton and D. Crystal (Editors), *op. cit.*, Volume II, p217.

59 D. Defoe, *Of Academies*, in W. F. Bolton (Editor), *op. cit.*, p91.

60 S. Potter, *Our Language*, p117, Penguin (1982).

61 R. Harris, *The Language Makers*, p178, Duckworth.

62 April 1982.

63 S. Victor, Citibank Paris, conversation with author (17 July 1982). For further discussion of limitations of the French attitude see M. Blume in *International Herald Tribune* (6–7 January 1979).

64 G. Orwell, *Nineteen Eighty-Four*, p7 and Appendix pp241*ff*, Penguin (1959).

65 A. Burgess, *1985*, Arrow (1980).

66 G. H. Vallins, *Good English*, p228, Pan (1951).

67 Compiled and edited by M. West, *A General Service List of English Words (with semantic frequencies)*, Longman (1974).

68 Two lexicographers (Betty Kirkpatrick letter 12 August 1982 and Patrick Hanks letter 17 August 1982) both suggested that there was an inclination to treat the dictionary too much like the Bible.

69 *Webster's Third New International Dictionary of the English Language*, Merriam-Webster, Springfield, Mass. (1961).

70 T. Augarde, conversation with the author (26 July 1982); see also J. Simon, *op. cit.*, p xiv.

71 BBC Radio 4 (27 January 1982).

72 Ephraim Chambers, 1680?–1740 (quaintly described by the *Dictionary of National Biography* as irascible and kind to the poor).

73 J. R. Hulbert, *Dictionaries British and American*, Andre Deutsch (1968).

74 *Ibid.*, p16.

75 J. Boswell, *The Life of Samuel Johnson, LL.D.*, pp111*ff*, Swan Sonnenschein, Lowrey (1888).

76 Among the most notorious is *oats*: 'A grain which in England is generally given to horses, but in Scotland supports the people'. For this and other entertainments see *Johnson's Dictionary: A Modern Selection* by E. L. Macadam and George Milne, Macmillan (1963) and Papermac (1982).

77 K. M. E. Murray (Sir James Murray's granddaughter), *Caught in the Web of Words: James Murray and the Oxford English Dictionary*, p167, Yale University Press (1977).

78 *Ibid.*, p88.

79 J. R. Hulbert, *op. cit.*

80 K. M. E. Murray, *op. cit.*, p167.

81 R. Quirk, *The Use of English*, p145, Longmans (1978).

82 For press comment on third volume, see *The Times* (Third leader), (15 July 1982) and P. Howard 'Pussivanting with pluck and prolly' (same day). The fourth volume is due in 1985 [*The Times* (10 May 1982)].

83 K. M. E. Murray, *op. cit.*, p296.

84 For the original version, see *The Oxford English Dictionary*, Volume I, p xxvii, OUP (1933). The version in Figure 48 is taken from the *Shorter Oxford English Dictionary*, p x, and has added Archaic.

85 H. Wentworth and S. Berg Flexner, *Dictionary of American Slang*, p vii, Thomas Y. Crowell. This is further described in Appendix 3.

86 *Shorter Oxford English Dictionary*, OUP (1973).

87 *The Concise Oxford Dictionary of Current English*, OUP (Seventh edition, 1982).

88 R. W. Burchfield, Presidential Address, The English Association (1979).

89 *The Concise Oxford Dictionary of Current English*, OUP (Sixth edition, 1978) with addenda pp1359–60.

90 *The Times* (10 May 1982). See also television advertising for Collins Concise, not considered here, featuring Frank Muir.

91 *Chambers Twentieth Century Dictionary*, Chambers (1977). (Next edition, 1983.)

92 Betty Kirkpatrick, letter to the author (12 August 1982).

93 A scrutiny of case-books and legal text books will show extensive reference to Chambers in court.

94 *Collins English Dictionary*, Collins (1979).

95 A particularly favourable review by Auberon Waugh, *Spectator* (15 September 1979).

96 P. Hanks, letter to the author (17 August 1982).

97 *Ibid.* In his otherwise eulogistic review cited at Ref. 95 above, Waugh took Hanks to task for his subjective, and possibly arbitrary, ordering of the senses. Hanks replied [*Spectator* (6 October 1979)] that the first sense of a sock was a light shoe worn by a Roman actor in comedy.

98 P. Hanks, letter to author (17 August 1982).

99 R. Burchfield, *Dictionaries and Ethnic Sensibilities*, in L. Michaels and C. Ricks (Editors), *The State of the Language*, p15 University of California Press (1980).

100 Johnson avoided all aponymous words such as *Arian*, *Socinian*, *Calvinist*, although he accepted the more general ones such as *Heathen*.

101 For further comments on Johnson and lexicographers in general, see D. Crystal (Editor), *Eric Partridge in His Own Words*, pp51*ff*, Andre Deutsch (1980).

102 K. M. E. Murray, *op. cit.*, p193.

103 T. Augarde, conversation with the author (26 July 1982).

104 K. M. E. Murray, *op. cit.*, p222.

105 P. Hanks, letter to author (17 August 1982).
106 *The Penguin English Dictionary*, Penguin (1979).
107 P. Hanks, review of Branford, see Ref. 12 above.
108 BBC Radio 3 (27 September 1981).
109 C.-J. N. Bailey and R. Shuy (Editors), *New Ways of Analyzing Variations in English*, pp340–71, Georgetown University Press, Washington (1974).
110 *Ibid.*, Figure 5.
111 *Shorter Oxford English Dictionary*, Volume II, p2287, OUP (1973).
112 *Roget's Thesaurus*, Longman (1982).
113 *The Sunday Times* (11 April 1982); *The Observer* (11 April 1982).
114 *The Times* (letters), (21 April 1982).
115 C. S. Lewis, *Studies in Words*, CUP (Second edition, 1967).
116 For example, *racial* in *The Times Law Report* (30 July 1982): (Court of Appeal *Manlla* v. *Lee*).
117 C. Barber, *Linguistic Change in Present Day English*, Oliver & Boyd (1964).
118 Kingsley Amis, *Girl 20*, Penguin (1980).
119 Seventh edition of *Concise Oxford Dictionary* marks the extended use of unique with their new marking of a bold D for a disputed usage.
120 Associated Television Corporation Ltd, *Annual Report and Accounts 1978*, p5.
121 G. H. Vallins, *Better English*, p29, Pan (1953).
122 B. Cottle, *The Plight of English*, p91, Arlington House (1975).
123 P. Hanks, letter to the author (3 January 1980).

Chapter 7 Pitching the report at the right level

1 E. Sapir, *Culture, Language and Personality*, p17, University of California Press (1949).
2 D. Crystal and D. Davy, *Investigating English Style*, p173, London (1979).
3 Nevertheless legal parlance is frequently used when more rudimentary language would be appropriate. An 11-year-old boy was being sentenced at the Old Bailey to which he had been exceptionally referred by the juvenile court. He was told that neither his parents or the local authority had 'the capacity to contain and inhibit your natural predilection towards crime' [S. Cortauld, *Spectator* (13 May 1978)].
4 S. Pit Corder, *Introducing Applied Linguistics*, p281, Penguin (1977).
5 G. L. Brook, *A History of the English Language*, Andre Deutsch (1977).
6 *The Guinness Book of Records*, Guinness Superlatives (1965).
7 *The Guinness Book of Records*, Guinness Superlatives (1982).
8 Kingsley Amis, *Ending Up*, p40, Jonathan Cape (1974).
9 D. Crystal, *A First Dictionary of Linguistics and Phonetics*, p301, Andre Deutsch (1980).
10 In the 14th Century, Lawrence of Aquilegia actually acknowledged this need by dividing correspondents into seven categories with combinations of phrases in which each could be addressed. [R. Harris, *The Language Makers*, p100, Duckworth (1980).]
11 Note the comment of Robert Robinson, BBC Radio 4 (9 May 1981): '. . . like all jargon and like all cant, it seems to pre-empt discussion by presuming that we are all agreed'. See also J. Kirkman, *Good Style for Scientific and Engineering Writing*, Pitman (1980), especially pp17–18 on the value and importance of jargon.
12 L. Bloomfield, *Language*, pp23*ff*, George Allen & Unwin (1979).
13 D. J. Allerton, *Essentials of Grammatical Theory*, Routledge & Kegan Paul (1979).
14 A. S. C. Ross, *U and Non-U: An essay in Sociological Linguistics*, in N. Mitford (Editor), *Noblesse Oblige*, p9, Penguin (1959). It was itself a condensed version of an article by Prof. Ross in the Finnish philogical periodical (1954), *Neuphilologische Mitteilungen*. Prof. Ross' *Don't Say It*, Hamish Hamilton (1973) attempted to update the subject. The less spectacular success of this work is further indication of changing attitudes.

15 N. Mitford (Editor), *Noblesse Oblige*, pp35ff, Penguin (1959).

16 T. Hardy, *Tess of the D'Urbervilles*, p22, Macmillan (1957): 'Mrs Durbeyfield habitually spoke the dialect; her daughter, who has passed the Sixth Standard in the National School under a London-trained mistress, spoke two languages, the dialect at home, more or less; ordinary English abroad and to persons of quality.'

17 B. Shaw, *Pygmalion*, p10 (Preface), Penguin (1959): 'Our West End shop assistants and domestic servants are bilingual'.

18 M. Drabble, *The Needles's Eye*, p135, Penguin (1973). Simon Camish's mother had a good regional accent which she had learned to adopt or dismiss at will.

19 D. Lodge, *How Far Can You Go?*, p193, Penguin (1981). Angela is described in that 'the family occasion had brought back a working-class timbre to her voice'.

20 Greenough and Kittredge, *Words and Their Ways in English Speech* (1901).

21 M. A. Lourie in M. A. Lourie and N. F. Conklin (Editors), *A Pluralistic Nation*, Newbury House (1979).

22 W. Empson, *Seven Types of Ambiguity*, Penguin (1977).

23 L. Bloomfield, *op. cit.*, p442.

24 See also I. A. Richards, *The Interanimation of Words* (1936) in D. Crystal (Editors), *The English Language*, Volume II, p171, CUP (1969).

25 This is demonstrated by its use on BBC Radio 4 *Today* (19 May 1982). A spokesman inadvertently spoke of 'the main area of *concern* which *concerns* us' before noticing the tautology and correcting it.

26 Lord Robens, *Human Engineering*, Jonathan Cape (1970).

27 National Consumer Council, *Gobbledegook* (1980).

28 Sir Ernest Gowers, *The Complete Plain Words*, described in detail at Appendix 3.

29 Plain English Campaign, Salford M7 0BD.

30 J. O. Morris, *Make Yourself Clear*, p149, McGraw-Hill (1980).

31 For instance, a programme on BBC Radio 4 on 27 January 1982 in which Ms Chrissie Maher of the Plain English Campaign was engaged in a discussion with Dr Robert Burchfield. The latter was describing the full richness of the language. Ms Maher's comments indicated a lack of appreciation of this wealth.

32 *The Daily Telegraph* (1 September 1980).

33 G. W. Turner, *Stylistics*, p21, Penguin (1979).

34 British Gas Corporation, *Annual Report 1980–81*.

35 Church Commissioners, *Report and Accounts 1980*.

36 Annual Reports Ltd, 4 Pembridge News, London W11 3EQ.

37 Cadburys Schweppes, *Annual Report April 1982*.

38 Granada Group, *Employees' Report March 1981*.

39 Black & Decker, *Employees' Report 1981*.

40 *All Ye Need to Know*, pp2–3, Annual Reports Ltd.

41 Price Commission, *Whitbread and Company Ltd – Wholesale Prices and Prices in Managed Houses of Beer, Wines, Soft Drinks and Ciders*, p viii, HMSO (1979).

42 Waste Management Advisory Council, Packaging and Containers Working Party, *Study of Returnable and Non-returnable Containers*, pp6–8, HMSO (1981).

43 Organisation for Economic Co-operation and Development, *Traffic Control in Saturated Conditions*, pp58–60, Paris (1981).

44 Esso Petroleum Ltd report, *Signature Verification System: position paper* (January 1981; unpublished).

Chapter 8 Style – and how to improve it

1 K. Waterhouse, *Daily Mirror Style*, Mirror Books, London (1981). See also, as an instance of newspaper style: on 20 September 1982 *The Daily Telegraph* announced its

266 HOW TO WRITE A SUCCESSFUL REPORT

intention to adopt 'the modern usage' of using the word *billion* to represent one thousand million as opposed to one million million.

2 N. E. Enkvist, *Linguistics and Style*, OUP (1964), uses the analogy of wearing brown shoes with black tie: 'its effects vary from the striking through the humorous, the awkward and the rude to the disastrous'.

P. Howard, *The Times* (9 September 1980), on old-fashioned expressions being like a bowler-hat or rolled umbrella.

G. W. Turner, *Stylistics*, Penguin (1973), speaks of linguistic as well as sartorial class uniforms.

3 Even here there are contradictory examples such as the styles of Thomas Carlyle and James Joyce, but neither is directly relevant to report preparation.

4 Ford Motor Company, *Guide Notes on the Processing of Correspondence* (unpublished).

5 Price Waterhouse, *Notes on Written Communication* (compiled by Simon Mort), (unpublished).

6 A. E. Darbyshire, *A Grammar of Style*, p24, Andre Deutsch, London (1979), talks about grammarians' grammar as a grammar of competence: 'Its generalisations can be statements of norm from which in the actual day-to-day uses, there might or might not be deviations'.

7 D. Crystal and D. Davy, *Investigating English Style*, p194, Longman, London (1979).

8 R. Hoggart, *The Uses of Literacy*, p103, Penguin (1977).

9 G. H. Vallins, *Good English*, p167, Pan (1951); *Shorter Oxford English Dictionary*, Volume I, p348, OUP (1977).

10 M. Drabble, *The Realms of Gold*, p169, Penguin (1979).

11 P. P. Read, *The Professor's Daughter*, Pan (1979).

12 R. Ingrams, *Spectator* (12 September 1981).

13 N. Atif, *The Listener* (29 July 1982).

14 A. C. Zijderveld, *On Clichés*, Routledge and Kegan Paul (1979).

15 A. C. Zijderveld, *op. cit.*, p7.

16 E. Partridge, *A Dictionary of Clichés*, Routledge and Kegan Paul (1978).

17 C. B. Williams, *Style and Vocabulary*, p5, Charles Griffin, London (1970).

18 P. Sprent, *Statistics in Action*, p116, Penguin (1979).

19 R. Gunning, *The Technique of Clear Writing*, p38, McGraw-Hill (Revised edition 1968); see also comments in H. A. Murphy and C. E. Peck, *Effective Business Communications*, p76, McGraw-Hill (Second edition 1976).

20 J. O. Morris, *Make Yourself Clear!*, p122, McGraw-Hill (1980).

21 B. M. Cooper, *Writing Technical Reports*, p92, Pelican (1964).

22 *Journal of Reading*, Vol. 21, p22 (December 1977).

23 Words per sentence; words per paragraph; words per punctuation pause; syllables per word.

24 J. O. Morris, *op. cit.*, p119.

25 T. Lupton, *Management and Social Sciences*, p81, Penguin (1971).

26 N. E. Enkvist, *Linguistics and Style*, p35, OUP (1964).

27 R. Jefferies, *The Amateur Poacher*, p97, Smith Elder & Co. London (1889).

28 C. Connolly, *Enemies of Promise*, p30, Penguin (1961).

29 W. Murray, *Happy Holiday*, The Ladybird Key Words Reading Scheme Book 7, *et al.*, Ladybird Books (1964).

30 National Computing Centre, *Impact of Microprocessors on British Industry*.

31 Argos Distributors Ltd, *Project Report on Training of Supervisors* (unpublished).

32 See also G. W. Turner *op. cit.* (Ref. 2 above), p234.

33 *Ibid.*, p71.

34 Argos Distributors Ltd, *op. cit.*

35 *Butterworths Yellow Tax Handbook* (annual), Butterworth.

36 M. Drabble, *The Needle's Eye*, pp198–200 and 218–20, Penguin (1981).

37 E. O'Brien, *Night*, pp73–7, Penguin (1980). (1,600 words).

38 H. Herd quoted in E. Partridge, *You Have a Point There*, p5, Routledge and Kegan Paul (1978). [Herd's work was *Everybody's Guide to Punctuation* (1925).]

39 See P. Howard, *New Words for Old*, p xiii, Hamish Hamilton (1977) on *The Times* rules for them. Also, Sir Linton Andrews, on seeing inverted commas around a cliché, would ask the journalist from what source they were quoted. (See G. L. Brook, *Varieties of English*, Macmillan, 1973.)

40 Department of Industry, *The Post Office* (White Paper: Cmnd 7292), (July 1978).

41 The Shell Transport and Trading Company, *Annual Report 1980*.

42 The National Trust, *Annual Report 1981*.

43 G. H. Vallins, *Pattern of English*, p158, Andre Deutsch (1956).

44 J. Stallworth, *Wilfred Owen*, OUP (1974).

45 J. Simon, *Paradigms Lost*, p143, Chatto & Windus (1981), quoting a view of Prof. O'Neil of Harvard.

46 General Council of British Shipping Draft Report (unpublished).

47 A. Tauber (Editor), *George Bernard Shaw On Language*, Peter Owen (1965).

48 T. Augarde, conversation with the author (June 1979); see also *The Concise Oxford Dictionary of Current English*, para VI, p xiv, OUP (Seventh edition, 1982).

49 G. H. Vallins, *op. cit.* (Pattern), p149.

50 P. Howard, *op. cit.*, p ix.

51 N. E. Enkvist, *op. cit.*, p19.

52 The analogy of chess is pursued at length by D. J. Allerton, *Essentials of Grammatical Theory*, pp11, 33 and 39, Routledge and Kegan Paul (1978).

53 J. Simon, *op. cit.*, p213.

54 A. E. Darbyshire, *op. cit.*, p95.

55 BBC Radio 4 (June 1981).

56 G. L. Brook, *op. cit.*

57 Bullock, *A Language for Life*.

58 *Ibid*.

59 Bank of America Senior Auditor's Report (unpublished).

60 See also Sir Ernest Gowers, *The Complete Plain Words*, pp206*ff*, Penguin (1977).

61 American Airlines, *Manager's exercise report* (unpublished).

62 Engineering Industry Training Board, *Employment and Training in the Telecommunications Equipment Manufacturing Industry*, RP/1/80 (1980; unpublished).

63 DHSS, *Report on the Joint Working Group on Oral Contraceptives*, HMSO (1976).

64 General Council of British Shipping. Draft Report (unpublished).

65 *Scarman Report*.

66 QANTAS Airways Ltd, Internal Report on Frensham Pond Sales Meeting (16 March 1979; unpublished).

67 W. Hazlitt, *Selected Essays*, p474, edited by Geoffrey Keynes, The Nonesuch Press (1942).

68 B. Foster, *The Changing English Language*, p17, Penguin (1976).

69 For further examples of this type of attitude, see R. Quirk, *The English Language and Images of Matter*, OUP (1972).

70 W. F. Bolton and D. Crystal, *The English Language*, Volume II, CUP (1969).

71 P. Howard, *Words Fail Me*, p88, Hamish Hamilton (1980).

72 'Of twenty yeer of age he was, I gesse': W. W. Skeat (Editor), *The Complete Works of Geoffrey Chaucer*; *The Canterbury Tales, The Prologue*, p420, line 82, OUP (1962).

73 S. Potter, *Our Language*, Penguin (1982).

74 *Ibid*.

75 *Ibid*.

76 *Ibid*.

77 S. Potter, *op. cit.*, p159.

78 See the rather perverse correspondence on Haigspeak (for Alexander Haig, Secretary of State) *The Times* (3 February 1981) *et al*. Yet many American words are accepted very

quickly into British English. P. Hanks describes (letter to author 17 August 1982) how frequently in the preparation of *Collins English Dictionary* the marker *US* had to be deleted as the word had become totally absorbed into British English.

79 *6,000 Words: A Supplement to Webster's Third New International Dictionary*, Merriam-Webster Springfield, Mass. (1976), shows some words which are ephemeral in the extreme.

80 C. Wain, *The Listener* (6 May 1982).

81 See, for example, Schering-Plough Annual Report for the rich variety of language to describe quite rudimentary functions.

82 *Webster's New Collegiate Dictionary*.

83 P. Strevens, *British and American English*, Cassell (1978).

84 J. Power, *International Herald Tribune*, (6–7 June 1979 and 10 June 1980).

85 E. O'Brien, *The Country Girls*, Penguin, (1980) *et al.*

86 For further comment in some detail on this area see J. and Z. Boyd in L. Michaels and C. Ricks (Editors), *The State of the Language*, pp43*ff*, University of California Press (1980).

87 M. Hennig and A. Jardin, *The Managerial Woman*, Pan (1978).

88 R. W. Shuy in M. A. Lourie and N. F. Conklin (Editors), *A Pluralistic Nation: The Language Issue in the United States*, p29, Newbury House (1978).

89 J. R. Hulbert, *Dictionaries British and American*, Andre Deutsch (1968).

90 *Debrett's Correct Form* compiled and edited by P. Montague-Smith, Debrett's Peerage and Futura (1979).

91 *Spectator* (17 July 1982).

92 A. S. C. Ross, *Don't Say It*, p105, Hamish Hamilton (1973), comments on the thoroughly fatuous use of the expression to describe '*so-called* Germans' in 1914–1918. It was quite certain that whatever else people may have thought about them they were Germans.

93 General Council of British Shipping. Draft Report (unpublished).

94 *The Times* (29 April 1978).

95 B. Levin, *The Times* (16 January 1980).

96 The Colt Car Company internal report on vehicles of various manufacturer (unpublished).

97 QANTAS Airways Ltd internal report on UK Cargo Sales Accounting System (unpublished).

98 P. Hanks, letter to the author (3 January 1980).

99 Interviewed by P. Howard, *The Times* (23 November 1978).

100 N. E. Enkvist, *op. cit.*

101 G. H. Vallins, *Good English*, Pan (1980).

Chapter 9   Using visual illustrations

1   Kingsley Amis, *I Want It Now*, p180, Panther (1969).

2   M. Kenny, *Thought for the Day*, BBC Radio 4 (23 April 1981).

3   T. Szamuely, *Spectator* (12 July 1980).

4   Department of Transport/Home Office, *Report of the Inter-Departmental Working Party on Road Traffic Law*, Green Paper, para 4, p3, HMSO (1981).

5   Ministry of Defence, *Statement on the Defence Estimates 1978*, Figure 6, p16, Cmnd 7099, HMSO (1978).

6   Department of the Environment, *Digest of Environmental Pollution and Water Statistics*, Figure 7, p4, HMSO (1980).

7   Engineering Industry Training Board, *Employment and Training in the Telecommunications Equipment Manufacturing Industry*, Figure 3.1, p15, RP/1/80 (1980; unpublished).

8   Prudential Corporation, *Annual Report and Accounts 1981*.

9   Northern British Properties, *Annual Report 1981*.

10 British Vita, *Report and Accounts 1981*.

11   S. & W. Berisford, *Annual Report 1981.*

12   Department of the Environment, *op. cit.*, Fig 30b, p40.

13   Ministry of Defence, *op. cit.*, Figure 5, p15.

14   *Ibid.*, Figure 3, p8.

15   *British Economic Survey*, Vol. 11(2), Figure 2(a), p46 (Spring 1981).

16   *Ibid.*, Figure 1, p45.

17   D. Huff, *How to Lie with Statistics*, p58, Penguin (1978).

18   Department of the Environment, *op. cit.*, Figure 43b, p58.

19   Argos Daventry Management Structure (detail), (August 1981).

20   Curry's Ltd, Financial Tree (unpublished).

21   W. S. Ryan, V. A. C. Willis and P. W. Brook, *The Increasing Use of Logical Trees in the Civil Service*, Civil Service Occasional Paper No. 13, HMSO (1975).

22   Monopolies Commission, *Hiram Walker-Gooderham and Worts Ltd and the Highland Distilleries* (1981).

23   *Central Office of Information Pamphlet 28* (Seventh edition, 1981).

24   Department of the Environment, op. cit., Figure 31, p23.

25   *Information Technology and Women's Jobs*, Table 10, p71.

26   Engineering Industry Training Board, *op. cit.*, Table A4, p43.

27   Department of the Environment, *op. cit.*, Figure 26, p34.

28   *Lyric Theatres Report.*

29   C. P. Snow, *In Their Wisdom*, Macmillan (1974).

Chapter 10   Organising the report

1   Esso Petroleum, *Initial Trials: Working Paper 2 (Signature Verification)*, April 1980 per Position Paper January 1981 (unpublished).

2   Bullock, *Industrial Democracy.*

3   Defence White Papers showing disposal of manpower, equipment and money around the world.

4   Department of the Environment, *Pop Festivals and their Problems, Second Report of the Working Group on Pop Festivals*, HMSO (1978). (Before Lady Stedman, the Chairman had been Lord Melchett.)

5   Kingsley Amis, *I Like It Here*, p81, Panther, (1958).

6   J. Keegan, conversation with the author (March 1977). This is a concept shared by J. O. Morris, *Make Yourself Clear!*, p174, McGraw-Hill (1980), who urges writers not to be put off by a bad first draft.

7   *The Spectator* (24 July 1982). (Chomsky, one of the most celebrated linguists in the world, is Professor of Modern Languages and Linguistics at the Massachusetts Institute of Technology.)

8   Kingsley Amis, *op. cit.*, p86.

Chapter 11   Typing or printing

1   Fraktur had some appeal as a Germanic type of script, but was repulsive to the occupied countries. Hitler finally ruled against it in 1941.

2   The westernisation of Turkish script was an obvious part of Attaturk's programme. Similar things have happened in more recent years in Malaysia.

3   *The Concise Oxford Dictionary of Current English*, OUP (Sixth edition, 1978 reprint).

4   *The Concise Oxford Dictionary of Current English* marks peculiarly British usages as | |. Chambers does not make this particular distinction, although the expression (*Scot*) prefaces a lot of their definitions. Collins has the note *Brit.*

5   *Information Technology and Women's Jobs*, para 1.3, p3.

6   Presidents of a sub-division of a print union.

7   *Hart's Rules for Compositors and Readers at the University Press, Oxford*, pp54–9 and technical bibliography on p60, OUP (Thirty-eighth edition, 1978).

8   *Scarman Report*, para 1.1, p1.

9   *Ibid.*, para 4.49, p60.

10   Hart's Rules, *op. cit.*, p43, say three is enough in any situation. E. Partridge, *You Have a Point There*, p84, Routledge and Kegan Paul (1953), says that six should be used for a complete sentence or more, but three for less than a sentence. The distinction seems useful.

11   Engineering Industry Training Board, *Employment and Training in the Telecommunications Equipment Manufacturing Industry*, RP/1/80 (1980; unpublished).

12   *In Place of Strife: A Policy for Industrial Relations*, para 119, p35, Cmnd 3888, HMSO (1969).

13   Health & Safety Executive, *Sizewell B*, para 3.3, p7.

14   P. Montague-Smith (Editor), *Debrett's Correct Form*, Futura Publications (1979).

15   *Ibid.*, Part II The Peerage, Part III Other Titles and Styles, Part VI American Usage, Part VII Usage in Other Foreign Countries.

16   The works of Milton and Bunyan illustrate this.

17   Hart's Rules, *op. cit.* See also G. V. Carey, *Mind the Stop*, Penguin (1958) who describes his own change of attitude over two decades: 'I feel less complacent about CAPITALS than when I originally wrote . . . (1939) . . . chiefly because of the present (1958) tendency to treat them as though they are slightly indelicate, or else extremely expensive'. Now, presumably we probably find them treated like the finest gold.

18   *The Oxford Dictionary for Writers and Editors*, OUP (1981).

19   See G. H. Vallins, *Spelling*, Andre Deutsch, (1973), especially Chapter 8, p150, for alternative spellings.

20   For example, Betty Kirkpatrick (letter to the author, 12 August 1982) suggests that press use of *tt* in *benefited* might soon give it respectability.

21   P. Hanks, letter to the author (17 August 1982).

22   J. Mace, *Working with Words*, p9, Writers and Readers Publishing Co-operative (1979).

23   French pronunciation caused some differences in spelling: *The English Language: its Beauty and Use*, Odhams Press London, unauthored and undated c 1930. *gh* in ghost is a Dutch import of Caxton's: D. G. Scragg *A History of English Spelling*, p66, Manchester University Press (1974). See also G. H. Vallins, *Spelling*, Andre Deutsch (Revised edition by D. G. Scragg, 1973).

24   A. Tauber (Editor), *George Bernard Shaw on Language*, Peter Owen (1965).

25   G. H. Vallins, *Better English*, p119, Pan (1953).

26   Bullock, *Language for Life*, p181.

27   See also Sir Ernest Gowers, *The Complete Plain Words*, pp200–203, Pelican (1977).

28   Hart's Rules, op. cit., pp34–7. A very few are shown in R. Ridout and C. Witting, *The Facts of English*, Pan (1964), (see under 'Printer's proofs').

Chapter 12   Binding and presentation

1   The paper-sizes in millimetres are:

SR A2 450 × 640	SR A4 225 × 320
A2 420 × 594	A4 210 × 297
SR A3 320 × 450	SR A5 160 × 225
A3 297 × 420	A5 148 × 210

2   Spicers Limited, Office Services Division, Sawston, Cambridge CB2 4JG.

3   Wiggins Teape (UK) Plc, 130 Long Acre, Covent Garden, London CS2E 9AL.

4   Esso Petroleum Ltd Report, *Signature Verification System: Position paper* (January 1981; unpublished).

5 Trustee Savings Bank Central Board (Computer Division), *Unipay-Future Developments* (December 1980; unpublished).
6 G. F. Smith & Son, Lockwood Street, Hull HU2 0HL, 2 Leathermarket, Weston Street, London SE1 3ET and Gazette Buildings, 168 Corporation Street, Birmingham B4 6TF.
7 National Coal Board, *Annual Reports* (1980 and 1981), *et al.*

Chapter 13 Appraisal reports

1 V. and A. Stewart, *Practical Performance Appraisal*, p56, Gower Press (1977).
2 *Ibid.*, p56.
3 As promulgated by J. Humble in *Management by Objectives in Action*, McGraw-Hill (1970) and *Management by Objectives*, Gower Press (1972).
4 V. and A. Stewart, *op. cit.*, p165.
5 V. and A. Stewart, *op. cit.*, p167.

Chapter 14 Accident reports

1 *Cardowan Colliery Report.*
2 A glance at a recent edition of Cross and Jones, *Introduction to Criminal Law*, Butterworth, or any other similar legal textbook will give some worthwhile guidelines on this.

Chapter 15 Abstracts

1 W. Shakespeare, *Richard III*, Act 1, Scene iv.
2 J. O. Morris, *Make Yourself Clear!*, p122, McGraw-Hill (1980).
3 J. M. Jackson, *Background Issues* in L. W. Porter and K. H. Roberts (Editors), *Communication in Organizations*, p86, Penguin (1977).
4 *The Times* (20 August 1982). Incidentally, apropos *The Times*, the Times Parliamentary reports are a model of concise writing. The accounts give the rub of every speech made in the Houses in sometimes only two or three sentences.
5 Department of Transport/Home Office, *Report of the Inter-Departmental Working Party on Road Traffic Law*, Green Paper, HMSO (1981).
6 *Ibid.*, para 77, p23.
7 The Prime Minister *et al: Industrial Democracy* (white paper) (Cmnd 7231) HMSO (May 1978).
8 BBC Radio 4.

Chapter 16 Telexed reports

1 *United Kingdom Telex Directory*, British Telecom (April 1982).
2 E. Thompson, Supervisor, *The Guardian* Wire Room, discussions with the author (July 1982).

Chapter 17 Reports of the future

1 *Information Technology and Women's Jobs*, para 2.1, p5.
2 H. M. McCabe and E. L. Popham, *Word Processing: A Systems Approach to the Office*, p6, Harcourt Brace Jovanovich (1977).
3 Research carried out in the USA by Datapoint Corporation shows 'Many senior executives were found to be averse to using a keyboard, particularly because they associated keyboards with lower level clerical staff. They believed that tapping at keys was beneath them.' [*Office Equipment Index*, No. 188 (July 1982).]
4 M. Berlins, *The Times* (Information Technology Supplement), (14 January 1982).
5 See, for example, the Open Files system which was introduced by Hackney Borough

Council (29 September 1982). It was criticised by the borough opposition for requiring an extravagant amount of handling and handlers. It was argued that the more information about people's circumstances that was made available, the more it would have to be segregated.

6   P. Virgo, *Cashing in On the Chips*, p25, Conservative Political Centre (1979).

7   J. W. Grundy and R. G. Rosenthal, *Vision and VDUs* and *VDU's* [*sic* with apostrophe] *and You*, The Association of Optical Practitioners.

8   See also S. G. Price, *Introducing the Electronic Office*, p14, National Computing Centre (1979).

9   'Now everyone can be a good typist no matter how many mistakes you make, you always get a perfect clean copy . . . no more waiting to have your material typed up.' (Phillips publicity material.)

10 As a broad generalisation, Wang estimate a 50% saving. Lynda King Taylor, *The Times* (14 January 1982) quotes a Civil Service study in 1981 which produced an improvement of between 43 and 72%, dependent upon type of office accommodation, specific equipment costs and so on.

11 *Mind Your Own Business*, Vol. 5(7), (July/August 1982).

12 A. Clark, *Office Skills* (Pitman Periodicals), (February 1980).

13 *Information Technology and Women's Jobs*, para 22, p8.

14 Department of Industry, *Microelectronics: the New Technology*, p23, HMSO (1981).

15 This point is expressed in S. Fedida and R. Malik, *Viewdata Revolution*, p64, Associated Business Press (1979).

16 *Business Equipment Digest* (May 1982).

17 A. Clark, *op. cit.*

18 IBM (UK) Ltd, PO Box 31, Birmingham Road, Warwick.

19 For example, Alpha Tantel.

20 J. Ellis, *Office Equipment Index*, No. 188.

21 Microwriter Ltd, Unit 2 Wandle Way, Willow Lane, Mitcham, Surrey.

22 4 inches wide, $8\frac{1}{2}$ inches long, $2\frac{1}{4}$ inches deep. Weight 24 oz.

23 *Business Equipment Digest* (May 1982).

24 *Computer Talk*, quoted by Microwriter Ltd, but date of the magazine is unspecified.

25 For example, FAX, Interscan Communication Systems Ltd, 39 Montrose Avenue, Slough, Berkshire.

26 Bell Laboratories, Murray Hill, New Jersey.

27 A. Berry, *The Daily Telegraph* (16 June 1981 and 7 October 1981).

28 Jensen Computer Systems Ltd, 30 Queen Square, Bristol.

29 *Mind Your Own Business*, Vol. 5(7), (July/August 1982).

30 D. J. Boorstin, *The Image*, p140, Weidenfeld & Nicolson (1962).

31 M. F. Bolt, *Computational Linguistics*, in J. Lyons (Editor), *New Horizons in Linguistics*, p222, Penguin (1977).

32 S. Fedida and R. Malik, *op. cit.*

33 Not only is this helpful with the itinerant recipient. It is also a valuable time-saver in overcoming telephone difficulties. BL Systems Readers Forum quotes a correspondent's study which showed that only 26% of his telephone calls went through first time. The rest were unanswered, engaged, refused to be interrupted and the subject of general telephonic frustration.

34 See B. L. Jones, *Welsh: Linguistic Conservatism and Shifting Bilingualism*, in E. Hangen *et al.* (Editors), *Minority Languages Today: A Selection from the Papers read at the First International Conference on Minority Languages held at Glasgow University from 8 to 13 September 1980*, p48, Edinburgh University Press (1981).

35 R. Burchfield, *The Daily Telegraph* (12 October 1979). See also R. Burchfield, *The Spoken Word: A BBC Guide*, BBC (1981). Although the slim (40 pages) volume was aimed at standards of spoken English, its lessons give a good indication of how Dr Burchfield sees an appropriate level of the written word.

36 *The Guardian* (28 December 1979).
37 R. Bridges, *The Society's Work* in W. F. Bolton and D. Crystal (Editors), *The English Language*, p93, Volume II, CUP (1969).
38 R. Hoggart, *The Uses of Literacy*, pp206*ff*, Penguin (1977).
39 N. Rogers, *Wessex Dialect*, p52, Moonraker Press, Bradford-on-Avon (1979).
    J. Simon, *Paradigms Lost*, p183, Chatto & Windus (1981).
40 A. E. Darbyshire, *A Grammar of Style*, p95, Andre Deutsch (1979).
41 H. M. McCabe and E. L. Popham, *op. cit.*, p148.
42 Marshall McLuhan, *Understanding Media*, Sphere Books (1967), *et al.*
43 A. Hodgson, *The Times* (2 October 1978).
44 I. McIntyre, *The Listener* (Langham Diary), (27 May 1982).
45 For expansion on these possible errors, see W. S. Davis, *Information Processing Systems*, Addison-Wesley (1978).
46 S. J. Teague (Librarian, City University, London), *Microform Publication* in P. Hills (Editor), *The Future of the Printed Word*, Frances Pinter (1980).
47 P. Geyl, *Napoleon For and Against*, Jonathan Cape (1957).

Appendix 2   Numbering systems

1 Organisation for Economic Co-operation and Development; Road Research, *Traffic Control in Saturated Conditions*, Paris (1981).
2 Devised M. Dewey, circa 1873.
3 Civil Service Department, *Manual for Civil Service Typists*, pp13–14, HMSO (1974).

Appendix 3   Selected suggestions for further reading

1 P. Howard, letter to the author (30 July 1982).
2 G. H. Vallins, *The Pattern of English*, p159, Andre Deutsch (1971).
3 A. Waugh, *The Sunday Telegraph* (27 July 1980).

Index

A large number of reports, published and unpublished, are discussed in the text. Decision on indexing of these many titles has constituted a problem. The following criterion has been used. The only reports included are those which, at the time of their publication, were likely to make front page news in national broadsheet papers. (For example, had they been available for comment when this book was written, the Franks Report, the Bishop of Salisbury's *Church and the Bomb* and the Serpell Report would have been treated in this way.)

References to authors of works described in Appendix 3 are only made here if the author's name appears in the body of this book.